Pedagogy Is Politics

Pedagogy Is Politics

LITERARY THEORY AND CRITICAL TEACHING

Edited by
Maria-Regina Kecht

UNIVERSITY OF ILLINOIS PRESS
URBANA AND CHICAGO

Manufactured in the United States of America
1 2 3 4 5 C P 5 4 3 2 1

This book is printed on acid-free paper.

Library of Congress Cataloging-in Publication Data

Pedagogy is politics : literary theory and critical teaching / edited by Maria-Regina Kecht.
p. cm.
Includes bibliographical references and index.
ISBN 0-252-01834-6 (alk. paper).—ISBN 0-252-06200-0 (pbk. : alk. paper)
1. Literature—Study and teaching (Higher)—United States.
2. Teaching. 3. Criticism—History—20th century. I. Kecht, Maria-Regina.
PN70.P44 1992
807.1'173—dc20 91-7603
CIP

CONTENTS

THE CHALLENGE OF RESPONSIBILITY: AN INTRODUCTION

Maria-Regina Kecht

> Education may well be, as of right, the instrument whereby every individual, in a society like our own, can gain access to any kind of discourse. But we well know that in its distribution, in what it permits and in what it prevents, it follows the well-trodden battle-lines of social conflict. Every educational system is a political means of maintaining or of modifying the appropriation of discourse, with the knowledge and the powers it carries with it.
>
> Michel Foucault, "The Discourse on Language"

> Criticism cannot assume that its province is merely the text, not even the great literary text. It must see itself, with other discourse, inhabiting a much contested cultural space, in which what has counted in the continuity and transmission of knowledge has been the signifier, as an event that has left lasting traces upon the human subject.
>
> Edward Said, *The World, the Text, and the Critic*

I

Though literary theory is frequently characterized as lacking significant social function, we should not forget, as Terry Eagleton reminds us, that modern criticism emerged in the early eighteenth century as a cultural force in the liberal, bourgeois, public sphere.[1] By the end of the nineteenth century, criticism gained professional legitimacy primarily through increased specialization and withdrawal from the politically "contaminated" social reality. Criticism thus acquired esthetic idealism, moral superiority, and ostensibly redemptive power by relinquishing social relevance and effectiveness. Literary inquiry still stressed its moral and cultural mission, but it became for the most part a merely textual matter. This trend continued into the twentieth century, which produced a growing technical refinement and diversity of method—self-absorbed, self-sustaining, and self-perpetuating—and though the sixties saw the critical practices and goals of "liberal humanism challenged as elitist, idealist, depoliticizing, and socially marginal,"[2] the following twenty years have shown no fundamental change for the better. True enough, the ideas of objectivity, rationality, and reason as guiding principles of human progress have been questioned, history has been seen as dissolved into a narrative, and the author's authority has been declared overthrown and replaced by the reader's willful deconstruction, but these and other assaults on concepts of hegemony and hierarchy have certainly not led to a democratization of criticism or an expansion of its social sphere of influence.

Considering how little impact the humanities have had on the development of world affairs and how little public attention has been paid to the accomplishments of the professional humanists, it is perhaps no wonder that many literary scholars have decided to forget about the ills of humanity and concentrate on their own well-being. Focusing on their narrowly circumscribed tasks, which define and determine survival in their labor market, most intellectuals in the humanities are perfectly satisfied with the professional rewards accruing to work that is not only highly specialized (if not arcane) and abstract, but also culturally insignificant and socially inconsequential.

In recent times, though, the status of academics as functionaries of the cultural order has been the center of much attention. Voices from the political right and left have expressed dissatisfaction with the performance of a profession that has promoted ever more refined expertise, indulged in elaborate textual techniques, and postulated esoteric theories, but neglected its fundamental duty to impart knowledge and skills to students. Clearly, these critical voices differ radically in how they characterize the nature of this knowledge and the kinds of skills that ought to be transmitted through teaching and scholarship in the humanities.

The public has been flooded with reform programs for reclaiming a legacy and for overcoming the crisis in the humanities, the closing of the American mind, and the lack of cultural literacy. And many have come to believe that our present problems in education can be solved by restoring the Renaissance ideal of *litterae humaniores*, returning to a core curriculum, and renewing the emphasis on the humanities as a "body of knowledge and a means of inquiry that conveys serious truths, defensible judgments, and significant ideas," as former Secretary of Education William J. Bennett recommends.[3] Others, however, claim such suggestions to rest on idealist and elitist assumptions that relegate literature and the arts to the realm of esthetics and ethics, negating their social and political embeddedness while simultaneously maintaining the myth of a neutral, objective, ideology-free pursuit of knowledge.

Humanists like Walter Jackson Bate, Allan Bloom, E. D. Hirsch, or William Bennett lament the humanities' loss of power in their, as it seems to them, self-evidently valid mission to instill the *fundamental* values and *great* ideas of our *Western* civilization in students. When they assert the necessity of teaching "important books" rather than confusing young minds with relativistic and abstract literary theories, and when they provide a detailed agenda of immediate steps to rescue the "institutional identity" of our universities, the "educational purpose," and the "essence" of university training, they pretend to be, or worse, *are*, oblivious to their ideological program. Their pretense of neutrality stems from ideological consensus, from having internalized and naturalized the conventions and norms that academic scholarship has declared legitimate in our social system.

Scholars of a Marxist persuasion agree with these humanists about the significant role that the humanities should assume in shaping social reality, but their concept of such involvement and moral commitment is radically different. Their vision of the function and the potential of teaching literature arises from an analysis of the fundamental political and economic forces that marginalize the humanities, from a critique of the dominant politics of culture, and from a scrutiny of the role that intellectuals play as carriers of hegemonic ideas. The left's suggested changes emphasize a critical investigation of the conventions and practices in the humanistic disciplines that will find where ideology, power, and knowledge converge. The historical and material positions of the institution, the discipline, the teacher, and the student all are to be taken into account when explaining the dominant structure of education and outlining alternatives. Most important to these counterproposals is their insistence on creating a critical consciousness among teachers and students that would reconnect the work inside the ivory tower with the world outside, underscoring the social and political relevance of literature and criticism, of reading and writing.[4] According to this view, theorizing need not be a narcissistic occupation but can be social praxis; the result primarily depends on the decisions and interests of the profession and its members.

Because literary studies are self-encased and hence out of touch with reality, their authority and consequentiality have eroded. Does this lament for lost power perhaps add impetus to the intense contentions among literary scholars, their relentless assaults on one another and their pathetic defense of tiny fiefdoms? Could one consider this struggle for victory before a small audience of insiders, this struggle virtually for its own sake, without any interest in a productive outcome or general relevance, as some ersatz gratification? And do the current, highly polemical debates among critics not create an aura of politics but, at the same time, successfully distract from the wider political responsibility of criticism? The desire for power within the discipline, frequently passed off as desire for truth, is clearly at work, no matter how limited the sphere of influence may be. To be right and attain the position of setting the rules for the critical game seem to be worth fighting for. (And judged by remuneration, it certainly has been worthwhile for a number of critical crusaders.) If ideology and politics have in some way become an integral and explicit part of current literary scholarship, it is quite disturbing to note that so much intellectual energy is wasted, for so little of this vigorous politicization is used to raise serious questions about the role, the function, and the practices of criticism. I find it distressing that, with a few exceptions, literary theory has still failed to turn into a meaningful, exciting cultural critique and action-oriented force outside the university's walls as well as inside.

Some observers may feel that it is not worth getting worried about the popularity and prestige of literary theory because, like any other professional fad, it will soon vanish without leaving any significant traces, and then it will be "business as usual." Some may agree with Gerald Graff's historical explanation of theory's inroads into the discipline, which makes it the latest stage in a recurrent pattern of incorporating or canonizing a hitherto eccentric or alternative intellectual interest.[5] Still others may find exactly that aspect of noninterference with the traditional practices of the discipline disconcerting or even dangerous. In all the theoretical activities, they see too much of the "business as usual." The rhetorical resistance to the tradition and the ensuing clamorous conflicts have not resulted in the discipline's critical self-examination. Even worse, many of the supposed targets of radical attack have only changed ownership rather than being destroyed. If dogmatism and orthodoxy, authority and hierarchy, privilege and exclusiveness were to be subverted, it is certainly ironic that literary theory, in its scholarly and institutional practices, has reaffirmed all of these things. What has flourished is the arrogance of self-righteous academics eager to impress and silence those who have not acquired proficiency in theoretical newspeak. What has increased are the class divisions between elite institutions providing star theorists with very high salaries for very low teaching loads, on the one hand, and schools employing Ph.D.s to teach the over-enrolled service courses in composition, on the other. What has grown are the gaps between critics and readers, critics and writers, and critic-teachers and students.

Perhaps this situation, full as it is of contradictions, oppositions, and struggles, can be assessed and examined as a refraction, a perfect manifestation, of our wider social, economic, and political world. Such a perspective encourages overcoming the disjunction between literary discourse and the material, historical human condition. Because our greatest need is to create and occupy the space of "worldliness," as Edward Said suggests, it seems reasonable to approach that project by raising serious questions about the basis of our professional practices, about the function and purpose of our work as intellectuals in an increasingly complex and powerful cultural order. If we can agree that language is situated in the world and thus always *interested,* that knowledge is socially produced and thus always determined by strategies of exclusion and containment, then we should also accept that as teachers and scholars we are engaged in social activities. Having gained some expertise in decoding structures of signification, we should be intellectually equipped to read our own practices, our institutions, and the world as a text.

Such cultural and political "acts of reading" can be carried out most productively when adopting Gramsci's concepts of "hegemony" and of "traditional" and "organic" intellectuals.[6] As soon as we recognize hegemony as a dynamic interaction between social, political, and cultural forces, namely, as a continual process rather than a homogeneous entity or monolithic system, we participate in that process either by validating and sustaining it or by resisting and transforming it. The whole social process is, according to Gramsci, organized by particular and dominant values that reflect a specific distribution of power and influence.[7] Domination and subordination are interrelated, constitutive aspects of the hegemonic process, which constantly attempts to modify, neutralize, accommodate, and integrate threatening forms of counterculture. Hegemony "has continually to be renewed, recreated, defended, and modified. It is also continually resisted, limited, altered, challenged by pressures not all its own."[8] So it is important to bear in mind that, no matter how much the dominant culture creates and determines all cultural activities, shaping and limiting alternative and even oppositional forms, it is possible to initiate "authentic breaks." Even as cultural functionaries we can make efforts that cannot easily be appropriated by, and thus rendered harmless to, the dominant order, efforts that are "irreducible to the terms of the original or adaptive hegemony, and are in that sense independent."[9]

Those literary scholars who consider their task of transmitting tradition, knowledge, and skills to be nonideological, and thus hygienically isolated from political interests, social constraints, or economic demands, are apparently quite blind to the powerful mechanisms of selection that define what will be the approved and accepted version of tradition, what will count as significant ideas, and what will be ratified as legitimate methods of inquiry. In the words of Frederick Crews, a former MLA president, complicity between the hegemonic process and the academic pursuit of knowledge can be diagnosed in the mere "congruency between ideologically useful attitudes and what scholars already believe."[10] The crucial question, then, is whether "ideology has helped to shape those beliefs without the scholars' conscious awareness." Crews, who was formerly interested in such issues, says that "this would be a relatively undramatic but quite serious politicization of learning, for someone who does not even know that he is thinking propagandistically is farther from objectivity than one who decides to suppress his real views."[11] Crews's judgment is aimed at the central trait of "traditional intellectuals," as we know it from Gramsci: their strong sense of their autonomy and independence, derived from their historical continuity and special qualification and confirmed by an *esprit de corps.*[12] The far-ranging social and political consequences of such a self-image are certainly manifest in our present academic situation, where even the voices of innovation and change offer merely ornamental alternatives to the traditional disciplinary attitudes and practices, and where the active contribution to the cultural hegemony is neither acknowledged nor even considered.

Once we understand that cultural hegemony is decisive in the noncoercive maintenance of any sociopolitical system, we must recognize what great responsibility rests on us as teachers and critics. Indeed, if our dissemination of the dominant beliefs and values helps preserve ideological unity, subdue class conflicts, and secure the political leadership of the powers that be, if we also serve the state's vital interest of manufacturing "free" consent to the existing law and order, then we had better admit that there is no boundary between the mystified ivory tower "inside" of academia and the real world "outside" of business and politics, social inequalities, and demagogic manipulation and exploitation.

The university is a marketplace of ideas, and we function as salesmen of cultural values.[13] We need to ask ourselves whether we want to be like Gramsci's "traditional" intellectuals, trying to uphold the myth of social autonomy and thus concealing any attachment to historical social formations, or whether we want to be "organic" intellectuals, seeing our professional activities as welded to political acts and thus sustaining a culturally adversarial position that is actually inscribed in the term "criticism." As teachers and scholars, we are bearers of critical knowledge that should empower others to make sense of their position in the world, become alert to the ideological workings of the cultural process, discover the neglected or suppressed aspects of the tradition, and seize the initiative to disrupt the hegemonic order. "Organic" intellectuals want to align themselves with various forces of resistance and opposition, reaching out for solidarity with those whose counterhegemonic efforts have been thwarted. "The mode of being of the new intellectual," Gramsci states, "can no longer consist in eloquence, which is an exterior and momentary mover of feelings and passions, but in active participation in practical life, as constructor, organiser, 'permanent persuader' and not just simple orator."[14] Even qualifying this description to avoid the dangers of what Paul Bové has identified as the undemocratic structure of the "leading" intellectual,[15] it should be clear that the foremost goal for an "organic" intellectual ought to be an oppositional practice rather than an oppositional rhetoric, action that challenges the social order to bring about more equality and justice.

A worthwhile attempt at becoming an "organic" intellectual could be the revaluation of journalism as a legitimate instrument to create a public sphere for the critic. This would require expanding one's specialization, going beyond textual studies, and recognizing the wider cultural field as a territory for active intellectual inquiry. The academic institution would be reluctant to give up its policy of "publish or perish," but solidarity of interest could effect a substantial revision. Ten scholarly variations of some marginal literary theme would then, perhaps, be less important for promotion than essays published in widely circulated papers and magazines. If we want to stop blaming others for the miserable state of the nation or the world, we must start acting, addressing wider audiences with our observations, insights, analyses, and suggestions. Our adversarial position toward given power structures should be voiced so that others can hear it, even those who will pretend not to listen.

If we are to play a role in bestowing some significance on the humanistic enterprise and turning it into a "force of persuasive dissent within our culture,"[16] we had better reflect on the validity of our academic practices and initiate a shift of the dominant paradigm. We need to examine how our activities as critics and teachers are marked by authoritarian, hierarchical, exclusionary qualities that reflect the nature of the hegemony and determine, among other things, our choice of texts for articles, courses, and reading lists; our relation to students; and our instructional strategies. Particularly, our position of power in the classroom requires close scrutiny. As long as the process of transmitting knowledge relies on inculcating our own ways of reading, suppressing alternative ways, and recruiting disciples, we certainly preserve undemocratic power relations. Our instructional methodology should not subordinate the students, ignore their specific identities and experiences, and deny their own social, historical positions; rather, it should establish a climate of dialogue in the classroom that allows students to represent their own worlds and perspectives, considers their nonacademic forms of knowledge, and promotes self-expression. To realize our social and intellectual ideals, our teaching practices should encourage forms of learning that foster critical judgment and healthy skepticism and serve to prepare students for responsibility and agency.

If we teachers of literature and criticism want to become a social force in our immediate environment, we still have a long way to go. When we look at our workplace, we need to ask ourselves several important questions: Do we succeed in presenting literature as a potentially emancipatory force in our students' lives, or do most of them regard reading "good" books merely as part of their liberal arts training? Do we succeed in contextualizing literature in its modes of production and forms of consumption, as part of historically changing ideological apparatuses? Do we succeed in illuminating the relation between analysis in the classroom and critical thought in general? Do we succeed in showing our students the power of culture as "a system of values *saturating* downward almost everything within its purview," and do we succeed in illustrating to them that "culture dominates from above without at the same time being available to everything and everyone it dominates?"[17] If we could answer a single of these questions with a firm "yes," we would see more students leave our schools with minds of their own and a critical awareness that might generate social change.

To get closer to such a goal, we ought to restructure the traditional curriculum in literary studies and set up alternatives to the present system of highly segregated disciplinary knowledge. It is necessary to question the function and validity of our standard course offerings, both in content and purpose. Without any doubt, the dominant curricular structures in literature departments do not encourage students to see connections between the text and the world, the classroom and the institution, the discipline and the cultural process. Neither do most courses promote the students' acquisition of knowledge that would lead beyond the hegemonic discourse of Western humanism, increase their perceptiveness concerning the link between power and truth, and expose them to the usually excluded images of otherness.

Rather than offering only genre, period, and author courses, we should, as several engaged teachers and critics have already suggested, structure our courses around issues.[18] We could have a freshmen seminar on *language*. Various interdisciplinary approaches could be presented, and recent literary theory would certainly be a good storehouse for explanatory models. The great educational value of such a project is, first, the vivid illustration of radically different, perhaps mutually incompatible, notions of language; second, the stimulation of student thought about something that may well be totally unproblematic to them; third, the augmentation of their intellectual preparation for any other course in any discipline; and fourth, the fostering of critical consciousness through a realization that our perception of reality is mediated and shaped through language. When students become aware of the power of language to constitute their identities and construct meaning, they also need, and will often desire, the training to examine the diverse codes surrounding them and molding their experiences.

In a similar vein, we could offer courses on the issues of *authority, history,* or *knowledge.* Furthermore, we should install *culture* courses whose interdisciplinary nature could introduce the students to the cultural process as torn by conflicting ideologies, challenging naive assumptions about social and political practices as well as counteracting dangerous historical amnesia. The overall purpose of such a course would again be the shaping of critical consciousness, so that our students would leave college with a belief in their own transformative abilities rather than passively accepting the forces around them. Perhaps we should see the purpose of our daily work, as Jim Merod put it, in the promotion of "an intellectual identity in students who in large measure are vulnerable to the pacifications of the common culture that organizes capitalist reality: advertising, commercial tv, and the onslaught of rock and Hollywood culture. The teacher's job is to breed the kind of critical capacities that allow students to resist such disabling forces."[19]

It may be easier to increase these critical capacities successfully when we develop more solidarity among responsible educators and recognize our potential to function as "micropowers" at our workplaces. Perhaps it is worthwhile trying to combine the role of Gramsci's organic intellectual with that of Foucault's specific intellectual. Foucault considers it the intellectual's role "to struggle against the forms of power that transform him into its object and instrument in the sphere of 'knowledge,' 'truth,' 'consciousness,' and 'discourse.' " And he regards theory as practice, a practice that is a "struggle against power, a struggle aimed at revealing and undermining power where it is most invisible and insidious."[20] The ubiquitous conflict between forces of domination and resistance may have a productive outcome when we focus on the operations of the power network in our work within the university. Reflecting on the history of our profession, examining our role as cultural functionaries, recognizing and understanding our involvement in "the regime of truth," and putting our intellectual efforts into the concrete, everyday struggle for a new, more democratic culture, we will meet the challenge of responsibility. After all, change does not occur by fighting the effects of power at large but by resisting domination at particular, local points. Only such resistance to specific exercises of power allows hope for emancipation.

If we manage to rouse our students from indifference and passivity, instill skepticism in them, encourage a questioning, inquisitive disposition to the world around them, broaden their understanding of themselves and others, enable them to recognize the dominant interests and socializing ideologies, and provide them with a language to articulate their critical findings—if we manage to accomplish all or even some of that, we might discover our vocation as critics. Literary theory would then definitely assume a noble task.

This collection of essays arises from the serious effort to bring together the voices of critics who believe in the significance of our vocation.

II

> Intellectual work is related to power in numerous ways, among them these: with ideas one can uphold or justify power, attempting to transform it into legitimate authority; with ideas one can also debunk authority, attempting to reduce it to mere power, to discredit it as arbitrary or as unjust. With ideas one can conceal or expose the holders of power. And with ideas of more hypnotic though frivolous shape, one can divert attention from problems of power and authority and social reality in general.
>
> C. Wright Mills, *Power, Politics, and People*

The volume has been arranged in three sections, each emphasizing different aspects of the issue of literary theory's relation to teaching. The essays in the first part, "Polemics," critically examine the rhetoric of poststructuralism that promises students and teachers emancipation from the bonds of traditional humanism. The inquiry into this alternative pedagogy—on the levels of both curriculum and classroom—is conducted from a radical perspective. It attempts not only to analyze the ideological premises and intellectual consequences of pedagogical strategies carried out in the name of Derrida and his followers but also to set directions for an antihegemonic teaching that is conscious of the connection between power and knowledge.

The second part, "Pragmatics," contains some specific examples of this kind of teaching. Notwithstanding the considerable differences among the contributors' suggestions for theory-informed change in the literary discipline as it affects undergraduate and graduate programs, course offerings, and course structures, all these essays express a conviction that students should be empowered to comprehend and criticize signifying practices as they determine the situation inside and outside the classroom. Each essay in this section provides concrete proposals for a pedagogy that addresses students as socially and historically inscribed subjects who can be agents of social transformation.

The diverse essays assembled in the third section under the heading "Positions" give voice to a belief in the relationship between the disciplinary discourse and the "regime of truth" in the culture at large. Scrutinizing the structure of English departments, the nature of writing classes, and the standard of close reading and other interpretive strategies, these essays point to some of the usually unidentified effects of ideology on conventions and norms of our profession. In each case, insights of current literary theory guide the critical argument toward a heightened awareness of hierarchies marking our cultural assumptions and, hence, our performance as teachers and scholars.

The first essay in this collection, Mas'ud Zavarzadeh's provocative "Theory as Resistance," introduces key issues: the need to connect academic work with the world, the obligation to examine the classroom as a text, the urgency to recognize the positions of teachers and students, the imperative to foreground the production and transmission of knowledge, and the desire to employ literary theory as an effective instrument of critique and emancipation. Zavarzadeh creates the framework for a comparison between hegemonic pedagogy and its subversive opponent, radical pedagogy, by illustrating the differences between Stanislavski's realistic theater and Brecht's epic theater. Whereas the former tends to make the audience (the students) passively submit to the pleasures of entertainment, thus forgetting the constructedness of the performance and their own situatedness in history, the latter strives to challenge the spectators' critical abilities, confronting them with conscious alienation of seemingly natural practices and thus drawing attention to how representation and reception are socially and ideologically embedded. Critical theory, according to Zavarzadeh, is to oppose and overcome the dehistoricizing nature of both humanist and poststructualist pedagogies. As long as these pedagogical models postulate meaning (and knowledge) as the creation of sovereign subjects or as a self-referential web of textuality, they fail to acknowledge the reality of the power/knowledge complex. Instead, they offer a "pedagogy of evasion," in which the student is "liberated" from his or her roots in class, race, and gender to approach discursive practices uncontaminated by social relations. As an alternative, Zavarzadeh proposes a "pedagogy of enablement" that would allow students to become aware of the cultural and political situatedness of the instruction itself. Teachers and students, breaking through the illusion of disinterested knowledge, would come to see their relationship as a struggle over authority. Furthermore, students would become alert to the social construction of meaning and recognize their power to criticize and even resist hegemonic codes. Once they acquire the theoretical tools to "make the world intelligible," the students could successfully defy the official standards of truth.

John Schilb's essay "Poststructuralism, Politics, and the Subject of Pedagogy" also deals with the development of emancipatory teaching principles. Schilb analyzes a series of poststructuralist essays on pedagogy to show that their rhetoric of subversion and emancipation is an empty promise, for in practice, poststructuralism fails to interrogate the traditional positioning of the student as a subordinate. Although poststructuralism presents the teacher as an intellectual rebel, an authority who is eager to challenge tradition by transmitting new and playful ways of reading, it also confines the pedagogical concerns to issues of textuality, and hence it does not lead students to a better understanding of the social dynamics as manifest in the classroom and the world at large. A highly contestatory theory that merely provides a source for exegetical techniques and academic methodology and fails to question its own usefulness for change at the site of its promulgation certainly does not promote democratization. To do that, Schilb maintains, it is necessary to establish a discourse of dialogue and collaboration in the spirit of feminism and Freire's pedagogy, which encourages students' critical inquiry into institutional, social, and historical contexts as well as into their particular experience as subjects.

In her essay "Subversion and Oppositionality in the Academy," Barbara Foley writes about the confirmation of hegemonic structures arising from seemingly adversarial and progressive practices. Foley specifically focuses on the revision and expansion of the literary canon, whose "oppositional potential" she certainly does not deny. Introducing marginalized writers to the records of literary history and thus reshuffling the canon's order does not, however, automatically weaken the power of tradition, and the frequently indiscriminate attempt to attribute subversive qualities to these writers in many cases is a gesture of professional up-to-dateness rather than a critical examination of their actual resistance to the dominant ideology. If, all of a sudden, subversion can be found in any text, the workings of ideology may be declared ineffectual, and we can stop worrying. Foley recognizes in this kind of "canon busting" a distressing lack of political responsibility on the part of neo-Marxists, feminists, and other "subversive" critics for whom the textual or scholarly opposition seems to challenge the tradition sufficiently.

The voices of harsh criticism in the first section of this volume are supplemented by the pragmatic observations of several critics in the second section. These commentators are less interested in describing what they find wrong with today's models of pedagogy than in proposing concrete alternatives that already have been either vigorously debated within departments or implemented in the curriculum or classroom.

Revising the curriculum and making literary theory the foundation for change is David Shumway's topic. In his essay "Integrating Theory in the Curriculum as Theorizing—a Postdisciplinary Practice," Shumway first examines the beliefs underlying most models for including literary theory in the instructional program and then discusses the merits of a totally restructured, theory-informed curriculum. He argues that the mere addition of theory courses to an otherwise unquestioned curriculum usually presupposes three basic assumptions: that students ought to be provided a variety of new "useful approaches," that a specific theory should be postulated as "interpretive policy," or that theory can be used to answer the discipline's "perennial questions." According to Shumway, none of these ways of exposing students to literary theory has any pedagogically sound effect. The students should learn *how* to "theorize," which means they should become proficient in an intellectual activity that questions the given, discerns the unsaid, discovers alternatives, and forgoes immediate practical usefulness. Teaching theory as an activity rather than a body of knowledge—teaching to theorize—fulfills the political need to arouse skepticism about structures of authority. Obviously, both a comparative examination of various theoretical practices and a reflection on their form and content are necessary to acquire competence in theorizing. Shumway says that such a project ought to be seen as postdisciplinary because the goal of translating the insights of theory into the curriculum can be attained only by transcending the traditional divisions and boundaries between literature, history, philosophy, and culture.

Kathleen McCormick presents a practical example of this model of theorizing in her essay "Always Already Theorists: Literary Theory and Theorizing in the Undergraduate Curriculum." Establishing theorizing as a corollary of pedagogy requires moving away from the traditional "banking system" of education and introducing "problem-posing education" (Freire) in a dialogic classroom. Advocating a self-conscious theoretical position for teachers and students alike, McCormick selects an "integrative approach" to theory-informed teaching, which she distinguishes from the "canonizing" and the "additive" approaches. Neither the strategy of creating a new canon by substituting masterpieces of theoretical texts for literary ones, which merely grooms new experts in theory and breeds a new elitism, nor the decision to hire theory specialists as departmental attractions (and proof of departmental pluralism) will help students become aware of the interests involved in producing knowledge. To attain this goal and to bring theoretical self-awareness to all courses, we must find new organizational principles and radically change the curriculum. In her discussion of just such a practice at her home institution (Carnegie Mellon), McCormick shows how courses at all levels of the curriculum can be arranged around issues of language, history, and culture rather than around periods or authors. Clearly, these categories are interrelated and permit using a variety of theoretical perspectives and reading materials as the contents of courses like "Discursive Practices," "Discourse and Historical Change," or "Reading Twentieth-Century Culture." If such a learning experience can effectively further the students' cognitive and cultural awareness—and the success of the Carnegie Mellon curricular development is good evidence for this—the enormous value of current literary theory for pedagogy will be recognized.

Susan Horton's essay "Let's Get 'Literate': English Department Politics and a Proposal for a Ph.D. in Literacy" suggests a major revision of graduate studies in English. Her concept of literacy as referring to "the relation between an individual and a signifying practice" allows her to design a comprehensive program that eliminates the traditional disciplinary boundaries and opens up the multiplicity of cultural significations as an object of study and analysis. In the course of such a program, students would become critical readers of cultural texts, examining the production and reception of these texts as well as assessing the given methodologies for their inquiry. Even more importantly, students would recognize the connection between literacy and the construction of the self; they would discern how instruction, for instance, develops different kinds of literacy and thus shapes their experience of the world. Being aware of the power of the cultural production of selves, students could develop suspicion of and resistance to their teachers' attempts to impose their own notion of academic literacy. Seeing differences in literacies as something to be valued rather than suppressed would promote more dialogue between students and teachers and thus contribute to intellectual growth. If the "politics of learning" and the "politics of cultural transmission" are made issues of academic concern and academic programs, teachers will be learners and share in a meaningful collective enterprise.

Providing yet another perspective on the complex relationship between teacher and students, Jim Merod, in "Blues and the Art of Critical Teaching," explores some pedagogical responses to structures of desire and defense in students' behavior. Unless we make the students' own worlds of desires, beliefs, and experiences a guiding principle in our approach to teaching, we will fail to establish a critical dialogue with them, fail to recognize and surmount their resistance. If we are to accomplish such communication in the classroom we need to question our own authority and our tendency to impose intellectual identities on our students while ignoring their culturally shaped minds. Merod's discussion of the Blues as a complex cultural ensemble whose artistic energy is conducive to an open exchange between teacher and students illustrates what he understands by "the art of critical teaching." By choosing as a "critical text" an important but academically neglected element of American culture that can evoke students' interest and spontaneous reaction, thus permitting desire to break down the barriers of defense, Merod thinks he succeeds in stimulating the students' critical strength and self-confidence. Apart from the Blues' pedagogical usefulness as a means of disarming resistance, encouraging the students' own hermeneutic power, and opening up dialogue, Merod thinks the form invites the teacher to focus on the textual, social, historical, and ideological frames and, as a consequence, on the contradictions in our society, conflicts that the hegemonic ideology tries to negate. Critical teaching is based on critical interrogation, a habit of mind that should be imparted to students so they can join the teacher's effort to destabilize fixed hierarchical positions and canonized notions of truth. If critical teaching makes use of some "oppositional practices of everyday life" as discursive structures to examine, it may very well succeed in bringing the world into the classroom and elevating the student out of traditional subjugation.

A critical sense of history is what Richard Ohmann hopes to develop in the politically engaged teaching he portrays in "Teaching Historically." Through two examples foregrounding the links between signifying practices on the one hand and social, historical, and economic structures on the other, Ohmann attempts to explain why his materialist "master narrative" may be an emancipatory pedagogical strategy that counteracts the official sense of history and increases the students' ability to scrutinize and understand historical processes. When learning how to read advertising as a vital element of capitalist consumer culture, for instance, students must have some idea of this genre's historical development to realize that, as Ohmann describes it, the familiar technique of "linking products to social ideals and personal dreams" is not a natural, intrinsic feature of ads. As soon as students become aware of the fact that discursive structures depend on particular, changing social formations, they may gain confidence in their power to affect the direction of history. This perception of their own social agency should also result from learning how to read literary texts as historically embedded and ideologically inscribed works. Ohmann's experience with the historical approach in a required literature class at his home institution (Wesleyan) has made him conscious of its inherent problems, but he is nevertheless convinced that a history-driven pedagogy is more radical and instructive than any model derived from the tenets of poststructuralism.

Whereas the essays in the "Pragmatics" section scrutinize literary theory's political impact on curriculum design and instructional strategies, those in the third and concluding unit, entitled "Positions," focus on the politics of various disciplinary practices, ranging from the organization of the *MLA Bibliography* to institutionalized methods of reading and writing. All the writers in this section share the belief that these ways of ordering the discipline help naturalize an undemocratic frame for the transmission of knowledge.

The metaphor of colonialism, in which hegemony is maintained by subordinating and marginalizing others, dominates the argument of Reed Way Dasenbrock's "English Department Geography: Interpreting the *MLA Bibliography.*" According to Dasenbrock, a series of hierarchical divisions extends throughout the discipline along the demarcations of language, nationality, and period. Dasenbrock uses a great number and variety of examples to illustrate on several levels that the given structure of the discipline no longer represents its actual constituencies. Because the basic organizational principle is still nationality (primarily, British or American), deriving its authority from some long-lost political (and cultural) supremacy, it has become increasingly difficult to situate fairly and categorize the prolific literary output in English coming from various other parts of the world. Dasenbrock discerns strategies of appropriation and marginalization that fail to give these important writings the status they deserve. Reconceptualizing the "map" of literature and choosing language as a guiding principle would enable something like a comparative literature in English, allowing a polycentric rather than ethnocentric view of the world to shape the curriculum, reading lists, or conference sessions. Furthermore, this new emphasis would open up critical discussions of the social and political role of language, thus alerting students to the power of the symbolic order.

John Clifford presents a political perspective on writing classes in his essay "A Burkean Critique of Composition Praxis." Clifford's argument rests on the premise that the instruction of writing is an effective socializing service of the ideological state apparatus providing students with "rhetorical conventions of various normative discourses" that in turn shape the students' minds and mold their identities. Notwithstanding the valuable theoretical insights into that matter by Gramsci, Althusser, and Foucault, it is Kenneth Burke's progressive views on language and its importance as a political instrument that Clifford thinks deserve more critical attention in discussions about self-conscious and responsible strategies of teaching writing. Burke's work on rhetoric certainly strengthens the belief in the teacher's (and the student's) power of resistance to the homogenizing dominant discourse. Once we challenge the validity (and supposed objectivity) of the standards and rules for form, style, and organization of composition, revealing their ideological intent and political consequences, we are in a position to produce a counterdiscourse, an alternative model of reality. As teachers who are interested in increasing our students' critical capacities, we need to share with them our theoretical consciousness about the correlation between language and power. Only such consciousness will enable the students to intervene in the process of constructing discourse. Like Burke, Clifford is confident that social change can be initiated and promoted from within the walls of the university.

The teaching of writing is a political activity, and so is the teaching of reading. Peter Rabinowitz, who wants to see the links between literature and the world strengthened, formulates his argument for diverse reading techniques in his essay "Against Close Reading." In Rabinowitz's view, the centrality of close reading as a standard method practiced in the classroom and a standard literary approach shared by critics of all persuasions needs to be challenged; its underlying assumptions need to be examined. The matter-of-factness in privileging close reading makes us overlook the effects of our choice. Otherwise, we would have to notice, for example, that the strategy of close reading looks for dense, opaque, figurative writing and is less applicable to realistic writing. The inherent valorization of this procedure makes some (usually canonical) texts more significant than others, a judgment of literary merit that can hardly be considered "objective." Rabinowitz deplores what he calls "the disease of figurization," which, arising as a favored interpretive device from close reading, turns everything concrete into a representation of something more general or abstract and thereby undermines the value of literature as a mediation of historical and political reality. Literary texts do have referential significance and can make us more deeply aware of a variety of human conditions, but close reading is hardly the best way to promote such a learning experience. A student's perspective can be expanded by extensive reading of heterogeneous materials, however, which may ask for a variety of interpretive strategies and a critical understanding of the authors' differing purposes in writing. Through new ways of reading—so says Rabinowitz—our students may gain a "breadth of vision" that any responsible pedagogue desires.

This collection of essays is aimed at a wide professional audience. The discussion of theory in the institutional context of our university and college system, with diverse suggestions for an integrative and transdisciplinary approach toward knowledge, should be helpful to teachers of English and foreign literatures on the graduate as well as undergraduate levels. It is hoped that all those who are in the process of redesigning their literature or writing programs, or about to install interdisciplinary culture programs, will find the essays in this volume thought provoking. Those who have specialized in theory during their graduate studies and are about to embark on their teaching careers may be interested in learning about the praxis of theoretical discourse.

Perhaps the strong sense of pedagogical and political responsibility that all the contributors of this collection share will strike sparks in the minds of the readers.

NOTES

1. Terry Eagleton, *The Function of Criticism* (London: Verso, 1984) 10.

2. Terry Eagleton 90.

3. William J. Bennett, " 'To Reclaim a Legacy': Text of Report on Humanities in Education," *The Chronicle of Higher Education* 29 (28 Nov. 1984): 16.

4. Among those whose work contains proposals for "critical teaching," I want to mention Paul Bové, Terry Eagleton, Henry Giroux, Jim Merod, Richard Ohmann, Edward Said, William Spanos, and Raymond Williams.

5. See Gerald Graff, *Professing Literature: An Institutional History* (Chicago: U of Chicago P, 1987). Graff traces the gradual institutional expansion from classical study to study of the modern languages. Once English was established, American literature became the new alternative. After that, modern literature was approved as an option alongside the study of older works. Literary theory has become the new contestant for a permanent position in academia.

6. See Antonio Gramsci, *Selections from the Prison Notebooks,* ed. and trans. Quinton Hoare and Geoffrey N. Smith (New York: International, 1971) and his *The Modern Prince and Other Writings,* trans. Louis Marks (New York: International, 1987).

7. For an excellent discussion and elaboration of Gramsci's concept of "hegemony," see Raymond Williams, *Marxism and Literature* (Oxford: Oxford UP, 1977) 108–27.

8. Raymond Williams 112.

9. Raymond Williams 114.

10. Frederick Crews, "Do Literary Studies Have an Ideology?" *PMLA* 85 (May 1970): 424.

11. Frederick Crews 424.

12. Antonio Gramsci, *Prison Notebooks,* 7.

13. Thomas R. Bates, "Gramsci and the Theory of Hegemony," *Journal of the History of Ideas* 36 (1975): 353.

14. Gramsci, *Prison Notebooks,* 10.

15. Paul A. Bové, *Intellectuals in Power: A Genealogy of Critical Humanism* (New York: Columbia UP, 1986).

16. Jim Merod, *The Political Responsibility of the Critic* (Ithaca: Cornell UP, 1987) 63.

17. Edward Said, *The World, the Text, and the Critic* (Cambridge: Harvard UP, 1983) 9.

18. Gary Waller, David Shumway, and Kathleen McCormick have—in articles and talks—described their "issue-oriented" curriculum in the English Department at the Carnegie Mellon University. The total revamping of their program by creating courses clustered around the topics of language, history, and culture can be regarded as real alternative teaching practice. (See the "Pragmatics" section in this volume for essays by Shumway and McCormick.) Henry Giroux has, on various occasions, suggested structuring courses around the issues of power, language, and history to transmit emancipatory knowledge; see, for instance, Giroux's essay (co-written with Peter McLaren) "Teacher Education and the Politics of Engagement: The Case for Democratic Schooling," *Harvard Educational Review* 56.3 (1986): 213–38.

19. Jim Merod 128.

20. Michel Foucault, "Intellectuals and Power." *Language, Counter-Memory, Practice,* ed. and intro. Donald F. Bouchard (Ithaca: Cornell UP, 1977) 208.

POLEMICS

1

THEORY AS RESISTANCE

Mas'ud Zavarzadeh

—For Terri, theorist and pedagogue

. . . and your view of theory as an abstract apparatus of mastery—a "metalanguage"—leads you to the conclusion, for example, that poetry is, by nature, atheoretical. Poetry, in your discourse, however, stands for a structure of understanding: the specificity of the "esthetic" experience in general. Paul de Man, in his discourses, regards this to be the particularity of the "rhetorical," but it operates as the strategy of a transhistorical general "literariness" that resists theory. I, on the other hand, understand theory to be what I call an "intelligibility effect"—a historical understanding of the material processes and contradictory relations through which the discourses of culture make sense. I therefore find it difficult to see how any cultural act that produces "meaning effects" could be outside such historical mediations and the workings of social intelligibilities and be atheoretical. To produce and to understand meaning effects is always already theoretical. Poetry is as much a theory of reality as any other discourse; it produces intelligibility/knowledge, and knowledge is always an effect of cultural and political institutions. To say, as you do, that poetry is by nature atheoretical amounts to saying that poetry is a transdiscursive act that is auto-intelligible—that it makes sense and is meaningful in and of itself outside any cultural mediations and without being entangled in the materiality of the signifying practices of society. Poetry, in short, is declared to be a transcendental moment of self-identity, panhistorical plenitude, and nonmaterial transparency. To say that poetry is atheoretical is a partisan political statement and not, as you seem to think, a disinterested defense of the human imagination against the totalitarianism of theory, because what you are actually stating is that (poetry as the synecdoche of) desire is outside ideology. That this is a political program becomes clearer when you consider that it is aimed, among other things, at producing a particular type of subject. Reading poetry as an atheoretical and transhistorical discourse produces the reader as a nonconstrained, self-same (speaking) subject who is marked by autonomy and a direct, unmediated access to the plenitude of the imagination: an instance of presence free from all social contradictions. This notion of the subject is necessary for the maintenance of the existing exploitative social arrangements.

Sense-full-ness, I believe, is the effect of cultural assumptions or frames of intelligibility and historical practices of knowing—in other words, a "theory." Such an understanding of theory makes it impossible for me to comprehend how anything could be "by nature" anything—poetry or nonpoetry. Nothing is inherently ("by nature") anything. Things become "something" when they are used in a culturally senseful way, that is to say, when they are situated on a cultural grid of intelligibility in a social location. It is the process of such situating—the use of discourses to enunciate them—that produces a "thing" as (socially) "something." There are, of course, modes of representation that suppress the material processes involved in producing this cultural something and consequently attribute the "something" to the "thing itself" (that is, to the "nature of things"), but this suppressing is itself a mode of cultural behavior and a consequence of the social situating of discourses. It is, in other words, the effect of a theory of the real.

In short, poetry is not "by nature" atheoretical; it is your "situating" of the discourse of poetry—its particular uses by you—that produces it as atheoretical and "by nature" resistant to theory. In other words, the atheoreticality of poetry is the effect of your use of poetry. Since the site in which you produce poetry as atheoretical is your classroom, I would like to focus on your theory of pedagogy.

1

In his writings on drama, Brecht speaks of a familiarizing drama and a familiarizing method of acting and, in contrast to them, proposes his own defamiliarizing drama and theory of acting. In the familiarizing drama, the "walls" of the theater are demolished and the experience on the stage is represented as life itself. The audience is removed from its habitual cultural situationality and is transported to a world other than the one in which it lives its routine life; consequently, for a short period of time, the audience is "liberated" from the drudgery of bourgeois life into a libidinal exuberance and autonomy.

The actor in this familiarizing drama also acts in a "transporting" manner: engaged in what Stanislavski called "method acting" (36), she forgets herself (is liberated from her self) in the role assigned to her. Brecht thinks that familiarizing drama and acting lull the audience into emotional submission and intellectual passivity. It is a drama that, in short, merely liberates the audience from its bourgeois life but fails, for ideological reasons, to emancipate it. His own theory of drama is based on the notion that the dramatic should not conceal itself but, on the contrary, mark itself as such—as a constructed act, a social use of codes and language, a textual entity—and never allow the audience to forget that it, too, is playing a cultural role (the role, that is, of "audience") while watching others ("actors") play their own cultural role (producing an "esthetic" experience). The purpose of such "marking" is to prevent the naturalization of social processes. "What is involved here," he writes, "is . . . taking the human social incidents to be portrayed and labelling them as something striking, something that calls for explanation, not to be taken for granted, not just natural" (Brecht 125). The goal of this drama is to give the spectator the chance to "criticize" what it encounters "from a social point of view" (86). The Brechtian actor involved in such dramatic performances has no urge for self-expression, for "making a part one's own," for a "spiritual experience" (22–29, 91–99). Rather than becoming one with his role, he stands outside it and points to his role and thus never allows the spectator to forget that he is watching an actor: such an actor is necessarily for Brecht a calculating actor, and not a spontaneous one; she stands "between the spectator and the event" (58). She has no use for such "artistic" marks popularized by the culture industry as improvisation, vision, originality, or the "mystic moment of creation" (95) in the sense that the Stanislavskian "method actor" employs them to emphasize his own inner life. Such a foregrounding of the inner life allows social meaning to evaporate. It is in the space between the actor and the role to which he gestures that the audience intervenes and begins its interrogation of the ideology and/or dramatic representation (125). Brechtian drama and acting, in short, are a process of denaturalization—a theater with heavy, thick "walls" (of discursive practices), a theater firmly situated in the texts of history.

2

The site in which you construct poetry as atheoretical, namely your classroom, bears an uncanny resemblance to what Brecht describes as familiarizing drama. And like that drama, it produces certain ideological effects such as the panhistoricity of textuality (whether we call it "poetry," as you do, or generalize it into "literariness," as de Man does) that are necessary for the maintenance of the dominant social arrangements. (By "your classroom" I mean the structure of pedagogy that you put forth as the ideal site for pedagogical activities.) Like the familiarizing drama, your classroom attempts to become one with reality itself and to liberate itself from its cultural situationality as a classroom. Like the familiarizing drama, it encourages its audience/participants to forget that they are being produced as subjects by their cultural positionality and to abandon not only their present but their past and future as well. This is the classroom without walls.

Despite their seeming differences, the dominant humanist and poststructuralist pedagogies are alike in having always attempted to remove the "walls" of the classroom, since to remove the "walls" is to remove all traces of their own historical constructedness and their limits as cultural and thus political institutions. The hegemonic pedagogy is articulated by the prevailing relations of production, which need its ideological effects for their own reproduction. But to operate effectively with the authority of (noninstitutionalized) Truth, it represents itself as the autonomous search for knowledge, and attempts to erase all traces of its connections with the dominant economic practices that in fact determine what it "discovers" as "truth" and legitimates as "knowledge." The "walls" are markers of "institutionality," that is to say, the ideological embeddedness of pedagogy (drama) in the ruling socioeconomic order. Bourgeois pedagogy has always made the eradication of these "walls" a professional priority for pedagogues. This project has been carried out at different historical moments according to varying strategies that are legitimated by historically convincing and up-to-date philosophical and theoretical discourses. Humanism is only one, although the most familiar, of these historical strategies for removing "walls" (denying the institutionality) of the classroom. It is so familiar in fact that, for many, humanist pedagogy is identical with bourgeois pedagogy itself. However, bourgeois pedagogy has many historical discourses, and, as I have already hinted by drawing a parallel between your idea of "poetry" and Paul de Man's notion of "rhetoric," the most effective form of bourgeois pedagogy at this historical juncture is articulating itself in terms of poststructuralist theory. Poststructuralist theory/pedagogy, in other words, is the most recent updating of the processes and discourses through which the dominant ideology is reproduced. In the familiar humanist pedagogy, the "walls" are removed by positioning the pedagogue and the student as sovereign subjects who are the origins of "meaning" (like the "method actor," who "creates" a "character" through her "vision" and "originality") rather than agents producing meaning through the mediation of institutional arrangements that make certain "effects" intelligible as "meaning." Poststructuralist pedagogy removes the "walls" (the traces of the political) by offering textuality as a panhistorical truth, which is considered to be beyond ideology just as is the "truth" produced in humanist versions of bourgeois pedagogy. On the surface this may seem rather obscure, since the whole point of "textuality," in the overt discourses of poststructuralism, is to locate, with analytical precision, the markedness of truth in all texts of culture—including, presumably, the text of the classroom/the classroom as a text. But textuality in poststructuralist pedagogy operates in such a manner as to place the classroom without walls (the classroom as text) beyond the reach of history and thus achieve ideological effects similar to those produced by other types of bourgeois pedagogy. The putative "war" between humanism and new theory (poststructuralism) is not a war between discourses that support and those that oppose bourgeois pedagogy. It is rather a family quarrel to determine which discourse represents the truth (of late capitalism) with authority and in an up-to-date and thus convincing fashion.

The real "foe" of bourgeois theory is "political" pedagogy/critique/theory, against which humanism and poststructuralism are in fact united. An even cursory look at the reconfiguration of the power structure of the academy will indicate how the "Young Turks" of poststructuralism (who have very quickly become "Old") are now ruling the academy in a coalition with the traditional liberal conservatives (antitheorists) and the reactionary elements of "creative writing" programs that strives to contain radical theory and pedagogy. This is the "foe" that Hazard Adams (the *humanist* editor of an anthology aimed at the wide dissemination of *poststructuralist* theory) warns against. Mapping the quarrels on the scene of interpretation today, he concludes:

> The quarrel is sometimes seen as one between old style interpreters and the new style poststructuralist theorists known as deconstructionists. *But what I am concerned about here is a third force*... the triumph of a reborn sociology. So complete has this triumph been prophesied to be that the term "literary theory" is completely smothered by the term "critical theory," which in turn means only sociological analysis. Before this triumph has its way completely, we should ask what it represses. In the question we may yet rescue what must always be rescued from abstraction and generalization in order to maintain sanity: the unique and individual. (441, emphasis added)

It is to rescue the unique and individual (the subject of patriarchal capitalism) that resistance to theory has come about. Your "poetry" and de Man's "literariness" are all part of this discourse that attempts to project theory ("concept") as the embodiment of a coercive totalitarianism so that it can demolish it and thereby "rescue" the unique, cellular, nomadic, and particular *experience* (of the subject). By removing *theory as the critique of intelligibility* from the scene of "reading" texts of culture, "experience" is represented as the site of the real. By positing experience as the real, the resistance to theory actually protects the dominant ideology. However, there is no such thing as "experience" in culture; what is made sense of as "experience" is actually an "experience effect" that is constructed, by means of a theory of the real (a theory that legitimates the ruling social order), in the discourses of ideology. The politics of resistance to theory is one of collusion with the oppressive ruling social regime. The unity of the discourses of humanism and poststructuralism in their resistance to theory and in their opposition to radical theory and its consequences does not, of course, mean that humanism and poststructuralism do not distance themselves from each other. In fact, it is through various devices of distancing that bourgeois theory differentiates its diverse products (as in its production of consumer goods) and thus endows each of its manifestations with a seeming apartness and represents them as individual and unique theories in conflict with all the others.

This represented difference gives each theory a local legitimacy by making it more responsive to specific regional demands on the conjunctural level, while at the same time it adds to the effectivity of the bourgeois pedagogy, as an ensemble of all differences, in its global operations. The diversity, in short, ensures that the hegemonic pedagogy's agenda is reproduced in all sites of culture.

I shall call the ensemble of all the strategies that the diverse theories and discourses of bourgeois pedagogy use to deny the historicity of pedagogical practices and the politics of its truth, thereby reproducing the exploitative relations of production, "the pedagogy of pleasure." It does not matter whether the pedagogy of pleasure removes the "walls" of the classroom through the agency of the theories of de Man, Jacques Lacan, Michel Foucault, Jean Baudrillard, Gilles Deleuze, Jacques Derrida, Hélène Cixous, Felix Guattari, and Jean-François Lyotard, or through those of Matthew Arnold, F. R. Leavis, Lionel Trilling, Stanley Fish, Richard Rorty, Clifford Geertz, Wayne Booth, Elaine Showalter, Sandra Gilbert, and Susan Gubar, since my concern is with the global political effects of theories and not with their local differences.

The pedagogy of pleasure aims at demolishing the "walls" of the classroom and promises spontaneity, originality, and vision. Then, by virtue of these qualities, it places the student in a position of intelligibility from which she believes she is an autonomous, unique, ethical being. The concern with ethics as a set of strategies of self-fashioning that produces the "freedom" of the subject is as much the concern of Leavis and Booth as it is the focus of attention in Lacan and Foucault. It operates in the discourses of both humanists and poststructuralists as a means for containing the "political." "Pleasure"—for all versions of bourgeois pedagogy—is an "experience" for attaining "ethical" goals and subverting the political.

In the classroom without walls all participants are liberated for a short period of time (as short, in fact, as the class) from their cultural situationality (students, teachers, class, race, gender, etc.) into a libidinal unboundedness, into an "other" space without oppressive social roles, into a "playfulness" that is at odds with the "serious" bourgeois workaday life. Their liberation is achieved, however, not through entanglements with the materiality of knowledge/knowing and the social order that underwrites it, but by suspending those involvements. What is at work in this classroom is not "imagination" but what

Coleridge called "fancy." "Fancy" (as opposed to "imagination") is a "mode of Memory emancipated from the order of time and space and blended with, and modified by that empirical phenomenon of the will, which we express by the word CHOICE. But equally with the ordinary memory it must receive all its materials ready made from the law of association." "Fancy," consequently, has "no other counters to play with but fixities and definites" (Coleridge 1:305). Like "fantasy" in Barthes (*A Barthes Reader* 477) and "desire" in Lacan (292–325), "fancy" is an instance of ceaseless slippage from one "fixity" to another "guided" only by tropes that establish associations, similarities, and coincidences among the "fixities" and thus conceal the social logic that makes them intelligible. The sliding of "fancy" from one "fixity" to another along the trace of tropes provides the subject in this classroom with the illusion of "freedom" and unboundedness, but what she or he experiences is more a "liberation" (a relief) than an "emancipation": the outcome of an active intervention that transforms the existing social relations and thus situates the subject in a different set of relations. "Fancy," like "desire," does not intervene in the "fixities" and the social logic. All that "fancy" does is to temporarily displace the dominant logic by pleasure and put the subject of pleasure in a position of intelligibility from which he can momentarily suspend the "law of the Father" and all its injunctive rules, regulations, and institutions. As long as the class lasts, the unleashing of "fancy" produces a pedagogical space that is at odds with the institution of the "classroom." In removing this institutionality, "fancy" provides a sense of "liberating" the subject from the constraints and "seriousnesses" of bourgeois life and its rituals such as "education." The working of both "fancy" and Lacan's "desire" are markers of "loss"—that estrangement that is inscribed in the culture of capitalism and that both the humanist pedagogy and Lacanian psychoanalysis attempt to sidestep. Humanist pedagogy posits "loss" not as the effect of social relations but as a lack in the individual, while Lacan posits it as the very condition of existence of the speaking subject and therefore as having little to do with the social.

One of the most significant political features of the pedagogy of pleasure is that it places power/knowledge relations fully in the background or completely conceals them. The power relations that always exist in a pedagogical (social) situation are treated as accidental, as false and unnecessary "extras" that can be thrown away. Thus freed from social constraints, the student and teacher can relate to each other on equal terms as if they were in a "lounge"—or, better still, in that privileged space in the bourgeois "home," a living room (which is, of course, itself a culturally constructed site). Together on equal terms, they can continue what Richard Rorty tellingly calls "the conversation of the West" (394). The suspension of power/knowledge relations in these "conversations" is the outcome of a locutionary strategy devised to protect exploitative social arrangements. This point becomes clearer in Roland Barthes's "Inaugural Lecture" (Collège de France):

> What I hope to be able to renew . . . is the *manner* of presentation of the course or seminar, in short of "presenting" a discourse without imposing it: that would be the methodological stake, the *quaestio*, the point to be debated. *For what can be oppressive in our teaching is not, finally, the knowledge or the culture it conveys, but the discursive forms through which we propose them.* Since . . . this teaching has as its object discourse taken in the inevitability of power, method can really bear only on the means of loosening, baffling, or at the very least, of lightening this power. And I am increasingly convinced . . . that the fundamental operation of this loosening method is, if one writes, *fragmentation*, and, if one teaches, *digression*, or to put it in a preciously ambiguous word *excursion*. (*A Barthes Reader* 476, emphasis added)

"Power" is suspended in the discourses of the Barthian classroom, which subsequently becomes, to use his privileged word, a space of pleasure, of playfulness, of "fancy," while diverting attention away from (and therefore shielding) the economics of social power underwriting all present relations, including those in pedagogical institutions such as a "course" or a "seminar." For Barthes (and bourgeois pedagogy in all its forms) it is not "knowledge" or "culture" that is oppressive but the manner of their representation! The "radicalness" of Barthes's pedagogy, like other modes of poststructuralist theory, is therefore in the "manner" in which the student is situated toward knowledge (regardless of the content of knowledge), that is to say, "how" the student comes to know. Poststructuralist pedagogy inquires into the "how" of knowing, thereby distinguishing itself from the humanist version of bourgeois pedagogy, which mostly concerns itself with "what"—the question of the canon, great books, and the like. Poststructuralism regards its displacement of the "what" of knowing to be a pedagogically radical move. However, this staging of the discussion between "how" and "what" rigorously avoids the question of the *why* of representation, that is to say, the politics of representation: *why* a particular representation at a given historical moment is acceptable as a representation of "something" to the members of a particular group of people with historically determined class/gender/race relations.

The initial difference between poststructuralist and humanist inquiry embodied in the varied focuses on the "how" and "what" of representation eventually vanishes, since the humanist preoccupation with "what" finally turns out to be a species of esthetics: *how* to know *what*—"how," in other words, to grasp "what" through the rhetoric of its particularity and uniqueness. Both humanist and poststructuralist pedagogy, as Adams points out, regard abstraction ("concept") to be an instance of pedagogical falsehood. What is preserved in the rejection of abstraction ("theory") is the uniqueness of the individual and the irreplaceable nature of "experience"—the sites of operation of the dominant ideology.

At their most ethical moment, humanist and poststructuralist pedagogies address questions about the ways in which a given discourse is "legitimated" in a given historical moment; they "read" it. Yet, there is a vast difference between examining "how" certain ideas get legitimated and asking radical questions about their "legitimacy." In fact, as I have already suggested, by diverting attention away from "legitimacy" (why) to "legitimation" (how), rhetoric represents all existing discourses as legitimate. A rhetorician thus can be interested as much in the rhetoric of the Ku Klux Klan as in the rhetoric of imprisoned black South Africans; for the rhetorician, all social phenomena are occasions for cognitive inquiries. And of course this fits right into the prevailing theory of pedagogy and knowledge in the academy in terms of which all inquiries are equally urgent. Barthes's focus on the "how" of representation, therefore, is not an eccentric feature of his pedagogy but an integral part of bourgeois pedagogy itself, which aims at concealing its embeddedness in the economics of power. By focusing attention on "how," dominant pedagogy eventually achieves its main goal, which is to replace "intervention" with "textualization." "Textualization" is thus a new form of politics.

By forgetting and suppressing the "authority" of the (knowledgeable), such a pedagogical situation proposes that knowing (knowledge) is itself a nonpolitical act: the outcome of the encounter between an object of knowledge and a natural subject (in other words, empiricism), rather than the effect of the contesting discourses of culture and the structures of power inscribed in them. The view of knowledge as contestation, on the other hand, inevitably leads to the sites of these contestations, which are social class, gender, race, and labor relations. In bracketing the power relations involved in the production of knowledge in the classroom, the liberationist, familiarizing classroom achieves a significant ideological function: it erases the awareness of meaning as conflict by substituting "difference" for contestation and replacing conflict with pluralism. Through this erasure it rejects the notion of history as the struggle between classes and denies that knowledge is an apparatus of political power. It is in this conflict-free, pluralistic classroom of the pedagogy of pleasure that poetry is produced as atheoretical, and atheoreticity is in fact the ideologically necessary discourse for securing hegemonic social relations.

The pedagogy of pleasure uses a number of strategies to remove social struggle from the classroom and liberate its participants from the dailiness (the historicity) of their lives. Chief among these is the realization of this libidinal liberation through "laughter," "parody," "pastiche," and "play." In other words, it brings to the foreground an ironic stance that safeguards the integrity and wholeness of the subject and guarantees disengagement. "Laughter" is a mode of deliverance from the mundane and the routine and the only way that politically conservative pedagogy knows how to place itself at odds with the "other" (engaged) pedagogy. In poststructuralist theory, laughter, parody, irony, and pastiche are regarded to be apparatuses of subversion and devices for radically decentering bourgeois life on which other practices of the social are based. Through "laughter" (and other decentering means), poststructuralism deconstructs the "serious" in bourgeois life by textualizing its solemnities: by demonstrating, in short, that the "serious" is the effect of "concept" (that is to say, an instance of illusory self-sameness and presence), which is itself a language construct. Thus the strategic uses of parody, pastiche, and similar devices expose the solemn beliefs of the bourgeois (and all the practices based on them) as moments of textuality, sites of slippage, and aporia. The solemn, in other words, is subject to the laws of *différance* and as such is at variance with itself. "Laughter" textualizes the "serious" and shows how what it takes to be a self-identical idea/concept/belief is in fact "reversible"—both inherently unstable and without access to a grounding logic. Without such a logic, the "serious" loses the protection of "reason" and becomes hopelessly "ridiculous."

This deconstructive move that deprives bourgeois beliefs of their authority is what poststructuralist theory and pedagogy regard as their contribution to radical change. In fact it provides the "foundation" for a new definition of "politics" in poststructuralism. Politics, as far as contemporary poststructuralism is concerned, is not discourses and practices of power and economics, for example, but a set of reading strategies through which the easy access of the signifier to the signified is blocked and thus the traffic of meaning in culture is deferred through its *différance.* This deferring and *différance* are the locus of radical politics for poststructuralism. Laughter, parody, and pastiche are some of the devices that make this problematization of "meaning" possible, and as such they are essentially political and subversive devices. Poststructuralist pedagogy—the classroom without walls—is the site of the joys of reversibility: the deconstruction of the serious in bourgeois life and the libidinal liberation of the student in relation to serious "knowledge."

The institutionalization of "laughter" in conservative postmodern pedagogy is now well under way, as demonstrated in Gregory Ulmer's notion of "lec(ri)ture." Ulmer's writings synthesize poststructuralist theories of pedagogy in an effective and imaginative way. He deploys "laughter" as his inaugural strategy for overcoming the "seriousness" of traditional teaching, thus realizing the ethical goals of postmodern pedagogy. He calls the space within which he sets up his program a "textshop," a site in which pedagogy as a process is itself textualized (52). The pedagogy of pleasure is always anxious to get out of the "classroom"; therefore, it often calls the space of its operation by such other names as "textshop," "humanities laboratories" (mostly by poststructuralists), "studio," or "workshop" (by humanist pedagogues). The main apparatus of subversive laughter in the textshop is what Ulmer calls "lec(ri)ture": a portmanteau joining "lecture" and "*ecriture*" (in the Derridean sense of inscription and textuality). What interests him in this macaronic punning is the foregrounding of "ri"—lec(ri)ture—which makes the new word echo with laughter (*rire:* to laugh, laughter). Lecriture, then, is a lecture that is textualized and thus decentered from within since now—its "seriousness" gone—it is a discursive space within which "happy knowledge" is born. "Lecture as texts," Ulmer writes, "is a certain kind of placing or spacing, the point being to refocus our attention, as composers or auditors, to the taking place of this place. At issue in these lectures is the extent to which the *performance* aspect of the lectures (the scene of lecturing, rather than the referential scene, the 'diegesis' of the lecture) is foregrounded, violating the students' expectation of information as message or content" (43). Lecriture as a pedagogical apparatus "operates by means of a *dramatic*, rather than epistemological, orientation to knowledge" (38). Lecriture is an anticonceptual mode of knowing that situates the student in the *experience* of knowing and attempts to change her contact with knowledge. What is at stake here is not knowledge as content but knowledge as relation, and this "radical" pedagogical act—the change of relation—is brought about by "laughter."

Poststructuralism's claim that laughter and similar devices are radical strategies demonstrating the "undecidability" of bourgeois beliefs—by displaying them as instances of textual "excess," as slippages within the system of representation—and that such an operation is therefore a means for change is itself an example of poststructuralism's collusion with the status quo. The reversal of concepts/ideas through parody, satire, jokes, and other textualizing means, far from being a strategy of decentering, is in fact the most common strategy for conserving (through renewal) the prevailing common sense. Common sense uses parody, pastiche, and similar strategies to reassert itself whenever its limits are transgressed by oppositional discourses. It not only parodies the intruding discourses but, at its most radical moment, in fact directs the parody at itself to jettison those elements in its knowledge repertoire that have become historically unviable. In other words, by reflexive parody, auto-pastiche, and self-mocking, the common sense conserves itself through these tactics of renewal. "Laughter" then is far from being "radical"; it is a very conservative device. Overthrowing bourgeois solemnities when they have become historically and politically counterproductive is in fact one of the pastimes of the bourgeoisie. Jettisoning the "serious" is one of the most conventional modes of rescuing the authority of an imperiled common sense.

For instance, on his election to the presidency, George Bush—who is keenly aware of the limits of his own seriousness and the transgressive potentials of seriousness to undermine the laissez-faire politics of conservative common sense—decided to subject the "serious" to the "excesses" of parody and to "reverse" the solemnities of the presidency itself: deconstructive practices that made another pillar of the common sense, the *New York Times*, proclaim: "Bush Stands up for Impish and Will Veto the Imperial" (5 December 1988). The "imperial" is, of course, totalizing and repressive "seriousness," the "solemn." The "impish" is the general name for all deconstructive reading strategies and, in this case, Bush's tactics for debunking the "official": eating popcorn and watching *My Stepmother Is an Alien.* His "funny" rewriting of the presidency and authority and Derrida's witty puns and parodies in his "disrespectful" readings of the presiding texts of Western philosophy both "reverse" and "reinscribe" the dominant. But these reversals do not transform the asymmetrical power relations in which they are involved. In fact, the unserious, the funny, and the parodic secure those relations in a more ecumenical, casual, democratic, and noncoercive (hegemonic) manner. Parody is a discursive detour for achieving consensus by building a "community" of the laughing and the amused. "Laughter" does not intervene in the reigning social relations; it merely subverts them and thus purges them of their unproductive elements. "Laughter," in other words, is a strategy of containment and is complicit with (not oppositional to) common sense. Contrary to the poststructuralist claim that "laughter" (the carnivalesque) dismantles the dominant, "laughter" in fact renews the dominant and gives it a new lease on life.

This becomes even clearer if we briefly examine Bakhtin's idea of the "carnivalesque," which in fact lies behind some of the poststructuralist theories of pedagogy. In *Rabelais and His World,* Bakhtin theorizes the "carnival" in a manner that clearly "justifies" the existing social contradictions by postulating a politics of laughter. Like the poststructuralist theory of politics-as-parody, the "carnivalesque" simply textualizes social contradictions, arguing that social contradictions are textual constructs and thus unstable and "other" than what they seem to be; they are not contradictions but instances of "difference." The carnival in Bakhtin is a moment of uproarious laughter in which "the entire world is seen in its droll aspect, in its gay relativity" (11), and this for Bakhtin is a subversive act. Laughter in the carnival, however, does not change the system and structures of domination; it merely changes, for a short time, the relation of terms within the system—it brings about a passing "reform." The system reemerges in full power after the carnival is over. However, the incoherence of Bakhtin's notion of the carnival begins to surface when he goes on to claim in the same text that laughter, which only temporarily suspends the operation of the system, produces "the utopian realm of community, freedom, equality, and abundance" (9). For laughter to be effective it must maintain the terms of the system, yet for change to take place (utopia), these very terms must be overthrown! It is only through a change without transformation that the carnival/laughter can function, and that is exactly what makes the notion of laughter/parody/pastiche so appealing to contemporary poststructuralism. Like poststructuralist "immanent critique," laughter/carnival conserves the system within which it operates. Instead of contesting the ruling system and its structures of domination, the carnival, through laughter, merely builds, in Bakhtin's own words, "a second world and a second life outside officialdom" (6). In other words, through laughter, parody, and pastiche, Bakhtin and poststructuralist pedagogy provide the illusion of change by retreating into a "second" world while the first world (the dominant one) goes on.

In the same manner, Ulmer's "textshop" constructs a "second world," a parapedagogy, that simply jettisons the obsolete elements of traditional pedagogy only to renew its ideological effects. Through "laughter" the textshop merely rearticulates conventional pedagogy so that it can carry on its ideological role in a new language and in a new setting. The pedagogy of "lec(ri)ture" becomes the pedagogy of evasion (parapedagogy) rather than a pedagogy of "practice": praxis means forming, grasping, and changing oneself and a historical world through collective productive work that mediates between the object and the subject. Parapedagogy focuses on the relation of the subject to the discourses of knowledge and quietly brackets the subject's relations to social practices. It thus separates itself from the division of bourgeois life into playtime and work time by turning the work time into playtime. In doing so it leaves work time outside the intervention of the subject of pedagogy; in other words, it establishes a Bakhtinian "second world." The division of life into play and labor is part of the practices that prepare "the enormous majority" to "act as a machine" under late capitalism, but Ulmer's program simply ignores the political economy of this division and turns the classroom into a place for restaging the imaginary, a place in which students and teachers dream the (fusional) dreams of André Breton, which are not dreamable in the course of the daily life of the bourgeois. Ulmer's "solution" of dissolving work into play is a repetition that (to use Marx's word) becomes, this time around, a "farcical" repetition of the Fourierist program in which "textshop" takes the place of "phalanstery" and, by a regress to the "imaginary" in a haze of idealism, suspends the social division of labor.

Transforming the "labor/play" distinction will come about only when the social division of labor as practiced in late capitalism is abolished by class struggle, not by delivering "lec(ri)ture" to desire-full fancy-ing students. The classroom that Ulmer proposes is the trivial space that Robert Bork articulated in his fall 1987 senate testimony. "In a classroom," Bork told his audience, "nobody gets hurt." But in real life—in the courtroom—"someone always gets hurt" (*New York Times,* 16 September 1987, A-28). The fact is people do get hurt in the classroom, because it is there that they are recruited into those subject positions that are necessary for maintaining existing social relations. It is to divert attention away from this ideological role of the classroom that Bork plainly declares its vacuity and Ulmer turns it into a ludic space of difference, thus suppressing its "conflicts." The "other" pedagogy—the pedagogy of enablement—uses the classroom with walls as a space of contestation and a site in which emancipatory knowledge of the reproduction of social subjectivities and its politics is constructed through theory as the critique of intelligibilities.

The regress to the imaginary is the condition of possibility of the classroom of pleasure, the classroom without walls. There is, of course, a variety of classrooms without walls. Again, the difference between, for example, the traditional humanist and the new deconstructionist pedagogy is one of strategy. Both are founded on the notion that learning (like watching a play) should at all times be "fun," that is to say, a deconstruction of the "dull," structured reality. Neither, therefore, interrogates that structure, but merely brackets it, thereby protecting it from the inspection and intervention of critical pedagogy. An interventionist pedagogy, as far as humanists and deconstructionists are concerned, is "propaganda" (the name that the bourgeois endows on the political practice that aims at dismantling its ideologically secured beliefs).

3

In contrast to this familiarizing classroom, in which the real loses its strangeness and acquires a nonthreatening sameness and familiar look, there is the defamiliarizing classroom, in which social difference is recovered. This classroom—in opposition to the familiarizing classroom, in which the discourses of culture are produced as instances of transparency—is the classroom that aims at making itself opaque, "strange," "different" from the world outside. In the words of Brecht's devoted reader, Roland Barthes, this classroom is "a mask which points to itself" (*Critical Essays* 98) and, in so doing, problematizes itself as a cultural (that is, a political) situation. In contrast to the situation in the familiarizing classroom, the power/knowledge relation between the teacher and student and among the students in this classroom is fully foregrounded and made visible; student and teacher know at all times that they are in contestation over the "interestedness" (cultural significance) of the knowledge being produced and that at various times during the class the power shifts from center to center but at no time is it absent. This classroom recognizes that "authority" and "power" are always present in social situations. The question for this classroom is not then to essentialize and thus conceal the existence of "authority" by "lec(ri)ture" and other bourgeois pedagogical devices but to mark it, to put it forth for interrogation in terms of the historicity of its uses. This classroom understands that the question is not the existence/nonexistence of "authority," as poststructuralist pedagogy proposes, but the uses of "authority." To occlude contestations of authority and to contain issues on political legitimacy, poststructuralism essentializes authority, it places authority outside the history of its uses. "Authority" removed from the specificity of its uses in the Paris Commune or in fascist Italy thus becomes one and the same. The question, however, is whether authority is used to oppress or to enable. It is only through such an inquiry that it becomes clear how pernicious are the uses of authority in the ludic classroom without walls, in which "authority" makes itself invisible in the ideological haze it generates.

The participants in the defamiliarizing classroom are produced socially by their "work," by their "practice," in the sense I proposed (the production of discourses that construct knowledge); those who are not enabled to work (to produce discourse) will not have knowledge, they will remain powerless. This is a classroom with thick walls constituted by social codes, political constraints, and cultural and ideological practices. This thick-walled classroom is always at variance with the "real world," and it is in its variance—in the space it deliberately and in full recognition of the world places between itself and that world—that it interrogates the practices of that world and produces (theoretical) knowledge about it. It is through such knowledge that a critique of the constituents of "experience" is produced. It is precisely because of its function as a critique of experience that "theory," as I have suggested, is attacked by both humanists and poststructuralists. This classroom, in short, is a very unnatural place, a highly constructed time and space, a very coded stage.

I have already mentioned Barthes's idea of the "mask" that points to itself and thus recognizes itself as a construct, but I would like to develop some of the political implications of that notion a little further here. To be in such an uncanny "masked" classroom is similar to reading some of the (nonrealistic) fictions of such postmodern writers as Vladimir Nabokov. In reading *Pale Fire,* for example, it is impossible to forget that one is reading "fiction"; in being constantly reminded of this fact one is made aware of one's situationality as a "reader," made aware of the cultural role one is given to play. For instance, by being denied the pleasures of "method acting," the Brechtian actor is placed in a post of intelligibility from which he sees the distance between the *subject* and the *subject position.* Furthermore, he realizes that the subject position is a highly political locus constituted by an ongoing social struggle over the meanings of signs of culture and the consequent definition of the real. The reader of *Pale Fire* and the participant in the self-situating classroom with walls are also denied the pleasure of mimesis and the self-sameness of their subject positions, whether the self-identity of realism (the identification of "method acting") or the simulation of realia of the ludic textshop. Both become aware of the way they are the sites through which structures of social conflicts produce meanings. Conscious of this cultural role, the reader knows she is playing the role of the reader and is not a natural discoverer of meanings. She becomes an interrogator of the ways that cultural practices turn the "actual" into the "real" and make the world intelligible. She, in short, becomes a "theorist" (in the sense that I suggested earlier) and is consequently empowered as an instance of resistance: resistance to the social classes that put forth the reality of their class as the universal reality of all classes by concealing the codes of intelligibility involved in constructing the(ir) "real."

The idea of theory as resistance that informs the defamiliarizing classroom is, of course, radically different from the founding notion of the familiarizing classroom: "the resistance to theory." The "resistance to theory" in contemporary pedagogy takes a number of forms from de Manian deconstruction to the various types of contemporary humanism. All these positions, however, have certain cognitive views in common: all, for example, oppose "theory" to "criticism," privilege the "local" and the cellular over the "global," and reject "concept" in the name of the "particular" (experience). More importantly, they also hold a common political agenda rooted in an ecumenical liberalism that restricts political struggles for social transformation by replacing "conflict" with "difference," thus naturalizing "pluralism" and "coalitionism." Humanism and deconstruction defend the same canon and the same eclectic (*inter*)disciplinary practices as opposed to a radical, committed *trans*disciplinarity. Contrary to commonsense discourses, deconstruction does not dismantle humanism or its liberal pluralism and ethics of self-fashioning; rather, deconstruction perpetuates this regime of truth by renovating it through new technological devices (that is, new methods of reading and interpretation and novel ways of organizing texts along *inter*disciplinary lines). The humanistic notion, for example, that poetry is atheoretical is not only supported by deconstruction but developed into a hermeneutic principle: poetry in deconstruction, as I have said earlier, becomes an inescapable "literariness" (a configuration of tropes) that always resists theory (the "concept" in argument). "Resistance to theory" is the effect of the aporia between the "figure" and "argument." Humanist discourse and the discourse of deconstruction support the same political regime, thereby making the institutional "center" of literary and cultural studies a coalition of humanists and deconstructionists.

The Brechtian classroom reunderstands "theory" itself, a reunderstanding that is different from both the traditional notion of theory and the deconstructive view. Humanism's resistance to theory is conducted in the name of the uniqueness of the autonomous subject; deconstruction's "resistance" to theory, as I have suggested, is based on its own hermeneutic proposal, which holds that theory is a coercive totalization violating the rhetorical particular. As a language construct, theory is, in the last analysis for deconstructionists, not an instance of "truth" but the site of tropological playfulness. The "argument" of theory, in other words, is always already "resisted" by the "literariness" of its own discourse. Again, such a resistance to theory is a defense of dominant ideology. It is based on an idealistic view of signification, a view that regards "tropes" to be inherently meaningful regardless of the frames of historical practices of intelligibility through which they are read. According to this approach, a "metaphor" is always panhistorically a "metaphor"—an instance of "excess" that disturbs representation by turning its identity into *différance,* thus subverting the argument of the text in which it occurs. But "tropes" acquire their tropicity (their recognition as metaphor and so on) only within a given historical and cultural frame of intelligibility: metaphors can cease to be metaphors and literal entities can lose their literalness and acquire metaphorical density. Similarly, "excess" is always made intelligible as "excess" within the historical limits of a system of representation. Tropicity, then, is not a natural, inherent attribute of certain linguistic entities, but the historical effect of their *uses.*

The question is not whether they are metaphors, but how metaphors mean within a particular historical/social discourse. Sense-fullness (in this case, the sense of a linguistic construct as "metaphor") is the outcome of cultural and historical assumptions and practices of cognition, that is, a theory of intelligibility. The *différance* that poststructuralism locates in textuality is thus not panhistorical, inherent in textuality itself, but is in fact historical and political. Language/textuality is the instance of *différance,* slippage, and aporia not because textemes are unstable in and of themselves—that is, outside systems of social representation—but because they are the objects of class struggle and social contestation. In *Marxism and the Philosophy of Language* Vološinov situates *différance* in the social:

> Existence reflected in the sign is not merely reflected but *refracted.* How is this refraction of existence in the ideological sign determined? By an intersecting of differently oriented social interests within one and the same sign community, i.e. *by the class struggle.*
>
> Class does not coincide with the sign community, i.e. with the community which is the totality of users of the same set of signs

> for ideological communication. Thus various different classes will use one and the same language. As a result, differently oriented accents intersect in every ideological sign. Sign becomes an arena of the class struggle. (23)

Difference, in short, is historical and material. Thus nothing (neither metaphor nor anything else) is in itself and "by nature" always already anything. Things become "somethings" when they are used in a cultural, senseful way, that is to say, when they are situated in a social location by struggle and as a result become part of social relations. It is the process of such situating that (socially) produces a thing as "something." The uses of a linguistic construct make it senseful as "metaphor" and endow it with the "subversive power" of *différance* that it has in contesting the argument of theory. This contestation is itself historically specific, since it is enabled only within the historically determined frames of understanding in which a particular linguistic entity is designated as a trope and thus seen as an antiargument—an antiargument that, by the way, is a mode of "argument" nonetheless. The force of the trope, in short, is part of its historicity: in a given historical moment the trope is endowed with subversive power, which is seen (as a consequence of social struggles) as a forceful "argument" against the *other* argument offered by those linguistic items of a text that are historically specified (as part of the same social struggle) as nontropic.

Inquiry into these processes of sense-making is an inquiry into the way things (metaphors and other cultural artifacts) make sense and become comprehensible. An understanding of this comprehension effect is what I proposed "theory" to be at the opening of this text. Theory, then, is not—as humanists and deconstructive critics alike write it—an abstract apparatus of mastery, but an inquiry into the grids of social intelligibilities produced by the discursive activities of a culture. Theory, in short, is a critique of intelligibility. As a result of such a critique, readers in a culture become aware of the ways in which signifiers are always organized so that through them the world is produced in such a manner that its "reality" supports the "reality" of the interests of state power, gender, race, and the dominant classes. Through such a recognition, theory enables readers to historicize the "reality" of the ruling class that is put forth in cultural texts as the universal reality (of all classes) and thus to engage in ideological struggle. Theory, as Gramsci has suggested (323–472), is an ally in political and ideological struggle: theory as resistance, not the resistance to theory, is what marks radical pedagogy and distinguishes it from the hegemonic pedagogy of "lec(ri)ture."

The defamiliarizing classroom intervenes in the reproduction of dominant cultural meanings that lend support to the continuation of existing social relations. Radical pedagogy thus goes "beyond" the humanism of common sense and the undecidability of deconstruction. This going "beyond" involves, among other things, a reunderstanding of the subject of knowledge as not merely the cognitive one "who is supposed to know" but as one situated in the grid of class, race, and gender relations, in other words, as a "critical" one. But this going "beyond" is prohibited in almost all the discourses of contemporary theory. The discourse of humanism posits common sense as the limits beyond which pedagogy should not move, and for Derrida a going "beyond"—striving for a "post" state—is merely an expression of a desire, an illusion of "progress," a logocentric wish to get even closer to TRUTH ("presence"). It is, of course, highly instructive that Derrida's injunction against going beyond has not deterred him from undertaking a rather violent move beyond. In recent pronouncements about his nonopposition to presence he has revealed a side of his work that accepts mysticism as a mode of authentic knowing (Sturrock 769). In this he has indeed gone "beyond" and in a manner similar to that of Julia Kristeva, Philippe Sollers, and other *Tel Quel* intellectuals of his generation who are embracing mysticism (through a new reading of Martin Heidegger) as the region of unbounded (ethical) knowledge and libidinal freedom: a region free from the rancor of the political.

In contrast, the going "beyond" of radical pedagogy is not undertaken to acquire transdiscursive (mystical) knowledge, nor to foster the illusion that cultural meanings are somehow authorized by a panhistorical Truth. The "beyond" or "post" of radical pedagogy is not so much the site proximate to Truth as it is the space of opposition to the reigning Truth. It is in this space that the radical classroom intervenes in readings of the texts of culture by inscribing opposition and conflict in the production of meanings. The apparatus of such an intervention is theory as critique, a practice that, as Marx explained, does not "dogmatically anticipate the world, but wants to find the new world through a critique of the old" (*Collected Works* 142). It is in this sense that theory, to quote Marx (*Early Writings* 251) again, becomes a "material force" . . .

NOTE

This essay previously appeared in *Rethinking Marxism* 2.1 (Spring 1989): 50–70. Reprinted by permission of the editor.

WORKS CITED

Adams, H. "The Dizziness of Freedom." *College English* 48 (1986): 431–43.

Bakhtin, M. *Rabelais and His World.* Trans. H. Iswolsky. Cambridge: MIT P, 1968.

Barthes, R. *Critical Essays.* Trans. R. Howard. Evanston: Northwestern UP, 1972.

———. *A Barthes Reader.* Ed. S. Sontag. New York: Noonday P, 1982.

Brecht, B. *Brecht on Theatre.* Trans. J. Willett. New York: Hill and Wang, 1979.

Coleridge, S. *Biographia Literaria.* Ed. J. Engell and W. J. Bate. 2 vols. Princeton: Princeton UP, 1983.

Gramsci, A. *Selections from the Prison Notebooks.* Trans. G. Nowell Smith. New York: International, 1976.

Lacan, J. *Ecrits: A Selection.* Trans. A. Sheridan. New York: Norton, 1977.

Marx, K., and F. Engels. *Collected Works.* New York: International, 1975. Vol. 2.

———. *Early Writings.* Trans. R. Livingston and G. Benton. New York: Vintage, 1975.

Rorty, R. *Philosophy and the Mirror of Nature.* Princeton: Princeton UP, 1979.

Stanislavski, K. *Stanislavski's Legacy.* Ed. and trans. E. R. Hapgood. New York: Theatre Arts, 1958.

Sturrock, J. "The Linguistics of Writing: A Colloquium." *Times Literary Supplement,* 769.

Ulmer, G. L. *Applied Grammatology.* Baltimore: Johns Hopkins UP, 1985.

Vološinov, V. N. *Marxism and the Philosophy of Language.* Cambridge: Harvard UP, 1986.

2

POSTSTRUCTURALISM, POLITICS, AND THE SUBJECT OF PEDAGOGY

John Schilb

Last year I taught a course for the adult education program at the Newberry Library entitled "The Battle for the American Mind: New Critiques of the Humanities." It covered Allan Bloom's *The Closing of the American Mind,* E. D. Hirsch's *Cultural Literacy,* and essays by feminist critics of the literary canon. In addition, it included Plato's *Phaedrus* as an example of a "Great Book" and Zora Neale Hurston's novel *Their Eyes Were Watching God* as an example of a "non-canonical" work now garnering attention. Naturally, the syllabus triggered debates about what should constitute the humanities curriculum, foregrounding Bloom's advocacy of the "Great Books," Hirsch's invocation of "mainstream" cultural references, and feminists' critiques of authorized knowledge. Although most class members did not teach the humanities, they spiritedly discussed these topics. The course therefore enabled me to see how an audience outside the academy might plunge into its controversies.

Above all, I was struck by how the more conservative members of the class slighted pedagogy. Endorsing Bloom and Hirsch in the name of a "shared" culture "we" all must uphold even if it marginalizes various groups, they resisted analyzing how different students actually learn. Instead, they embraced the osmotic theory of education, assuming students can and should acquire knowledge merely from exposure to certain hallowed texts. They agreed with Bloom that students must simply let the "Great Books" speak to them, as if various mediating forces did not affect how various readers construe texts. They assented to Hirsch's implicit "building block" model of the mind, wherein the learner merely accumulates one item of culture after another; they tolerated his failure to discuss how students might form concepts for themselves instead of simply ingesting certified data.[1] Even those who questioned aspects of Bloom and Hirsch joined the rest in envisioning a freshman humanities core course that included practically every famous text ever written, as if students could rapidly assimilate one after another on a daily basis. At one point, most deemed it all right for junior high students to be bored by *Romeo and Juliet* because at least they would be "exposed" to Shakespeare.

The course strengthened my belief that reflection on curriculum should also involve reflection on pedagogy, especially given that a model of curriculum that reinforces inequity might be intertwined with dubious notions of how teaching and learning can proceed. To use the title of this volume, "pedagogy is politics," both in the sense that teaching can have political effects and in the sense that political analysis of the academy must encompass teaching practices as well as curricula. At first I thought certain class members failed to consider pedagogy because they were not experienced teachers, let alone humanities teachers, but then I recalled that it was two veteran teachers of the humanities whose best-selling proposals for education disturbed me. I recalled as well that most graduate programs and tenure committees in the humanities still do not value inquiry about teaching nearly as much as they do traditional scholarly research. Even so-called radical critics can prove reluctant to consider issues of pedagogy. Talking at the 1988 MLA convention with a scholar wishing to transform English studies into cultural studies, I was jolted when he showed far less interest in the praxis of teaching—and especially when he dismissed the potential validity of class discussion by sneering, "Oh, do you mean that sixties interactionist stuff?"

An exchange at the 1989 convention further underscored how curriculum theory can get distanced from pedagogy in the name of progressive causes. Addressing "The Political Responsibilities of the Teacher of Literature," Paul Smith emphasized course content, urging that literature be studied as an exclusionary discursive formation. In contrast, Jane Tompkins emphasized classroom process, calling for teachers to analyze how they wield authority. As the session ended, they grudgingly acknowledged that their agendas might dovetail, but until then they questioned each other's stance, and though both their emphases seemed worthwhile, the audience clearly found Tompkins's the more difficult to ponder and enact. Although she was hardly the first literary scholar to link politics with matters of classroom authority— several feminist critics preceded her—the reactions she provoked from Smith and others suggested how pedagogy can be an unexplored and even unwelcome challenge for those otherwise dedicated to transforming schools.

In recent years, however, several poststructuralist theorists have devised explicit pedagogical models geared to progressive social change. In particular, deconstruction has been tapped as a potential source of liberatory teaching principles. I myself have drawn on deconstructive theory in suggesting ways to improve composition instruction, finding especially useful its critique of the ideologies of textual realism ("Deconstructing Didion"). Nevertheless, I worry about certain calls for a poststructuralist pedagogy. When I read them I experience the same reservation I feel when I hear class discussion categorized as fruitless "interactionist stuff." They strike me as deriving far more from theoretical trends within the field of literary criticism than from intensive study of classroom circumstances, thus maintaining the traditional hierarchy of academic concerns.[2] For even though they challenge the "subject" of traditional teaching in the sense that they propose new texts and new modes of interpretation, they fail to probe how traditional teaching constructs the *student* as subject. If progressive champions of curricular reform are not to lapse into their own sterile version of the osmotic theory, however, they need to consider how their classroom actions might reinforce subject positions they wish to subvert. I believe advocates of poststructuralism or cultural studies need to pay sustained attention to *these* processes of subjection, contemplating them in ways that will ultimately lead students to work for the liberation of other people.

Changing how the student is constructed as subject entails a number of related teaching practices. It means considering how social differences can affect the interests, backgrounds, learning styles, and degrees of confidence that students bring to the classroom. It means examining how authority operates there as well as in the larger society, analyzing how traditional power relations might be rethought or merely reinforced when teachers and students meet. It means taking students' accounts of their own experiences as at least potentially legitimate avenues to knowledge. It means recognizing that learning can involve intuition and emotion, not just cold, hard logic. Overall, it means taking as a central classroom aim the empowerment of students as conscious, active subjects in the learning process, thereby enhancing their capacity to develop a more democratic world.

My thinking is influenced by the literacy teaching of the Marxist theorist Paulo Freire, whose ideas grew out of his work with laborers in Brazil. This project compelled him to recognize that illiterate people must actively investigate their own world to identify and articulate the social forces that have silenced them. Hence, he came to espouse a "dialogic" method of education, involving both students and teacher as co-inquirers into the conditions of their existence; this is opposed to the traditional "banking" method, which merely seeks to "deposit" information in their minds. I have also been inspired by Henry Giroux and Ira Shor, two of Freire's American followers. Both have sought to involve students by fostering "an intelligent engagement and reflective dialogue that considers the interrelated dynamics and effects of social class, gender, race, power, and history on their lives" (Giroux 50).

I am influenced even more, though, by the tradition that Tompkins in effect endorsed: the models of feminist teaching propounded over the last two decades. The political movement from which they emerge has long viewed the classroom as a potential site of democratic praxis. Of all the current schools of literary theory, only feminist criticism has consistently sought to develop a democratic pedagogy, in particular calling for greater recognition of how women students actually respond to texts. Although theorists of feminist pedagogy differ somewhat one from another, Frances Maher summarizes their recurring principles when she writes that

> a pedagogy appropriate for voicing and exploring the hitherto unexpressed perspectives of women must be collaborative, cooperative and interactive. It draws on a rich tradition going back to Paulo Freire, John Dewey, and even Socrates, of involving students in constructing and evaluating their own education. It assumes that each student has legitimate rights and potential contributions to the subject-matter. Its goal is to enable students to draw on their personal and intellectual experiences to build a satisfying version of the subject, one that they can use productively in their own lives. Its techniques involve students in the assessment and production, as well as the absorption of the material. The teacher is a major contributor, a creator of structure and a delineator of ideals, but not the sole authority. (30)

As Maher indicates, theorists of feminist pedagogy resemble Freire in criticizing the teacher who would simply dispense knowledge instead of helping the class dialogically produce it. They emphasize how such practices often reproduce patterns of domination, even when the content is supposed to liberate. Of course, they especially attend to "the hitherto unexpressed perspectives of women," examining how transmission models of teaching slight their viewpoints in particular, but this critique has grown to encompass other social differences that pedagogy has long treated invidiously, including ones of race, class, nation, and sexual preference. Feminist pedagogy thus opposes the habit of lumping students together and deeming them all empty vessels needing the teacher's authorized wisdom. It challenges not only conservative educators who demand that students acquiesce to the "Great Books" but also leftist ones who identify their students only with a social blindness they must set out to remedy.

Note that Maher still acknowledges subject matter and still encourages teachers to help their classes investigate it. In the classroom that she and other feminist theorists envision, students do not revel in sheer relativism (the conservatives' fear) or false consciousness (the leftists' fear). The collaborative approach Maher calls for in fact enables a more rigorous, nuanced, and socially responsible attention to course content than is possible when the teacher strives to be "the sole authority," for it allows students to assess carefully the diverse slants they and their teacher bring to the course topic. Furthermore, they continually ponder the conditions and procedures of their inquiry—struggling to understand what makes for truly democratic relations of knowledge, praxis, and power not only in the classroom but in the larger world.

The lenses of poststructuralism might find defects in the principles I have sketched. Indeed, it has increasingly questioned the concept of "experience" that has pervaded theories of feminist pedagogy, often accompanied by one form or another of the slogan "The personal is political." Critiquing from a deconstructive stance the anthology in which Maher's essay appears, Barbara Johnson comments that "on the one hand, it would be impossible to deny that female experience has been undervalidated. On the other hand, the moment one assumes one knows what female experience is, one runs the risk of creating another reductive appropriation—an appropriation that consists in the reduction of experience *as* self-resistance" (46). Johnson's warning implies three by-now familiar concerns about appeals to "experience": (1) they presume immediate access to reality, thus ignoring how ideologies and subject positions shape knowledge of it; (2) they consider the self to be homogeneous, thus ignoring its internal conflicts; and (3) they often wind up generalizing about a category like "women," ignoring differences between its members. But students bear in mind these reservations even as they relate their personal experiences. Feminist pedagogy has indeed privileged autobiography as a mode of classroom interaction, but it has done so precisely because it questions how the academy has universalized certain perspectives over others that personal testimonies might reveal. In soliciting them, it seeks through communal inquiry to disclose the cognitive limits as well as the cognitive advantages of the students' own social roots. If it encourages students to exchange their stories as potential sources of knowledge, it also encourages them to study how and why these stories differ, as well as how and why people not in the classroom might have other stories to tell. Thus, even as Diana Fuss agrees with Althusser that "experience can never be a reliable guide to the real," she contends that "such a position permits the introduction of narratives of lived experience into the classroom while at the same time challenging us to examine collectively the central role social and historical practices play in shaping and producing these narratives" (118). Even as the class invokes the stories of women students in particular, it can recognize with Teresa de Lauretis that "the female subject is a site of differences; differences that are not only sexual or only racial, economic, or (sub)cultural, but all of these together, and often enough at odds with one another" (14).

Certain readers of Foucault who emphasize the strains of pessimism in his work may insist that teachers' authority can never be seriously challenged and that students can never hope to thwart oppressive social structures.[3] But without denying how power can persist in the classroom and the larger world—and without taking the one as a simple mirror of the other—classes nonetheless can experiment with various distributions of authority, analyzing their differing effects on students' capacities for thought and action. Moreover, a sense of agency is required for students to undertake political analysis in the first place, even if it must be continually tempered by an awareness of constraint. Trying to slough off the more deterministic tendencies of Foucault and Althusser, many theorists now emphasize how resistance to hegemonic regimes and discourses is always present and at least potentially efficacious. This claim need not entail a romantic view of human beings as autonomous shapers of their own destiny, ultimately capable of surmounting all forces that hamper them. Paul Smith, for example, proposes that continued adherence to the notion of "subject position" can on its own terms breed hope because of the value in thinking about the conflicts between the various subject positions that comprise identity (*Discerning*).

As these remarks indicate, I think we should consider how poststructuralism might refine the model of teaching I have described, yet I also think we should acknowledge that poststructuralism itself has inadequately theorized how students get subjected in classrooms. To support this claim, I will look mostly at essays from the anthology edited by Atkins and Johnson, *Writing and Reading Differently: Deconstruction and the Teaching of Composition and Literature.* The book was published in 1985, and some of its contributors have altered their positions since then, yet it continues to influence the profession's thinking about how critical theory and pedagogy should relate. Although the authors even then were neither completely unified in their views nor responsible for what each essay said, I think it fair to critique what emerges as a central motif of the collection: much faith in deconstructionists' ability to liberate their students, little regard for how students could experience traditional modes of subjection even in the avowedly deconstructive classroom. In examining passages from certain of the book's essays, I will bring in the principles of teaching I have outlined to suggest how these writers' confidence in deconstruction needs to be qualified if the political effects they seek are to be produced.

Note how questions of students' agency, background, and authority get simplified in the very first essay, Vincent B. Leitch's "Deconstruction and Pedagogy":

> Out of such deconstructive thinking comes a certain strategic stance and practice for pedagogy. Nothing is ordained, natural, unalterable, monumental. Everything is susceptible to critique and transformation. "Arrangements," whether traditional or contemporary, can be "rearranged." To criticize is to cause crisis. In order to be successful, this teaching—suspicious, critical, discriminating, optimistic—must pass to students. What distinguishes such

> pedagogy is its grounding in *writing*. It is precisely the power of *writing*—to ordain, create, naturalize, and monumentalize—which produces the grounds for critique and transformation.
>
> As classroom discourse, deconstructive teaching ought in turn to submit its own language to depropriation. There might follow tactical assaults on and transformations of pedagogical grammar and syntax through excursive rhetorics and impure styles. Socratic dialogue, dialectical conversation, would probably be disrupted. Intelligibility would be put in constant jeopardy. If not "depropriated," pedagogical discourse risks ordaining and naturalizing its own critiques. In this case, criticism would remain discreet cultural conversation. (23)

In content, the passage apparently celebrates radical challenges to traditional classroom processes and epistemologies; more striking, however, is its own "pedagogical grammar and syntax." Although it calls for revolutionary deconstructions of habitually accepted phenomena, it curiously fails to invoke human subjects who might perform these maneuvers. It cites many actions, but it does not really specify their agents. Only once does the passage even allude to human beings, when it declares that "this teaching . . . must pass to students." Even here, though, it portrays students as recipients or objects of an action, not as agents. Moreover, the passage leaves unclear what "passing" might entail. Does the teacher transfer something to the students, bestow something on them, model something? Does the teacher's personality emerge as significant during the "passing" of "this teaching"? Can "this teaching" itself be transformed in "passing"? By referring to "teaching" as a substance "passed" rather than as a process involving students to begin with, Leitch suggests that the class should accept his principles as automatically valid. Yet whatever the legitimacy of these ideas, a teacher seeking to implement them would need to consider how and why various kinds of students might have various reactions to them, including hostility and fear. Such analysis would presumably involve studying the personal situations that students bring to the classroom as well as the roles they might find encouraged there, intentionally or not.

In other words, Leitch valorizes the "classroom discourse" of "deconstructive teaching" at the expense of attention to the particularities of context—the wide spectrum of purposes, situations, and degrees of agency that students may experience during this discourse. He does state that "deconstructive teaching ought in turn to submit its own language to depropriation," but what follows in the passage is merely a renewed burst of deconstructionist vocabulary, not various languages that students may present along with their various social implications. Leitch thereby seems to exemplify a tendency that Barbara Foley associates with Derrida. Contrasting Derrida with Marx, she suggests that he privileges the discourse of deconstruction itself as the prime engine of resistance to oppression rather than focusing on "a historically specific class-subject" as the agent of change (127). Similarly, Leitch concentrates far more on "the power of writing" than on the varying power of students to engage in "critique and transformation." And there is no need to share Foley's concept of the proletariat as the subject of history to question Leitch's neglect of social class along with gender and race in referring to "students." By making that reference so brief and bare, he in effect posits a generic student as well as a passive one, even though deconstruction supposedly affirms heterogeneity. As I have emphasized, students do not experience social reality in generic ways; they might operate from very different positions even when they collectively seek to alter it. Because he does not actually explore the relations of teachers and students to one another and to the deconstructive activities he cites, Leitch does not actually help his readers understand how courses might enhance students' political consciousnesses and result in their developing strategies for political change. Although I think he sincerely desires these effects for teaching, he engages in apocalyptic rhetoric generated by the scholarly world of literary criticism, not strategy based on careful analysis of how various forms of stratification affect everyday lives. As Foley remarks in her treatment of Derrida, "if words could kill, the last vestiges of Western metaphysics would now be six feet under" (18–19).

In the second essay of the anthology, "Textshop for Post(e)pedagogy," Gregory Ulmer also curiously neglects to invoke human subjects when he writes early on that "classroom discourse is now responsible for experimenting with its own realist, representational conventions and for taking into account its own heterogeneous nature (being a scene that is rich in nonverbal and performance supplements to verbal communication)" (38–39). If the sentence had said more about who in the classroom does the experimenting, supplementing, and communicating—and what the relations might be among the various parties allowed to engage in these actions—Ulmer conceivably might have transcended his own rhetorical performance here in a way that would have illuminated how students ultimately can be empowered by "post(e)pedagogy." To be fair, he does go on to mention specific classroom activities and students' potential responses to them, but the two main actions he writes about—his parodic introduction of Harold Bloom to an audience and his design of a "textsheet" also soliciting parody—seem to involve mostly his own "pleasure" (59), with no details provided of how particular students got much out of it.

Ulmer's failure to elaborate how students might gain at least some authority for themselves instead of merely reveling in his ludic virtuousity derives, I think, from his identification of contemporary teaching's basic challenges. For Ulmer, "the principal pedagogical problem of our era" is "the discontinuity brought about by modern science separating formal space (the space in which we think) from phenomenological space (lived experience)" (49). He claims "the real issue of our material" that students must confront to be "not what literary works mean, but why one writes in the first place; not the work of analysis, but first of all, the pleasure of the creative process" (56). Leaving aside the possible oddity of an avowed poststructuralist's using such metaphysically flavored terms as "the principal pedagogical problem" and "the real issue," Ulmer disregards sexism and other kinds of oppression as he focuses on the supposedly intrinsic validity of particular esthetic talk. Certainly gender differences have been closely interrelated with traditional dichotomizations of "formal space" and "phenomenological space." Certainly sex/gender economies throughout history have differentially affected people's ability to cultivate "the pleasure of the creative process" within the public sphere. Furthermore, reflecting on how men and women might react to a male instructor as authority figure—whether he tries to impress on them the canon of the Renaissance or the celebrated precepts of Barthesian *jouissance*—might have led Ulmer to consider the chance that his strategies would not fill all his students with a sense of their own potential for meaningful action. By implying, as Leitch does, a generic student, Ulmer can be said to enact the separation of "the space in which we think" and "lived experience" that he otherwise decries. One way to overcome this breach is to consider, through the group dialectic encouraged by feminist pedagogy, the situational differences between people routinely masked by references to "we."

In a subsequent article, "Textshop for Psychoanalysis: On Deprogramming Freshmen Platonists," Ulmer gives more details of classroom praxis, but in a way that still marginalizes how power has involved gender differences. Discussing how his sense of the surrealists' accomplishments leads him to have his students create readymades, he reports that "the students are surprised to find themselves laughing throughout the entire exhibit as each artist presents his or her work in turn, framed in a brief narrative describing the process of composition. One object—a vise with a letter addressed to the artist's mother clamped firmly in the grip, swathed in a pair of men's briefs with the screw lever protruding through the flap, entitled 'The Whore Moans' —quite stunned the group with its provocative implications" (763). Yet Ulmer does not spell out these "provocative implications." Did all the students "find themselves laughing" while at the same time being "quite stunned"? Given the strong possibility that male and female students reacted differently, Ulmer's failure to elaborate is even more frustrating. Addressing the possibly different responses within the class might have led Ulmer to "provocative implications" raised by the students rather than by the object. In turn, Ulmer's tendency to evoke a universal student as the subject for his teaching might have been weakened.

Part of the problem here is that Ulmer again assumes the ultimate validity of his planned course content, so that his theory of pedagogy focuses on its delivery rather than on the various ways that students might incorporate it into their own lives. Moreover, Ulmer's certainty prevents him from contemplating the authority he adopts in the classroom and the ways that students might share authority with him. They may get to create their own art objects, but the doctrine of "deprogramming" he pushes them to accept threatens to objectify *them* by rooting them in traditional subject positions as students. Ulmer laments that students "still resist the claims of the original surrealists" (762), and with reference to psychoanalysis he proceeds to discuss how the classroom must involve "transference" so as to "deal with" their "resistance" (763). What he himself does not confront is the possibility of countertransference, of his own "resistance" to contingencies that might disrupt his complacency. Without analysis of this sort, the students might be far more conscious of the teacher's authority than they are of the putatively radical ideas the teacher is advocating.[4]

In their later essays in *Writing and Reading Differently,* Andrew P. Debicki and Jasper Neel also fail to consider that poststructuralist teachers might inadequately contextualize the alleged subversiveness of deconstruction, possibly even growing authoritarian in their effort to transmit allegedly liberatory content. Debicki's comparative essay "New Criticism and Deconstruction: Two Attitudes in Teaching Poetry" concludes that "a deconstructive perspective will make the students work harder on developing their own readings and at confronting other readings creatively; it will help them to transcend simplistic visions of literary texts, of other systems of signs, of the world around them" (181). But Debicki fails to explain how his own students moved from interpretation of literature to interrogation of social structures—if they did—once they adopted a deconstructive stance. Indeed, the only result of his teaching that he identifies, along with the generation of class discussion, is his students' privileging of texts like Pedro Salinas's, which "offered the richest play of difference and . . . provided the greatest opportunity for . . . extension of the text's possibilities" (181). The outcome seems merely the shifting of various works and interpretations on the literary stock exchange.

As with Ulmer's valorizing of play, Debicki's faith in the power of multiple perspectives does not include sustained reflection on the broad network of social forces that deconstruction must contend with to be effective outside the literature classroom. Indeed, it would have been useful for Ulmer and Debicki to have considered how play and multiplicity frequently have been co-opted. For example, the state, in its general domination, has often encouraged the Bakhtinian carnival as a cathartic moment, and late capitalism has wanted the popular mind decentered enough to embrace the products of a consumer economy. Furthermore, as Peter Dews has pointed out, text-based modes of interpretation such as deconstruction can do only so much to clarify how institutions work. Dews rightly observes that "deconstruction is centrally concerned with exposing the mechanisms whereby texts generate effects of meaning and truth while, at the same time, undermining them—in other words, with logical contradictions. Political antagonisms, however, cannot be reduced to logical contradictions" (35). As feminist criticism and pedagogy have repeatedly suggested, textual study can eventually lead students to analyze how "political antagonisms" influence the very acts of reading, writing, and thinking, but a class probably will not reach this point if it is encouraged simply to appreciate how textual meanings abound rather than to ponder how social circumstances might cause its members to interpret a work differently.

Debicki avoids this latter approach when he neglects to explore the effects on his female students (and his male ones, for that matter) of several references to women in Salinas's poems. Although he notes with some apparent misgivings Salinas's comparisons of sand to a flirting woman, electric light to a submissive princess, typewriter keys to nymphs, and spring to a model/mannequin, he does not indicate how his students reacted to these analogies and how discussion of them might illuminate cultural practices reinforcing gender inequities. The omission is especially evident when he writes that "the hypothetical New Critic, who saw in the metaphor of sand as woman a means of embodying the theme of fleetingness, was seeking closure; the deconstructionist, who viewed it as a 'seam' and an invitation to explore diverse implications that were engendered by it, was providing for the openness and the multiple possibilities of the text" (175). Note again that Debicki valorizes the traditional object of literary study, even though he wants to replace the dominant postwar approach to the text with another theory of interpretation. Students would broaden their awareness of culture and politics, however, if they used their responses to examine how schools and other institutions "engender" people through stereotypes like "the flirt."

Such an altered focus would have the additional virtue of enabling students to draw on their own encounters with men and women, so that cognitive authority in the classroom gets distributed more widely than is usually the case. Although he alludes to student discussions, Debicki does not describe a classroom structure that would render his own beliefs vulnerable. Indeed, I suspect he exerted significant control over the students he mentions, even though he suggests that his favorite theory of literature inevitably confers power on them. As with Leitch's pedagogy, the actual scene of teaching remains conveniently vague. Prior to analyzing the first Salinas poem in his essay, Debicki identifies it as one that he "recently taught to a group of students influenced by deconstruction" (171). But was he not the influencer? Later he reports that "this new view of Salinas's poetry emerged very strongly when I studied it with a class that had been reading deconstructive criticism" (180). But was not he the one who had them read it? Shortly afterward he remarks that "once the class was conscious of the ways in which a play of differences is produced within a text, it by necessity came to see its task, not as the arrival at definite interpretations, but as the extension of the text's possibilities" (181). But was not he the shaper of the consciousness, the "necessity," and the task? Debicki seems disingenuous, therefore, when he goes on to state that a class influenced by New Criticism "will be more likely to expect an authoritative solution to all of its problems on the part of the teacher" (181). Most likely, a teacher's authority has been very much at work even in Debicki's deconstructionist class, establishing a framework in which certain "problems" are likely to arise and certain others beyond the traditional purview of literary studies are not. Yet that authority must be confronted by both students and teacher to begin even a rudimentary analysis of how power operates in society.[5] Significantly, most of Debicki's essay is occupied by his own textual exegeses—just as descriptions of how actual students learn and how they can act in wider public realms are virtually absent from the entire book.

In "Plot, Character, or Theme?: *Lear* and the Teacher" Neel unwittingly indicates the chance of a poststructuralist teacher's communicating authoritarian metamessages through the essay's interesting repetition of certain language. At one point, he declares that

> *Lear* is, in fact, unreadable in any sort of permanent way. The pedagogy of the twentieth century, however, is founded on the assumption of permanent readings. Students know intuitively that such readings are *forced* on the text. Their response is normal: "That's the teacher's opinion. My opinion is just as good, but I need the grade." Or, "There is no way Shakespeare could have known all the stuff the critics say." (198, my emphasis)

But note the words he uses at the end of his essay:

> Students expect the *Lear* of plot, character, and theme. As these terms are deconstructed, a process of reading literature is deconstructed also. More than that, a way of reading life is deconstructed, for without plot, character, and theme to obscure the forever rereading which is reading, students are *forced* into a labyrinth of linkages where they *give up* the expectation of origins and endings and enter the realm of the signifier where

> fools quote the wizards who will live after them. (201–2, my emphasis)

At first, the word *forced* receives its usual negative connotation, for Neel associates it with the attempt to promote false closure in interpretation. At the conclusion, however, it does not strike him as negative at all, for he associates it with a teacher's alleged success in getting students to adopt deconstructive thinking. Yet even here a term like *forced*—and its companion term *give up*—ought to raise questions about how democratic the teacher's classroom really is, no matter how unconventional the school of literary interpretation being promulgated. For example, who is doing the deconstructing in Neel's second paragraph? Once more, a human agent is missing. Because "students" are mentioned only as the passive objects of "forcing," and because the essay has barely referred beforehand to what *they* might do in the classroom, Neel implies that the teacher is the sole initiator of learning, being the disseminator of a particular critical methodology. The student who feels "forced into a labyrinth of linkages" might very well want to say again, "That's the teacher's opinion. My opinion is just as good, but I need the grade." At the least, Neel has failed to sketch here what a truly deconstructed classroom praxis might look like, choosing instead to suggest that students will gain radically new benefits in their education if they simply heed their teacher's assaults on orthodox conceptions of literary texts.[6] In addition, Neel resembles Debicki in moving easily from "reading literature" to "reading life," as if complex social dynamics could be deciphered through the exegetical techniques currently nurtured by a particular academic discipline. As I have suggested regarding Debicki, teachers stand a better chance of getting their students to investigate "life" if they encourage those students to investigate collaboratively their own views and circumstances. A text like *King Lear* might still be used to provoke discussion, but students would also discuss the contexts of their lives and the development of their present inquiry, thereby testing claims for the liberating power of literature and its deconstructions.

Paul Northam's essay "Heuristics and Beyond: Deconstruction/Inspiration and the Teaching of Writing Invention" puts in starkest form the premises that disturb me in these contributions to *Writing and Reading Differently.* Above all, he attributes to deconstruction an inherent capacity to enhance students' powers of critical thinking, regardless of their particular backgrounds and the deconstructing teacher's own classroom behavior. Barely hedging with the syllogistic connection he wishes to draw between deconstructive teaching and students' cognitive growth, Northam writes that "deconstruction is (potentially) a powerful aid to inspiration. The student who reads so closely has a greater chance of finding in an essay . . . the inspiration to write about some element of that text; she or he is likely to discover a new outlook worth exploring, worth considering, worth caring about. It is therefore likely . . . that such a student will write an essay more noteworthy than will readers not trained in deconstruction" (122). Northam provides no examples of student writing to support his assertion; even if he had, he would have needed to elaborate his concept of "noteworthiness," especially given the recent attention of composition scholars to the effects of social context on criteria for "success" in writing (see, for example, Bizzell). What counts as "noteworthy" for some people or situations may differ from what counts as "noteworthy" for others. But Northam must be acontextual here, because to consider the effects of deconstruction in a range of teaching contexts might be to weaken the universal status of its appeal for him. Similarly, to confer preeminent status on a certain kind of "training" in "reading," he needs to slight other factors that can boost or constrain a writer's inspiration, including the different kinds of social circumstances the writer might face inside and outside the classroom.

Committed to a particular form of "training" popularized by literary studies even as he professes concern for students' liberation, Northam suggests that he wants to impose contours on how they achieve it. Note how the parenthetical observation that concludes the following statement clashes with what precedes it: "Students who read deconstructively are thus trained to approach a text with *freedom,* to see the text as intertwining threads of signification that they are as *free* to unravel as anyone else (such readings *cannot* be arbitrary, of course—a deconstructive reading *must* begin with the univocal or logocentric interpretation, which it then proceeds to unravel by a more or less *definable mechanism*)" (122, my emphasis). When he explains how a deconstructive reading "must" begin, Northam confuses deconstructionists' actual processes of thought with how they eventually structure their arguments; Derrida does not necessarily examine a text through the same steps he cites in his printed analysis of it. By setting up deconstruction as a "mechanism" for students' "freedom," Northam fails to consider how any "mechanization" of teaching praxis might not only stultify particular students' thoughts but also preclude their developing an intuition of "freedom," making them sense instead their subjection through traditional classroom relations.[7] Moreover, the belief that "freedom" can be produced through a "mechanism" once again renders a key term acontextual, for it ignores how "freedom" can take on different meanings, potentialities, and impediments for different people in different situations. Students' and teachers' recognition of this seems crucial if they are to work for their own "freedom" and that of others. I, for one, thus react with a great deal of skepticism to Northam's claim that "obviously, a deconstructive habit of mind changes things" (123). As I have suggested, I think a deconstructive habit of mind might actually be quite limited in its ability to change things if it is not combined with attention to gender and other differences; to the role of all authority, including the teacher's; to the ways in which students themselves might create valid approaches to knowledge; to students' personal investments in their learning; and to the encouragement of students as vigorous and aware agents, working for a more equitable and inclusive democracy.

At this point, I feel compelled to address a question my argument may have stirred: am I not confusing what people say about their teaching with that teaching itself? Is it possible that the theorists I have criticized teach as I would like them to teach, and my criticisms merely apply to some unfortunate signals given off by their descriptions of their ideal classroom? I suppose so, but when they keep gliding past issues that feminist pedagogy has raised, I grow less inclined to dismiss their evasion as oversight. At any rate, whatever the realities of the classroom practices from which their texts have emerged, readers have only the descriptions to attend to and be influenced by. Moreover, just as performative elements in these texts are at odds with the revolutionary content they are designed to express, so the poststructuralist teacher's classroom performance can wind up giving students customary impressions of pedagogical authority instead of enhancing their personal talents for critique.

Of course, by calling attention to possible discrepancies between what a text says and what it does—to what a teacher says and what that teacher does—I could be said to rely on an approach heavily identified with poststructuralism, especially of the de Manian variety.

It could even be argued that the theorists I have questioned fail in not being as rigorous as de Man himself—that he, too, would have had problems with their depictions of the classroom. Indeed, I can imagine him scorning Ulmer's vision of it, for example, as "programmatically euphoric utopianism," words that come from "The Resistance to Theory" (in *The Resistance to Theory* 12).

Yet even though many admired his teaching, de Man also failed to reflect on students as the subjects of pedagogy, choosing to concentrate instead on the elements of literature he thought needed to be promoted. In "The Resistance to Theory" he asserts that "to the extent . . . that they are theory, that is to say teachable, generalizable and highly responsive to systematization, rhetorical readings, like the other kinds, still avoid and resist the reading they advocate" (18). In other words, deconstruction can betray itself if it turns its emphasis on the indeterminacy of textual meaning into a predictable classroom procedure. Truly deconstructive teaching, de Man intimates, would question its own propensity for lapsing into predominant routine. Otherwise, though, he resists thinking much about teaching here. He makes his most direct comment about it at the start: "Overfacile opinion notwithstanding, teaching is not primarily an intersubjective relationship between people but a cognitive process in which self and other are only tangentially and contiguously involved. The only teaching worthy of the name is scholarly, not personal; analogies between teaching and various aspects of show business or guidance counseling are more often than not excuses for having abdicated the task" (4). The bulk of his essay then explains the nature of literary language, suggesting that "the task" of teaching is its elucidation. By trivializing sensitivity to teacher-student relations as a perilous lapse into "show business" and "guidance counseling," however, de Man himself seems "overfacile." In fact, what he writes soon after about resistance to theory seems to characterize his own attitude toward matters of classroom interaction: "It is a recurrent strategy of any anxiety to defuse what it considers threatening by magnification or minimization" (5). What gets threatened here is de Man's identification of the purpose of teaching: if this aim is to be defined and controlled simply by the interests of literary scholarship, teacher and student must be seen as "only tangentially and contiguously involved." Such a move threatens to keep students in their traditional positions within the classroom, however, maintaining them as generic beneficiaries of the teacher's transmitted wisdom instead of elevating them to the role of co-inquirers with various needs and orientations.

Moreover, the attempt to make teaching responsive only to the literariness of language marginalizes the issue of students' ability to effect social changes responsive to a wide range of people. It dodges the task of building, in the classroom and the world, relations between "self" and "other" that can empower both. In "The Return to Philology" (in *The Resistance to Theory*), an essay that celebrates Reuben Brower's New Critical method of teaching, de Man claims that it is "deeply subversive" (24). But subversive of what? As with other terms in the essays I have discussed, the idea of "subversion" here is vague and acontextual. Although the wording carries an apocalyptic charge, the connection between Brower's "subversion" and a student's capacity to effect more conspicuous "subversion" of political orthodoxy is left untheorized. To explore it, however, would be to relate de Man's model of teaching to more issues of social context than he apparently wished to confront.

Responding to accusations against de Man that have emerged with the rediscovery of his wartime collaborationist writings, critics like Barbara Johnson, Jonathan Culler, and J. Hillis Miller have insisted that he steadily became a keen analyst of fascist ideology. To consider him so, I think, is to confer on his career a tidy narrative shape that a deconstructionist would ordinarily suspect, yet de Man's late essays do turn toward issues of ideology, especially as it is buttressed by principles of esthetics. What troubles me is that his remarks on teaching serve to defer reflection on it as a praxis—more specifically, on how it can encourage students to support particular ideologies and to undermine others. His approach to texts can indeed be adopted to critique the "programmatically euphoric utopianism" of particular theorists promoting deconstructive education, but his own programmatic advocacy of deconstruction as a pedagogical force should not go unchallenged.[8]

Even though I have used the tools of deconstruction to identify the political limitations of certain works endorsing it, I have tried to keep in mind Peter Dews's warning that "political antagonisms . . . cannot be reduced to logical contradictions." For that matter, I suspect that teachers can help their students to a sharper awareness of political antagonisms and political affiliations only by encouraging them not simply to celebrate "logical contradictions" in texts but also to understand how they and others are influenced by complex social processes. I want to emphasize that these include processes operating in the classroom, for despite the claims of the osmotic theory, students are the subjects of pedagogy, and if pedagogy is not merely to enforce their continued subjection, they need the chance to subject *it* to their own active scrutiny.

NOTES

1. Hirsch himself may argue that he recognizes concept formation through his emphasis on schema theory; see Scholes, however, for a cogent demonstration of how Hirsch misuses the notion of schemas, equating them with accumulations of vocabulary rather than with concepts.

2. Of course, the boom of the New Criticism stemmed in part from its being a teaching methodology suitable for returning World War II veterans and other new student constituencies presumably ignorant of traditional literary history. Nevertheless, the reward system of the university has continually privileged research over teaching.

3. Both several followers and several critics of Foucault have associated his thought with political paralysis, but he does offer grounds for hope, even though it could be a more consistent theme in his work. In *Power/Knowledge*, for example, he observes that "there are no relations of power without resistances; the latter are all the more real and effective because they are formed right at the point where relations of power are exercised; resistance to power does not have to come from elsewhere to be real, nor is it inexorably frustrated through being the compatriot of power. It exists all the more by being in the same place as power; hence, like power, resistance is multiple and can be integrated in global strategies" (142).

4. For another critique of Ulmer, focusing upon his politics of "pleasure," see the first essay in this volume, Mas'ud Zavarzadeh's "Theory as Resistance." It should be noted that Ulmer has more recently pointed out implications of feminist theory for pedagogy ("Teletheory"). He deals only with postmodern feminist art and performance, however, thus continuing to show what is for me an excessive faith in the political potential of the avant-garde.

5. I do not mean to suggest that what goes on in the literature classroom is devoid of political character—only that the teaching of literature should not be taken as the best means of exploring the complexities of institutions on the larger global scene or of combatting their abuses.

6. Neel offers a more sustained and nuanced analysis of students' perceptions in his recent book *Plato, Derrida, and Writing*.

7. More recently, in "Psyche: Inventions of the Other," Derrida has sought to distinguish the terms "deconstruction" and "invention," in part because he associates the latter with institutionalized mechanisms he questions.

8. For another analysis of "The Resistance to Theory," particularly as it bears upon theories of teaching, see Johnson (42–46).

WORKS CITED

Atkins, G. Douglas, and Michael L. Johnson, eds. *Writing and Reading Differently: Deconstruction and the Teaching of Composition and Literature.* Lawrence: UP of Kansas, 1985.

Bizzell, Patricia. "Cognition, Convention, and Certainty: What We Need to Know About Writing." *PRE/TEXT* 3 (1982): 213–39.

Bloom, Allan. *The Closing of the American Mind: How Higher Education Has Failed Democracy and Impoverished the Souls of Today's Students.* New York: Simon and Schuster, 1987.

Culler, Jonathan. "It's Time to Set the Record Straight About Paul de Man and His Wartime Articles for a Pro-Fascist Newspaper." *Chronicle of Higher Education* 13 July 1988: B1.

Debicki, Andrew P. "New Criticism and Deconstruction: Two Attitudes in Teaching Poetry." Atkins and Johnson 169–84.

de Lauretis, Teresa. "Feminist Studies/Critical Studies: Issues, Terms, and Contexts." *Feminist Studies/Critical Studies.* Ed. de Lauretis. Bloomington: Indiana UP, 1986. 1–19.

de Man, Paul. *The Resistance to Theory.* Minneapolis: U of Minnesota P, 1986.

Derrida, Jacques. "Psyche: Inventions of the Other." Trans. Catherine Porter. *Reading de Man Reading.* Ed. Lindsay Waters and Wlad Godzich. Minneapolis: U of Minnesota P, 1989. 25–65.

Dews, Peter. *Logics of Disintegration: Post-structuralist Thought and the Claims of Critical Theory.* New York: Verso, 1987.

Foley, Barbara. "The Politics of Deconstruction." *Rhetoric and Form: Deconstruction at Yale.* Ed. Robert Con Davis and Ronald Schleifer. Norman: U of Oklahoma P, 1985. 113–34.

Foucault, Michel. *Power/Knowledge: Selected Interviews and Other Writings 1972–1977.* Ed. Colin Gordon. Trans. Gordon, Leo Marshall, John Mepham, and Kate Soper. New York: Pantheon, 1980.

Freire, Paulo. *Pedagogy of the Oppressed.* Trans. Myra Bergman Ramos. New York: Seabury, 1970.

Fuss, Diana. *Essentially Speaking: Feminism, Nature and Difference.* New York: Routledge, 1989.

Giroux, Henry A. *Schooling and the Struggle for Public Life: Critical Pedagogy in the Modern Age.* Minneapolis: U of Minnesota P, 1988.

Hirsch, E. D., Jr. *Cultural Literacy: What Every American Needs to Know.* Boston: Houghton Mifflin, 1987.

Johnson, Barbara. *A World of Difference.* Baltimore: Johns Hopkins UP, 1988.

Leitch, Vincent B. "Deconstruction and Pedagogy." Atkins and Johnson 16–26.

Maher, Frances. "Classroom Pedagogy and the New Scholarship on Women." *Gendered Subjects: The Dynamics of Feminist Teaching.* Ed. Margo Culley and Catherine Portuges. Boston: Routledge and Kegan Paul, 1985. 29–48.

Miller, J. Hillis. "Commentary on the Heidegger/de Man Debates." *Times Literary Supplement* 17–23 (June 1988): 676.

Neel, Jasper. *Plato, Derrida, and Writing.* Carbondale: Southern Illinois UP, 1988.

———. "Plot, Character, or Theme? *Lear* and the Teacher." Atkins and Johnson 185–205.

Northam, Paul. "Heuristics and Beyond: Deconstruction/Inspiration and the Teaching of Writing Invention." Atkins and Johnson 115–28.

Schilb, John. "Deconstructing Didion: Poststructuralist Rhetorical Theory in the Composition Classroom." *Literary Nonfiction: Theory, Criticism, Pedagogy.* Ed. Chris Anderson. Carbondale: Southern Illinois UP, 1989. 262–86.

Scholes, Robert. "Three Views of Education: Nostalgia, History, and Voodoo." *College English* 50 (1988): 323–32.

Shor, Ira. *Critical Teaching and Everyday Life.* 1980. Chicago: U of Chicago P, 1987.

Smith, Paul. Address. Div. on The Teaching of Literature. MLA Convention. Washington, D.C., 29 Dec. 1989.

———. *Discerning the Subject.* Minneapolis: U of Minnesota P, 1988.

Tompkins, Jane. Address. Div. on The Teaching of Literature. MLA Convention. Washington, D.C., 29 Dec. 1989.

Ulmer, Gregory L. "Teletheory: *A Mystory.*" *The Current in Criticism: Essays on the Present and Future of Literary Theory.* Ed. Clayton Koelb and Virgil Lokke. West Lafayette: Purdue UP, 1987. 339–71.

———. "Textshop for Post(e)pedagogy." Atkins and Johnson 38–64.

———. "Textshop for Psychoanalysis: On De-Programming Freshmen Platonists." *College English* 49 (1987): 756–69.

3

SUBVERSION AND OPPOSITIONALITY IN THE ACADEMY

Barbara Foley

My topic in this essay is the rhetoric of subversion—or rupture, or disruption—that so frequently appears in critical discourse these days; my purpose is to raise some questions about the implications this rhetoric carries for a politically oppositional practice in the academy. I will address some important features of poststructuralism and deconstruction, as well as certain components of feminist theory, but I will try to minimize my treatment of theory as such and instead stress a related concern that has increasing influence on our everyday critical practice and pedagogy—namely, the matter of challenging (whether opening up, jettisoning, or, as my former colleague Michael Warner calls it, *busting*) the literary canon (Warner). When I use the term "new scholarship" in this essay, I refer primarily to this canon-busting activity, in conjunction with its roots in poststructuralist, deconstructive, and feminist theory.

Before tackling these critical and literary-historical questions, however, I need to summarize briefly the historical context within which our current discourse about theory and pedagogy is taking place, for any recommendations about political oppositionality necessarily address themselves to a specific situation. This context is profoundly anomalous and contradictory. On the one hand, we seem to be inhabiting a wasteland that makes T. S. Eliot's spiritual desert a comparative oasis. The developments are many: the supersession of Cold War rivalries by a race for newly opened markets that will align emergent and declining superpowers in highly competitive—and increasingly warlike—alliances; the desperation of a declining U.S. empire that is doggedly supporting fascist regimes around the world while creating a massive new poverty class among its own proletariat; the reestablishment of gross inequalities of race and gender, even after decades of popular resistance; and the reconversion of the campuses into centers for CIA recruitment and war research. These and other phenomena signal the deepening of a capitalist crisis that can only result in increasing repression and impoverishment for most of the globe's inhabitants.

On the other hand, although CIA recruitment is on the increase, in the academy we seem to be experiencing an exciting and progressive development that signals a very different sort of trend: the number of canon-busting scholars and poststructuralist theorists is also on the increase. A generation of scholars in their forties, whose social and political consciousnesses were shaped in the crucible of the 1960s, has now reached full maturity, is writing many of the books and articles we now read, and is attaining (or seeking to attain) tenured positions in English and literature departments. Academic Marxism is experiencing a popularity and prestige unprecedented since the 1930s. Where fifteen years ago it was heresy to treat literary works as anything other than apolitical, ahistorical, transcendental, and privileged, now, in the wake of poststructuralism, deconstruction, and feminism, it is almost a new orthodoxy to proclaim that everything is ideological, that everything is textual and political. And in the wake of the canon-busting movement, the literary tradition emerges as variegated and full of pockets of resistance, not monolothic and hegemonic. Ethnic minority, female, and working-class writers now draw the attention of many of the best younger scholars, and even the stodgy mainstays of the canon are discovered to have been secretly in rebellion against the dominant ideologies of their times. As a result, the humanist's role as the gatekeeper of tradition seems to have undergone a profound alteration. Where once we were charged with pointing up the uniqueness of works of undisputed genius and the darkness and ambiguity of the human condition, we are now empowered—indeed, encouraged—to relativize, historicize, and contextualize. Subversion is the new order of the day, and we appear to inhabit a decidedly oppositional stance in relation to dominant ideology. Allan Bloom and William Bennett may be building up a dangerous case for cultural traditionalism among the populace at large, but we in the academy know that pluralism and decentering constitute a truer and better (kinder and gentler?) approach to cultural matters.

Does this anomalous disjunction between the situation in literature departments and that in the body politic indicate that the academy is exempt from the previously described rightward drift? Do we in fact look to semiotics and poststructuralism for political guidance in the moral limbo exemplified by Tammy Bakker and Geraldo Rivera, Donald Trump and George Bush? Is the Chapel Perilous located in departments of comparative literature? Is the canon-busting scholar the Fisher King? Or does the apparent progressiveness of contemporary literary scholarship make for only thunder over distant mountains, but no rain?

My irony no doubt signals my skepticism. Before explaining the reasons for this irony, however, I should acknowledge the most significant achievements of the canon-busting movement. First, and most obviously, the movement has profoundly democratized literary study, for students are now asked to not only read but also understand and respect significant numbers of previously marginalized writers and traditions. Of course, no major shakeup occurs when a few women writers or writers of color are given grudging admission to course syllabi or when old analytical paradigms remain intact. (I think here of a professor who incorporated Charlotte Perkins Gilman's "The Yellow Wallpaper" into his survey of American literature but taught it as an instance of Nabokovian unreliable narration!) Nonetheless, careful attention to those very features of neglected literary texts that caused their exclusion from the canon can help create a profound rupture in literary study—not only with inherited models of literary history but also with the elitist politics undergirding traditional notions of esthetic value. For example, Cleanth Brooks's valorization of literary texts as setting forth not ideas but what it would feel like to hold certain ideas can take shape not merely as an expression of an esthete's disdain for political commitments in general but as a conservative's reaction against the leftist politics that many texts of the 1930s had worn openly on their sleeves (Brooks 731).[1]

Second, the canon-busting movement invites us to rehistoricize canonical writers as well, thus rescuing them from the toils of the New Critical and archetypal interpretations in which they have been enmeshed for so many years. It becomes difficult indeed to stress Melville's metaphysics to the exclusion of his materialism when "Benito Cereno" is taught not with "The Turn of the Screw" but with Frederick Douglass's *Narrative of the Life of an American Slave* or Harriet Wilson's *Our Nig.* Viewing *Adventures of Huckleberry Finn* in conjunction with Charles Chesnutt's *The Marrow of Tradition* or Du Bois's *The Souls of Black Folk* requires the critic to address questions quite different from those invited when comparing it with *Walden*. As Carolyn Porter has pointed out, Emerson's early essays gain a crucial social dimension when seen in the context of the author's anguished reactions to the commodification and alienation of labor in New England mill towns of the 1830s (*Seeing and Being*). After decades of a critical hegemony exercised by the intentional and affective fallacies, paradox and ambiguity, epistemological skepticism, and archetypal patterns of Adamic innocence in a fallen world, history reenters the domain of literary study, not simply as background or source, but as a constitutive component of discourse and textuality. (See also the recent excellent revisionary readings in Karcher, Sundquist, Arac, and Wilding, as well as Reising's theoretical study of the politics of traditional American literary scholarship.)

Despite the significant achievements of the canon-busting movement, however, I believe that in many ways it falls short of its emancipatory rhetoric and frequently ends up reconfirming those very structures of authority it purports to oppose. Indeed, this process of co-optation and reincorporation occurs along a number of axes; it is to a scrutiny of these that I now turn, focusing first on more exclusively critical issues and then exploring their implication for our political practice in the academy.

First, the maneuver of opening up the literary tradition—and the curriculum—to previously silenced or marginalized voices is often conflated with the notion that these voices, *because* excluded, must somehow constitute a significant threat to the hegemony of dominant social groups. Now, I am certainly not saying that works such as Jessie Redmon Fauset's *Plum Bun* or Rebecca Harding Davis's *Life in the Iron Mills* fail to query important facets of class, race, and gender inequality in American culture and in the discourses by which that culture represents and validates itself. But I am bothered by the argument that these writers, simply by virtue of their race or gender positioning, articulate a counterdiscourse that is intrinsically subversive of dominant power relations.

For an instance of this phenomenon—more examples of which appear every day—I refer to Sandra Gilbert's introduction to the recently issued Penguin edition of *The Awakening*. This essay is in some ways politically astute but also, in my view, injuriously one-sided. Gilbert argues with considerable force against Susan Wolkenfeld's antifeminist reading, which would invoke standards of "realistic" plausibility and would accordingly treat the novel's conclusion as " 'a defeat and a regression, rooted in a self-annihilating instinct, in a romantic incapacity to accommodate . . . to the limitations of reality.' " Accordingly, Gilbert claims that Edna's final act of suicide represents instead "a resurrection, a pagan female Good Friday that promises a Venusian Easter." The protagonist's final gesture thus "expresses not a refusal to accommodate to reality but a subversive questioning of both reality and 'realism' " (31).

I am in considerable sympathy with Gilbert's desire to point out the oppositional, even triumphant, aspects of Edna's rejection of a patriarchal society that would restrict her possibilities for growth. I also agree with Gilbert's corollary assumption that feminist criticism should address itself not simply to textual patterns of victimization but also to representations of defiance. I would, moreover, second the view that the presumably "realistic" invocation of probability and common sense as criteria for evaluating Edna's character carries with it a freight of conservative patriarchal judgments. But I also think that by treating Edna Pontellier as a kind of transcendent pagan goddess Gilbert profoundly distorts the contradictory nature of Chopin's portrayal of her protagonist—a woman marked by considerable weakness of intellect as much as by greatness of spirit, by a narrow selfishness as much as by a generous identification with cosmic regenerative forces. In short, by arguing that Edna engages in a "subversive questioning of both reality and 'realism' " Gilbert mistakes the part for the whole, substituting a univocal—and somewhat anachronistic—celebration of female sexual identity for what is, in my view, a highly tension-filled and ambivalent representation of the cost of woman's emancipation. In particular, it is precisely at the text's moment of closure that this conflict emerges most sharply. For in her attempt to synthesize the divergent claims of individual and social identity, Chopin's valorization of her protagonist's courage is substantially qualified by profoundly ambiguous patterns of symbolism and imagery that suggest infantile regression at least as much as they suggest Venusian transcendence.[2]

The problem I have pointed out in Gilbert's introduction to *The Awakening* is repeated, I believe, in a substantial number of works of the new scholarship. Recent critics are often eager to demonstrate that a noncanonical—or in this case, a recently canonized—writer occupied (and occupies) an oppositional stance in relation to dominant institutions of power. In arguing their case, however, these critics too frequently select various subversive moments in the text but overlook the ways in which these moments are frequently subordinated to larger narrative patterns (most particularly patterns of closure) that negate or at least blunt the text's sporadic querying of hegemonic conceptions of character and social relations. The critic's own brand of oppositional politics, in other words, becomes conflated with authorial intention.[3]

Second, practitioners of the new scholarship too often conclude not only that noncanonical writers possessed subversive politics but also that long-canonized writers authors either experienced significant sympathy with oppressed social groups or at least ironized or otherwise problematized the more reactionary ideas that their texts appear to assert. As I mentioned before, Carolyn Porter's discovery of Emerson's awareness of the alienation of labor in 1830s New England mill towns and her postulation that this awareness was centrally involved in his formulation of a transcendentalist epistemology put Emerson's philosophical enterprise in a badly needed historical context. Nonetheless, this discovery does not in itself demonstrate that Emerson had any particularly strong sympathy for the oppressed masses, who figure in his essays as a somewhat rowdy and undesirable presence—"the unintelligent brute force that lies at the bottom of society [and] is made to growl and mow" (960). In Emerson's complex political epistemology, the great unwashed masses contribute to the anguish suffered by the all-seeing "eye" at least as much as they themselves suffer from a comparable alienation. Nor does demonstrating Emerson's awareness of alienation in itself prove that, in his own philosophical practice, Emerson managed to contest or overcome the commodification that he perceived and decried. Moreover, Porter extends her analysis of Emerson as a radical—which, given his association with Fuller and other progressive transcendentalists, is at least plausible—to James, Adams, and Faulkner as well. "Each of them [the four cited above] responds critically to his society," she declares, "and the related terms in which these several radical critiques take shape reveal at once the deepening structure of reification in American society as it moves from the nineteenth century into the twentieth, and the exemplary efforts of four of America's most formidable critical minds to overcome and resist that reification" ("Reification" 188–217). Emerson, James, Adams, and Faulkner did indeed offer compelling analyses of the costs of living in modern industrial society, but their criticisms were largely articulated from a conservative viewpoint. It hardly helps clarify these writers' political stands to treat them as sympathetic participants in an essentially Marxist critique of capitalist commodification (for an interesting discussion of the distinctly nonradical aspects of Emerson's thought, see Grusin).

I invoke the example of Porter's *Seeing and Being* not to negate the value of her discoveries about the centrality of alienation in the works of Emerson and other American writers but simply to point out a certain lack of dialectical thinking that is prevalent in a number of works of the new scholarship, even the most valuable. In the attempt to pull canonical writers down from the clouds of idealist critical discourse and reground them in history, writers who for decades have been seen as bearing the standard of traditional moral values are suddenly seen as querying these values. By a curious turn of the wheel, then, the effort to historicize produces a new kind of dehistoricization, albeit on a different plane. To be sure, writers are no longer seen as espousing human truths divorced from time and space, but in their insertion into time and space they frequently take on an aura of anachronistic political correctness. Their firm commitment to elitist, sexist, or racist social values is waved aside so long as their works contain the germ of a concern with decentered subjectivity or the problematics of reference.[4]

Indeed, such a privileging of postmodernist concerns can result in a very troubling bypassing—verging on whitewashing—of reactionary politics in canonical texts. Andrew Parker, for example, argues that Ezra Pound's virulent hatred of Jews stemmed from his perception that "Judaism, writing, money and rhetoric . . . all belong to the same tropological series, each term functioning analogously as a figure of 'excess,' as an inscription that deflects any immediate connection between the sign and its intended referent" (81). Although Parker claims that his argument "will enable us to reject the widely-held critical position that considers Pound's anti-Seminitism as a merely 'contingent' phenomenon, ancillary to his poetic achievement" (71), I remain skeptical of a rehistoricizing that virtually collapses politics into poetics. Parker is certainly not arguing that there is anything progressive about Pound's anti-Semitism, but his contention that Pound worked out his poetic anxieties through his social attitudes has the effect of dignifying those attitudes. Pound's obsessive concern with the relation of signifier to signified makes him "one of us"; even his repellent politics take shape as a protest, however distorted, against the epistemological dilemma of modern humanity.

I can anticipate various objections to these arguments. It might be claimed, for example, that by invoking critical categories such as "larger narrative patterns," "closure," and "intention" it is I who am reproducing dominant ideology, especially when I apply these notions to noncanonical texts. Concepts of totality, coherence, and authorial subjectivity can be seen as Aristotelian or Jamesian mediations of phallogocentric hegemony. Counterinvoking Derrida or de Man, the canon-busting critic might argue that oppositional ideology necessarily asserts itself in gaps, fissures, and discontinuities in the text, that opposition is by definition a marginalized phenomenon. It is enough for the text to have flaunted the logocentric conventions that support patriarchy and racial domination; subversion consists not in the *negation* of this hegemony, but simply in its interrogation.[5]

I am bothered by this argument, even though we hear it often enough these days, uttered in a tone of radical panache. For what it amounts to is an admission that subversion and oppositionality are essentially formalistic operations, maneuvers whose target and goal remain unspecified. The *act* of rupture is valorized, but what this act is subversive *of* and oppositional *to* is too often left unclear—as is the *extent* of the text's commitment to its disruptive stance. The enemy seems to be an epistemological nexus defined by stability, fixity, and realism, but beyond this we know little else. The result of this insistently structural definition of the antagonist is that we are left with only a hazy notion of the actual political praxis involved in textual subversion. Power, in this critical paradigm, lurks everywhere, but it is not always clear where power comes from or whose interests it serves. There is no cause for despair, however, for polysemous subversion waits everywhere in ambush, forcing dominant ideology continually to cover its flanks against guerrilla harassment from what Derrida calls the "marginalized other" of the West (Derrida 134–35). There are romantic echoes here of the discourse and practice of Regis Debray, so popular among certain elements of the New Left in the 1960s. We may wonder, however, whether such a formulation of subversion and oppositionality is as sure a safeguard against reincorporation as it claims to be.[6]

It is not necessary, I believe, to throw out the subversive baby with the traditional bath: to recognize that texts do not always succeed in negating dominant ideology is not to deny that they may try to do so. Such notions as intention, totality, and closure do not rule out the importance of considering *contradiction* in literary texts; indeed, they enable us to view the text as an ideological battleground where contradictions in representation fight out the broader struggles of the society at large. Within the dialectic of the text's unity, however, there are nonetheless primary and secondary aspects of contradiction. If the "pockets of resistance" in a text constitute a secondary aspect—as is, in my view, most often the case with works written in the bourgeois tradition, even with noncanonical texts—so be it, and let us appreciate these pockets for all they are worth and point out their significance to our students. But this does not mean that other aspects of authorial consciousness may not end up winning the battle, however unfortunate that victory may be. Indeed, to posit that an insurgent, secondary aspect of a contradiction is, simply by virtue of its existence, a primary, essence-determining phenomenon is to end up trivializing the very urgency of the political issues that the canon-busting movement invites us to consider. Such a contention makes battles that have been bitterly waged in the historical world—and often continue to be waged—appear to have been won comparatively easily in the realm of literary discourse.

As a kind of fall-back position, it might also be objected that even if I am right about the limited subversiveness of the majority of texts produced in the bourgeois tradition—or even at its margins—I am misconstruing literature's relation to ideology when I hold writers accountable for the formulable social views that their texts project. Some, invoking a more traditional distinction between the languages of science and poetry, might maintain that literary discourse is pseudostatement. Others, calling on the post-Althusserian description of literary discourse as positioned midway between ideology and ordinary propositional discourse, might declare that literary texts are distanced from the politics they appear to articulate. To hold Emerson as a "subject" accountable for the views he expresses is to miss the point, for the new scholarship is demonstrating how subjectivity is constructed by discourse. Rather than affix praise or blame to the formulable politics explicit or implicit in a text, the critic's task is to reveal how the multiplicity of language continually disrupts ideology as such; indeed, the real subversiveness of literature (and of the criticism that treats it) resides in precisely this antipathy to the confinements of univocal meaning and reference.[7]

In response to this argument, I claim it quite illogical to assert that, on the one hand, "literary" texts must be understood within the fuller context of contemporaneous discourse and that, on the other, there is something distinctive about "literary" language that overturns the text's apparent commitment to the ideological content it appears to set forth. Indeed, what this argument does is not to foreground but to bracket—or at least to marginalize once again—the issues of politics and history. For if poets and novelists necessarily become rebellious when they start tangling with literary language, then there must be something intrinsically subversive about literary discourse per se. Politics thus becomes an abiding feature of discourse rather than a historically specific matter of social analysis and intervention. Writers might in their personal lives (which after all are historical lives) adhere to politically retrograde beliefs, for example, Faulkner on the subject of black equality. Nonetheless, when such writers take pen in hand, they become deft interrogators of dominant ideology. Ideological contradiction is thus displaced from within authorial ideology (where I, for one, think it belongs) and inserted into the epistemological space between literature and ideology (see Eagleton, Macherey, and Bennett). Despite its insistence that everything is both political and textual, then, much of the new scholarship—even in some of its neo-Marxist variants—ends up hypostasizing the realm of the esthetic as a terrain somehow exempt from the political constraints that ordinarily shape the operations of consciousness. Perhaps Cleanth Brooks has not, after all, been completely left behind.

I can now address the implications that this critique of the politics of the new scholarship has for our practice as citizens of the world and, in particular, as teachers in the universities and colleges of the empire whose troubled situation I touched on in the opening part of this essay.

There is, I believe, a distinct oppositional potential in the critical movements I have been describing here. In challenging both the canon's makeup and the values that sustain it we *are* in a position to subvert key tenets of dominant ideology. We therefore occupy a potentially adversarial position in relation to the centers of power in U.S. society—centers that are represented, among other places, on the boards of trustees of the colleges and universities that pay our salaries. And though it is our colleagues in the physical and social sciences who are called on to do weapons and couterinsurgency research for military escapades in Central America, we should not minimize our importance to ruling-class hegemony. After all, it is our job to furnish—and make compelling, beautiful, and inevitable—views of the human condition that, if they do not glorify, generally justify and permit social inequality and the separation of personal morality from public policy. The humanities, Herbert Marcuse once observed, serve to inure people to their own and others' want of bread by demonstrating that man does not live by bread alone (109). If we successfully undermine such assumptions, pointing up their specious universalism and ahistoricity and bringing to our students' attention entire submerged subcultures that have queried such values, then we do pose a threat to ruling-class hegemony.

But if this is the case, why do our boards of trustees generally tolerate—indeed, actively cultivate—our presence? Why, indeed, has the move for integrating race, gender, and class into the curriculum been promoted over the objection of harshly hostile elements at major universities such as Duke and Stanford, where the sons and daughters of the wealthy receive their training? This happens, I believe, not because financiers and industrialists shed their crude commercialism when they enter the groves of academe, but because we oppositional scholars by and large make ourselves safe and because, to some extent at least, the captains of industry actually *need* us to do much of what we do. I will now translate my earlier criticisms of the canon-busting movement and the new scholarship into a critique of the political practices, both liberal and neo-Marxist, that they imply.

To begin with, the movement to open up the canon to new voices and traditions is easily assimilable to the myth of American democratic pluralism: the melting pot has simply made it to the academy at last. What a celebration it is of U.S. "representative" institutions if female and minority writers now receive "representation" in anthologies and course syllabi! Even if the largest poverty class in the United States consists of families headed by single women, and even if millions of unemployed and working-class peoples of color confront continually worsening prospects for housing and jobs, what a testament the new cultural pluralism is to the "sensitivity" of the leading institutions in our society! My sardonic tone here should not be taken to signify that I think this opening up to have been *negative* (on the contrary, we should always recall that the decisions about inclusion and exclusion that take place nowadays in the quiet halls of W. W. Norton are the fruits of very unquiet decisions—and demonstrations—about inclusion and exclusion that took place in other halls some twenty years ago). My point is simply that if we really want to "politicize" the study of literature, we should juxtapose Richard Wright's *Uncle Tom's Children* with William Faulkner's *Absalom, Absalom!* in a way that fully acknowledges the fundamental antipathy between the two. For unless we incorporate a re-creation of *social struggle* into our presentation of these writers to our students, we are simply perpetuating, and certainly not subverting, quintessentially logocentric conceptions of the American body politic. Wright and Faulkner are not simply two sides to the democratic coin. The social views articulated in their texts are as irreconcilable now as they were in the 1930s. Any pedagogical strategy that simply juxtaposes them in a pluralistic exploration of literary representations of race and racism violates the motives that prompted both writers to take pen in hand.

By no means, however, are all scholars involved in opening up the canon so conventionally liberal as I have just suggested. Some of the new scholars would claim that they are not validating the myth of the melting pot but rather blasting it open, demonstrating that social life and discourse are constituted not by unity and consensus but by difference, alterity, and heterogeneity. Indeed, they would argue, the politics implied by their critical practice is emancipatory, even revolutionary, for they are seeking out pockets of resistance and envisioning social change coming from autonomous groupings of dispersed elements—women, blacks, Hispanics, Native Americans, homosexuals—who fashion what Stanley Aronowitz calls a "micro-politics of oppositional movements" or what Felix Guattari calls the "proliferation of marginal groups" that will bring about "molecular revolution" (Aronowitz 123–36; Guattari 268–72).[8] According to this analysis, traditional Marxism is logocentric and authoritarian because it posits the primacy of production in determining social relations, situates change in the class struggle rather than in the activities of "interest groups" such as those cited above, and makes the fatal mistake of supposing that a "third term"—revolution—will synthesize and resolve the destructive binary oppositions on which bourgeois society founds itself and by which it justifies itself. In short, true resistance *can* come only from "pockets" that take the "refusal of mastery" as a guiding political principle. If these pockets should turn into phalanxes, even armies, then the margins would become the center, and logocentric structures of authority would reassert themselves, albeit in a different guise. According to this argument, which is endorsed by a number of feminists and neo-Marxists involved in the new scholarship, the goal of overturning the canon is neither to reaffirm liberal democracy nor to contribute to a class-based movement for social revolution but rather to carry on rear-guard guerrilla actions that will interrogate hegemonic discourses without superseding or replacing them.[9]

Such a politics amounts to little more than a rewarming of the liberal pluralism I mentioned before, although its adherents would strenuously disagree with me. To be sure, many feminists and neo-Marxists are quite correct to point out the Old Left's fatal failure to understand the centrality of questions of race and gender within the overall class contradiction. And a class-based Marxism need not—indeed, should not—seek the eradication of plurality, which is not at all the same as pluralism. Nonetheless, to concede that race and gender cannot simply be collapsed into class does not mean that the class struggle is no longer the main contradiction shaping historical processes. Nor does it mean that provisional coalitions of dispersed and molecular interest groups can successfully confront the powers that be, which have proven themselves remarkably efficient in accommodating demands for cultural self-determination, at least rhetorically. Indeed, our political experience of the last decade or so reveals that this presumably radical politics of heterogeneity and difference is readily enough absorbed into the conservative pluralism of *e pluribus unum,* which celebrates the openness and flexibility of American capitalist democracy while guaranteeing the continuing segregation and subjugation of the great number of its citizens. Interrogation from the margins is kept safely at the margins.

Indeed, the extreme form of this politics of decentering and marginality actually enshrines impotence as a positive good. The "refusal of mastery," apparently an act of heroic disengagement from the epistemology that fosters oppression, can lead to a kind of defiant passivity. This passivity may console the conscience of the individual, but it precludes the possibility of engagement in a praxis that will encounter hegemony on its own turf. The adherents of this refusal of mastery become avatars of Eliot's Fisher King—incapable of determinate action, but by their very presence continually emanating the promise of a redemptive rain that will magically fall from the sky. In fact, some practitioners of the new canon-busting scholarship seem actually to relish the continuing existence of ruling-class hegemony, at least insofar as they take their own marginality as a condition of their scholarly being and conceive of themselves as a kind of loyal opposition. Fearing that, should the margins become the center, they would be transformed into sites of a new power that would be, *qua* power, as oppressive as the old, these scholars prefer to engage in skirmishes that never take as their goal the actual reconstruction of textual value and literary tradition—let alone the seizure of power in the society at large—according to a new plan.[10] Better, they counsel, to drop in our lines from the dock behind the gashouse, turn our backs on the devastation of the global wasteland, and restrict ourselves to setting in order our own lands, demarcated by the new pluralistic geography. What starts out as a radical refusal to engage in the co-opting discourse of power can easily enough end up as a resort to the solaces of the word processor and the conventional prestige rewards of the profession.

At any rate, such questions of how most effectively to oppose the machinations of power are frequently rendered moot for liberals and neo-Marxists alike by what I have argued to be the greatest drawback of much of the new scholarship—namely, the tendency to find subversion under every textual bush. If it is true not only that marginalized texts subvert the established canon but also that canonical texts subvert the traditional and conservative ideologies they seem to endorse, then bourgeois ideology—at least when embodied in literary texts—poses no threat at all. It self-destructs when touched, or at least, when touched by the poststructuralist critic or pedagogue. The scholar who holds this view of literature actually ends up bolstering bourgeois hegemony, however inadvertently. For if the deconstruction of literature, *qua* literature, offers such a trenchant critique of dominant values, and if it takes the oppositional scholar to point out the full extent of this critique, then what are universities and colleges if not privileged zones where the mysteries of textual subversion can be plumbed? The logic of the new scholarship *ought* to extend to a critique of those institutions that help maintain hegemony. But it can actually end up legitimating the hegemonic view that campuses are apolitical centers where disinterested research and pedagogy take place and, moreover, where the future leaders of society can receive the humanistic enlightenment that will equip them to respond effectively to the discursive plurality of the citizenry, if not its material needs. Poststructuralist scholarship thrives on the perception of ironic incongruities. I can think of no more ironic incongruity, however, than the situation of the poststructuralist scholar who affirms the latently self-critical capacities of bourgeois culture while his or her campus administration is recruiting students for the CIA or training officers to lead working-class G.I.s into battle in the Middle East—or, on the more mundane level, preparing a new generation of business leaders to meet the challenge posed by an increasingly multicultural work force. For the view that both literature and criticism subvert and disrupt dominant ideology carries the implication that the discourse carried on in departments that teach literature and criticism is somehow not complicit with the discourses and operations in which the university as a whole is engaged. Despite its up-to-date post-Saussurean dress, then, and its insistence that literature purveys not sweetness and light but counterhegemonic subversion, much of the new scholarship ends up valorizing literary study on grounds that are hardly unfamiliar. As I noted before, the numbers of both canon-busting scholars and CIA recruiters are increasing on our campuses these days; let us not be content with a conception of either literature or literary study that facilitates a peaceful coexistence between the two.

NOTES

This article previously appeared in *College Literature* 17.2/3 and is reprinted with permission. © 1990 West Chester University.

1. For a discussion of the problems minority and female writers have encountered with the ideological premises encoded in inherited genres, see, respectively, Reilly and Abel. The *locus classicus* of the relation of questions of esthetic value to the activity of canon revision remains the final chapter of Tompkins.

2. Similar dynamics and difficulties underlie McDowell's recent introduction to the reissued edition of Fauset's *Plum Bun:*

> *Plum Bun* has the hull but not the core of literary conservatism and convention. . . . It passes for conservative, employing "outworn"

> and "safe" literary materials while, simultaneously, remaining suspicious of them. . . . *Plum Bun* dares to explore questions about unconventional female roles and possibilities for development using the very structures that have traditionally offered fundamentally conservative answers to those questions. Fauset's answers were risky, in the literary marketplace, but powerful, liberating alternatives nevertheless, both for herself as a writer and for the image of blacks and women in literature. (xxii)

(For this example I am indebted to conversations with Carla Kaplan during our joint explorations of Harlem Renaissance literature in a graduate independent study course at Northwestern University.) There are abundant examples of these sorts of radical claims in recent feminist scholarship, one of which occurs in Edwards, who encounters a dilemma frequently found in works of scholarship that aspire to demonstrate the oppositionality of a submerged tradition in women's writing. On the one hand, Edwards asserts that her study, unlike Gilbert and Gubar's *Madwoman in the Attic* (1979), finds not "covert reappraisals" of patriarchal domination, but "overt and radical attacks" (15). On the other hand, she is forced to conclude that, in work after work of nineteenth-century fiction, the female hero ends up a "heroine," safely reincorporated into the dominant system of patriarchal marriage. I agree that many nineteenth-century novels featuring woman heroes *do* exhibit this contradiction and therefore wonder at Edwards's claim to be discussing works that unequivocally contain "overt and radical attacks." For a considerably more dialectical assessment of the strengths and limitations of the "cult of domesticity" in nineteenth-century women's fiction, see Baym, especially 22–50.

3. See the final chapter of Foley (*Telling the Truth*) 233–64; for a discussion of ideological reincorporation in Afro-American literature, see Hogue; for a description of the ways in which an excluded cultural tradition develops its own oppositional poetics and countertraditions, see Gates. In stressing the issue of ideological reincorporation, I am not denying that it has been a salutary development in feminist criticism to move from analyses of women's distorted lives, anxious authorship, and conservative social roles (e.g., Heilbrun) to explorations of their strategies of cultural survival and resistance. I am simply arguing that it is crucial that we not heroize the achievements of victims of oppression in such a way as to end up minimizing the nature and extent of that oppression. What seems to me a very sensible analysis of the relationship between oppositionality and reincorporation is presented in Radway.

4. For arguments along similar lines regarding the presumably self-reflexive (and hence antilogocentric and antiauthoritarian) quality of the American

literary tradition in its entirety, see Dauber and Riddel. Porter avoids the solipsism of Dauber and Riddel but mistakes the *foregrounding* of the problem of reification in classic American literature with a *radical opposition* to that reification.

5. For divergent views on the extent to which the novel form itself is irrevocably patriarchal, see, on the one hand, Jehlen and Fetterley, and, on the other hand, Tompkins.

6. For a valuable critique of the pseudo-oppositionality of the leftist panache accompanying much poststructuralist criticism, see Graff, Meyerson, and Larson. It is important to note, however, that poststructuralism can produce the diametrically opposed claim that literature—or at least narrative—is intrinsically so co-optative as to preclude opposition of any kind, whether deriving from an author's explicit politics or his or her implicit subject position; see Davis.

7. See Rabinowitz for an intelligent discussion of literary conventions as carriers of ideology, a discussion that both acknowleges the force of dominant ideology and at the same time allows space for oppositional activity.

8. Interestingly, Guattari notes that "it is impossible to make a clear-cut distinction between the fringe ideas that can be recuperated and those that lead down the slippery slope to authentic 'molecular revolutions.' The borderline remains fluid, and fluctuates both in time and place" (269). This argument is similar to Foucault's contention that power and opposition are often indistinguishable from each other (Foucault 141).

9. See Foley's "Politics of Deconstruction" and, for the poststructuralist/Marxist critique of dialectics, Ryan. Among the poststructuralists/Marxists who attempt to retain dialectics as an analytical category, a common operation is to assert the importance of identity rather than struggle within contradiction, thus evading the necessity of determining which aspect of the competing tendencies determines essence. See, for example, Jameson (281–99), who argues that utopian gratification and ideological manipulation often become virtually indistinguishable from each other in both literary texts and social experience. It seems to me crucial for the Marxist critic—for any critic—to make distinctions in this arena.

10. For an instance of a critical stance that takes the refusal of mastery as both premise and goal, see Craig Owens's description of Martha Rosler's photographs of the Bowery, in which she purposefully undermines her own authority as photographer to impress upon her audience "the indignity of speaking for others" (Owens 69, her words). There is an urgent need for further inquiry into the extent to which such statements articulate not simply antipathy to hegemonic discourses but also an unacknowledged anticommunism, one that conceives of Marxism as a reductionist discourse threatening to engulf all difference not immediately subsumable to class. Until such

inquiry is undertaken, there is the continual possibility that current research into the intersections—textual and historical—of race, gender, and class will be inhibited by the assumption that these intersections are merely conjunctural, with the consequence that the last of these categories will, by a curious turn of the wheel, almost automatically be subsumed to either of the former two.

WORKS CITED

Abel, Elizabeth, et. al. *The Voyage In: Fictions of Female Development.* Hanover: UP of New England, 1983.

Arac, Jonathan. "The Politics of *The Scarlet Letter.*" Bercovitch and Jehlen 247–66.

Aronowitz, Stanley. *The Crisis of Historical Materialism: Class, Politics and Culture in Marxist Theory.* New York: Praeger, 1981.

Baym, Nina. *Woman's Fiction: A Guide to Novels by and about Women in America, 1820–1870.* Ithaca: Cornell UP, 1978.

Bennett, Tony. *Formalism and Marxism.* London: Methuen, 1979.

Bercovitch, Sacvan, and Myra Jehlen, eds. *Ideology and Classic American Literature.* Cambridge: Cambridge UP, 1986.

Brooks, Cleanth. "Irony as a Principle of Structure." *Literary Opinion in America.* Ed. Morton D. Zabel. New York: Harper, 1951. 729–41.

Dauber, Kenneth. "Criticism of American Literature." *diacritics* 7 (March 1977): 55–66.

Davis, Lennard J. *Resisting Novels: Ideology and Fiction.* London: Methuen, 1987.

Derrida, Jacques. *The Margins of Philosophy.* Trans. Alan Bass. Chicago: U of Chicago P, 1982.

Eagleton, Terry. *Criticism and Ideology.* London: Verso, 1976.

Edwards, Lee. R. *Psyche as Hero: Female Heroism and Fictional Form.* Middletown: Wesleyan UP, 1984.

Emerson, Ralph Waldo. "Self-Reliance." *The Norton Anthology of American Literature.* 3rd ed. 2 vols. New York: Norton, 1989. 1: 956–72.

Fetterley, Judith. *Provisions: A Reader from 19th-Century American Women.* Bloomington: Indiana UP, 1986.

Foley, Barbara. "The Politics of Deconstruction." *Genre* (Spring–Summer 1984): 113–34.

———. *Telling the Truth: The Theory and Practice of Documentary Fiction.* Ithaca: Cornell UP, 1986.

Foucault, Michel. *Power/Knowledge: Selected Interviews and Other Writings 1972–77.* Ed. Colin Gordon. Trans. Gordon et. al. New York: Pantheon, 1980.

Gates, Henry Louis, Jr. " 'The Blackness of Blackness': A Critique of the Sign and the Signifying Monkey." *Black Literature and Literary Theory,* ed. Henry Louis Gates, Jr. New York: Methuen, 1984. 285–321.

Gilbert, Sandra. Introduction. *The Awakening.* By Kate Chopin. Harmondsworth: Penguin, 1986. 7–33.

Graff, Gerald. "American Criticism Left and Right." Bercovitch and Jehlen 91–121.

Grusin, Richard A. " 'Put God in Your Debt': Emerson's Economy of Literature." *PMLA* 103 (January 1988): 35–44.

Guattari, Felix. *Molecular Revolution: Psychiatry and Politics.* Trans. Rosemary Sheed. Harmondsworth: Penguin, 1984.

Heilbrun, Carolyn. *Reinventing Womanhood.* New York: W.W. Norton, 1979.

Hogue, W. Lawrence. "Literary Production: A Silence in Afro-American Critical Practice." In Weixlmann and Fontenot 2:31–45.

Jameson, Fredric. *The Political Unconscious: Narrative as a Socially Symbolic Act.* Ithaca: Cornell UP, 1981.

Jehlen, Myra. "Archimedes and the Paradox of Feminist Criticism." *The Signs Reader: Women, Gender, and Scholarship.* Ed. Elizabeth Abel and Emily K. Abel. Chicago: U of Chicago P, 1983.

Karcher, Carolyn. *Shadow Over the Promised Land: Slavery and Violence in Melville's America.* Baton Rouge: Louisiana State UP, 1980.

Larson, Neil. *Modernism and Hegemony: A Materialist Critique of Aesthetic Agencies.* Theory and History of Literature 71. Minneapolis: U of Minnesota P, 1990.

Macherey, Pierre. *A Theory of Literary Production.* Trans. Geoffrey Wall. London: Routledge and Kegan Paul, 1978.

Marcuse, Herbert. *Negations: Essays in Critical Theory.* Trans. Jeremy J. Shapiro. Boston: Beacon, 1968.

McDowell, Deborah. Introduction. *Plum Bun.* By Jessie Redmon Fauset. New York: Pandora Books, 1985. ix–xxiv.

Meyerson, Gregory. Review of *Universal Abandon: The Politics of Postmodernism.* Ed. Andrew J. Ross. *Ariel* 20 (October 1989): 192–96.

Owens, Craig. "The Discourse of Others: Feminists and Postmodernism." *The Anti-Aesthetic: Essays on Postmodern Culture.* Ed. Hal Foster. Port Townsend: Bay Press, 1983.

Parker, Andrew. "Ezra Pound and the 'Economy' of Anti-Semitism." *Postmodernism and Politics.* Ed. Jonathan Arac. Minneapolis: U of Minnesota P, 1986. 70–90.

Porter, Carolyn. *Seeing and Being: The Plight of the Participant Observer in Emerson, James, Adams, Faulkner.* Middletown: Wesleyan UP, 1981.

——. "Reification and American Literature." Bercovitch and Jehlen 188–217.

Rabinowitz, Peter J. *Before Reading: Narrative Conventions and the Politics of Interpretation.* Ithaca: Cornell UP, 1989.

Radway, Janice. *Reading the Romance: Women, Patriarchy, and Popular Literature.* Chapel Hill: U of North Carolina P, 1984.

Reilly, John. "History-Making Literature." Weixlmann and Fontenot 85–120.

Reising, Russell. *The Unusable Past: Theory and the Study of American Literature.* London: Methuen, 1987.

Riddel, Joseph. "Decentering the Image: The 'Project' of 'American Poetics.'" *Textual Strategies.* Ed Josue Harari. Ithaca: Cornell UP, 1979. 322–58.

Ryan, Michael. *Marxism and Deconstruction: A Critical Articulation.* Baltimore: Johns Hopkins UP, 1982.

Sundquist, Eric J. "Benito Cereno and New World Slavery." *Reconstructing American Literary History.* Ed. Sacvan Bercovitch. Cambridge: Harvard UP, 1986. 93–122.

Tompkins, Jane. *Sensational Designs: The Work of American Fiction 1790–1860.* New York: Oxford UP, 1985.

Warner, Michael. "Recanonization." Paper delivered at the Midwest Modern Language Association, Chicago, November 1986.

Wilding, Michael. *Political Fictions.* London: Routledge and Kegan Paul, 1980.

Weixlmann, Joel, and Chester Fontenot, eds. *Belief vs. Theory in Black American Literature.* Vol. 2 of *Studies in Black American Literature.* 2 vols. Greenwood: Penkevill, 1986.

PRAGMATICS

4

INTEGRATING THEORY IN THE CURRICULUM AS THEORIZING—A POSTDISCIPLINARY PRACTICE

David R. Shumway

Because the movement named *literary theory*—or just *theory,* as I will refer to it here—is by some accounts more than twenty years old, it is not surprising that people should have begun to think about how this research practice might be reflected in pedagogy and the curriculum. It perhaps also should not be surprising that much of what has been written on this topic has almost nothing to do with concrete attempts to integrate theory into our courses. In this respect, the first volume of essays on theory and teaching, a 1982 issue of *Yale French Studies,* is representative. Here, teaching is a trope, a theme, or an object for theoretical reflection—anything but a practice. This is not to say that such a discussion of teaching is uninteresting; Shoshana Felman's "Psychoanalysis and Teaching," for example, makes important theoretical points in reading teaching through the lens of psychoanalysis, opening a line of inquiry that Constance Penley develops significantly in "Teaching in Your Sleep: Feminism and Psychoanalysis." But Penley's essay is also symptomatic. It ostensibly discusses the problems of teaching a course of feminism and psychoanalysis, but in fact, mention of the course is significantly absent from the essay, which is devoted to theoretical problems raised by the intersection of teaching, feminism, and psychoanalysis.

I will try to avoid the trap of doing theory at the expense of addressing issues of curriculum design. Thus, my primary focus is not on what to do tomorrow in your survey of British literature to make it theoretical but rather on how theory might be the basis for a major curriculum revision in English and other literature departments. First, I focus on problems associated with current ways of integrating theory into the curriculum; second, I present a positive proposal, a project for integrating theory in the form of theorizing, a postdisciplinary practice.

The relationship between theory and the curriculum has remained largely undiscussed and unquestioned. Perhaps because there has been so little written specifically on theory and the curriculum, theory has begun to be integrated into the curriculum in terms of one or more of three sets of (usually unstated) assumptions. I name these sets of assumptions, or metatheories, *useful approaches, interpretive policy,* and *perennial questions.* Because I think each of these metatheories is inadequate for realizing the most important insights of poststructuralist theory in curriculum design, I claim that they should be avoided. I must qualify in advance these "do nots," however, for I do not mean that we should always and everywhere avoid useful approaches, or questions that have come to be perennial, or even interpretive policy. Rather, I mean that each of these is to be avoided precisely as a theory of theory in the curriculum. Furthermore, another qualification is needed. The issue of theory in the curriculum is not identical to the issue of theory in the classroom, for curriculum design is not simply a matter of pedagogy. The notion of theorizing does have important pedagogical implications, but my focus here is on theory as something to be taught rather than as a source of ideas about how to teach. I choose this focus in part because most of the discussion of theory and education to date has focused on pedagogy. Books by Nelson, Greg Ulmer, and Douglas Atkins and Michael L. Johnson all take as their fundamental assumption that theory will have its major impact on the way literature is taught rather than on what it is that gets taught. This is not to say that these books completely neglect the curriculum, but that it is a marginal concern, treated in one or two essays or by implication.

Atkins and Johnson's *Writing and Reading Differently* takes deconstruction as its theoretical focus. Although the book was published in 1985, the apolitical and textual (rather than cultural) emphasis of the book already seems dated.[1] Nelson's collection, *Theory in the Classroom,* takes all contemporary theory as its starting point, but the essays have an explicitly political and cultural cast to them that makes the book more pertinent than *Writing and Reading Differently.* (The inclusiveness of the term *theory* does make for some strange bedfellows: the first essay in the volume, by William Schroeder, out-Hirsches

Hirsch by arguing that we lack complete interpretations of most literary works and that we should be teaching students the most complete interpretations possible.) That this collection focuses on interpretation is suggested by the list of questions entitled "Problematizing Interpretation" that Nelson places before the essays, and this focus mitigates the potential curricular implications that the topic "theory in the classroom" ought to carry. Despite arguments by critics as diverse as Jonathan Culler (in "Beyond Interpretation") and S. P. Mohanty (see his critique of "reading" in Nelson's volume), the assumption seems to be that the interpretation of literary texts will remain what gets taught in our classes.

Greg Ulmer's *Applied Grammatology*—for which his article in Atkins and Johnson is a kind of preview—is more successful as theory than as pedagogy. The first section of the book, "Beyond Deconstruction: Derrida," is an important corrective to the almost exclusive identification of Derrida with deconstruction. Ulmer proposes "grammatology" as the more important Derridean project, and he describes it as "a name designating a new organization of cultural studies" and as "a new mode of writing whose practice could bring the language and literature disciplines into a more responsive relationship with the era of communications technology in which we are living" (4). This is, of course, a suggestion for curricular revision, and an important one at that. Nevertheless, Ulmer never gets specific enough about what a grammatological curriculum would look like, and many of the specific proposals he does offer fail precisely because they differ too little from deconstruction. The second part of the book, "Post(e)-Pedagogy," attempts to outline a "pedagogical practice that is designed to overcome the logocentric limitations of discourse" (5). This is an enormous task, and it is not so much a criticism as a recognition of the inevitable to say that he fails. What Ulmer does best, especially in the chapter on "Models," is to catalog the moves that Derrida and other poststructuralists typically make. What he does not successfully address is how these moves might actually be implemented in course design or classroom practice.

The implication of many of the essays in the Nelson and Atkins/Johnson volumes is that theory will find its way into the curriculum on the basis of one or more of the assumptions I will attack here. In general, however, theory has been entering the curriculum without any explicit theory of its place there. Usually, the introduction occurs on the basis of one or more of the three previously mentioned sets of implicit assumptions: useful approaches, perennial questions, and interpretive policy. In practice, these three metatheories tend to result in two strategies. Either students are presented with exemplary interpretations of texts based on new theoretical assumptions, a practice that most often results from useful approaches or interpretive policy, or they are offered a course that treats literary theorists either historically or as members of a contemporary movement. This latter sort of course can have as its rationale either the need for interpretive policy or the desire to expose students to timeless issues of esthetics, rhetoric, and hermeneutics. Neither kind of course requires any basic changes in the curriculum as a whole. The exemplary interpretations method has obvious parallels to teaching practices derived from New Criticism, and it need not alter the basic literature curriculum at all. The theory course may differ from anything offered recently in many departments, but it can simply be added, leaving the rest of the sequence of periods, genres, and authors just as it was before theory was introduced. Contemporary theory should cause us to rethink the curriculum as a whole, but so far theory has merely been added to it. The current metatheories are inadequate in other ways, however, besides the fact that they would leave the current curriculum more or less intact.

Useful Approaches. It may seem perverse to recommend avoiding anything one can call useful, but it is only so if utilitarianism is assumed as the norm. The useful-approaches metatheory treats theories as machines for producing interpretations, as J. Hillis Miller and Barbara Johnson's "new rhetoric of reading" treats deconstruction. Much reader-response pedagogy shares the useful-approaches metatheory. The question that must be asked here is "approaches to what?" The text, of course, but how can something that one's theory holds to be unstable, indeterminate, or always already deconstructed be "approached"? The approaches metaphor assumes that the text is an independently existing object that can be walked around, examined from different perspectives, and, like a mountain, scaled via the best or even the most challenging route. But poststructuralist theory holds that we are always already on top or at least on our way to the top. We have an interpretation before we ever choose a method. We need not share Fish's view that one can have only a single interpretation to acknowledge that one is never without any interpretation.

The mountain metaphor also helps expose the second faulty assumption of useful approaches, that the texts of the canon are permanent features of our intellectual landscape that we must perennially reclimb because they are there. Again, contemporary literary theory cannot support this assumption. Feminist theory has taken the lead in attacking it, although feminists often call merely for addition or replacement rather than for a thorough reconception. Which texts get taught ought to be determined by the issues one hopes to raise in a particular course. That is, choosing texts is itself a theoretical project. To teach theory as a set of approaches is in fact to avoid many of most important implications of poststructuralism.

One of these implications is to question the boundaries that we usually take to separate both literature from other kinds of discourse and theory from practical criticism. These boundaries tend to put the literary work on a pedestal: the work is held above more utilitarian or mundane texts, but at the same time it is prohibited from being understood as performing a function other than providing esthetic pleasure or moral edification. The implication of poststructuralism, however, is that fiction and poetry are themselves *theoretical*, just as theories themselves are understood as fictions. Thus, texts we usually consider theoretical, such as the philosophy of Hegel or Rousseau, can be treated as "literature," while *A Portrait of the Artist as a Young Man* or "Dover Beach" can be read as theory.

Once the literary work is removed from its pedestal, its ideological function becomes the major issue, not one approach among others. This calls attention to another significant defect of the useful-approaches metatheory, its pluralism. If theory is understood as providing a selection of different interpretive strategies, it will generally not be understood as a way of discriminating among those strategies. Thus, although the useful-approaches metatheory need not be explicitly pluralist, that is, it need not assume that all approaches can yield some truth, theory taught as useful approaches in practice will come across as pluralist. Students will not be taught to understand why they might prefer a humanist theory to a psychoanalytic one, for example, except to the extent that the text might be said to "lend itself" better to one theory than to another. But this move abandons theory, and we find ourselves relying on the intrinsic character of the text. Pluralism is objectionable not only because it denies both the reality that we all have commitments to some positions and not others and the possibility that some theories may be wrong, but also because it renders theory uncritical of its own project.

Interpretive Policy. If integrating theory into the curriculum as useful approaches is pluralist, incorporating it as interpretive policy tends toward the opposite, the assumption that a single theory can allow us to interpret literature correctly. In their infamous essay "Against Theory," Knapp and Michaels assume that all theory—or, to read them charitably, all theory that they are against—is meant to establish interpretive policy. (Their essay should have been titled "Against Prescriptive Hermeneutics," but no one would have published— much less read—an article with this title.) This understanding of theory is not without support from the dictionary or from the characteristic role that theory has played in the development of the academic disciplines. One commonly accepted definition of theory identifies it with natural *law.* Perhaps more importantly, especially in the social sciences and humanities, *theory* and *method* are often used interchangeably, so that the theory a student learns takes the form of instructions or prohibitions. Theory used in this way is an explicit form of governance and performs the kind of police action that Knapp and Michaels attack. Their attack, however, is itself a police action, asserting that because any interpretation *must* be a statement of what the author intended, theory should be prohibited as a waste of effort. What they seem to be saying is that theory is unnecessary because of the nature of interpretation, which is both necessarily governed and ungovernable. Theory, they argue, can have no effect; it is based on a series of pseudoproblems deriving from the belief in "mistakes" such as the ambiguity or indeterminacy of language, the arbitrary character of language, and so on. What Knapp and Michaels fail to acknowledge, however, is that these judgments are themselves theoretical, interpretation being neither a natural nor a self-evident activity, and that their prohibition of theory will govern the practice of members of the profession just as surely as any particular theory of interpretation.

To be sure, much theoretical debate is carried on as if interpretive policy were what is at stake, but theory has other meanings that cut against its association with law. The most important of these meanings is *speculation.* As Paula Treichler shows in her review of the OED definitions of "theory," the word begins with speculation as derived from sight or spectacle—it is etymologically linked to seeing—

and ends with the popular extension of the term to mean "hypotheses, conjectures, ideas, and individual views and notions" (88–89). To deconstruct the term *theory,* to reverse our usual valorization of law over conjecture, is precisely what poststructuralist theory does, not only in its opposition to established practices within literary studies but also in its opposition to the scientism and positivism rampant in our culture, especially in the social sciences. If we are to convey this important role for theory to our students, we cannot teach it as the rules and regulations for interpretation. Rather, theory should be understood as the space of the possible and taught as a group of ways such a space may be constructed.

Prior to its recent rise under the influence of French and other foreign schools of thought, theory was understood almost exclusively as policy, although "literary theory" might be understood as the project of governing literary practice—parallel to the project of music theory—as well as interpretation. Under this assumption, theory played only a very minor role in the curriculum. Because it was assumed that undergraduates would learn correct interpretation by imitating their teachers or that they would naturally interpret literature in the right way if given the opportunity to do so, literary theory became a subject suitable for graduate students, who needed some rationale for the activity that they were planning to make their careers. Even at this level, literary theory was mainly intended to keep the neophytes from straying into extraliterary matters. Wellek and Warren's *Theory of Literature* served as the law in American literary studies by demonstrating the error of all approaches save the "intrinsic," or as it should have been called, the New Critical. If one of the new theories were to be integrated into the curriculum as interpretive policy, the results would be similar. One theory would be taught, but it would be taught to undergraduates as if it were not a theory but the truth. Of course, such a new theory might cause major changes in the curriculum, but it would not make theory itself a more important part of it.

Perennial Questions. If "theory" is used as a shorthand expression for "literary theory," then we are most likely to associate it with the two previous metatheories. When we begin to think of theory as a transdisciplinary project traceable back to the Greeks, we are more likely to think of a pattern familiar from philosophy, a group of questions about which theorists have always disagreed and will always disagree. The questions that have characterized the discipline of philosophy at least since the Enlightenment should be familiar to all: the mind/body problem; the other minds problem; the problem of representation; the relation of subject and object; the nature of Being; and so on. Some of these issues—for example subject/object and representation—also crop up in literary theory, but others are characteristic of it: the significance of the author's intention, the nature of literary language, and the necessity of tropes. If theory were to become dominant over literary texts in the language disciplines, then these questions might well become their preoccupation, and literary theory would imitate the mistakes Rorty accuses professionalized philosophy of making, mistakes that have removed philosophy from the larger culture and made Rorty idealize literary criticism.

Philosophy is not the only guilty party here. Academic disciplines in the humanities are typically defined by both a canon of texts and a group of perennial questions. Students learn the questions by reading either their history or their expression in the works of the "fathers." There is thus a strong connection between the theoretical canon and the questions a discipline raises. In the natural sciences, which lack a canon and which have a history of developing questions—Stephen Toulmin calls it a genealogy, but he has neither Nietzsche nor Foucault in mind—the symbiosis between major figures and questions is not nearly so strong. The poststructuralist critique of humanist privileging of Western, upper-class texts should make us seek to rethink the role of canons in cultural studies. Its critique of foundationalism or essentialism should lead us to realize that there are no perennial questions, only context-dependent ones. We do not want to build theory into the curriculum in such a way that students will be still raising poststructuralist questions 400 years from now as philosophy students are still debating Cartesian questions today.

Nevertheless, there is nothing in either poststructural theory or elsewhere to suggest that culture studies could imitate the sciences even if it wanted to. As Foucault argues, many of the major discursive formations of poststructuralism—psychoanalysis, Marxism, Nietzschian genealogy—depend on a "founding father" for their identity and development. Feminism, which as Treichler points out lacks a Femina, a founding mother, is one exception that ought to be a model for theorists of culture studies (90). Feminism and other theories that are tied to particular social struggles seem less likely to fall into asking perennial questions, but the history of Marxist theory suggests that it is not impossible for them to do so.

There remains a great danger that perennial questions, in spite of assumptions that ought to prohibit them, will come to structure theory courses and curricula as the discourses of poststructuralism become institutionalized. This will be especially true if theory becomes institutionalized as a discipline. Humanities disciplines are defined not by their methods or even their content but by the objects they deal with and the kinds of questions they ask of those objects. Thus, philosophy is defined by a canon of philosophy texts and by the specifically philosophical questions it seeks to solve. Literary study is defined by a canon and by the interpretive questions it asks. If theory were to become a discipline or subdiscipline, it would doubtless be defined in the same way. Theory, of course, does have both a canon and its own kinds of questions, but as a discipline, its canon would become increasingly fixed and its questions would be continually under the influence of the canonical theorists. That is why theory should not seek to become a discipline or to be included in the curriculum mainly as a subdiscipline taught in courses separate from those on other texts.

My task in this section is to set out the assumptions on which theory should be integrated into courses. I argue that theory should be incorporated as a postdisciplinary practice and taught as theorizing, an activity characterized by an attitude of skepticism toward accepted beliefs, a willingness to play with alternatives, a focus on what is entailed and not merely stated, and a lack of immediate practical application. Theorizing is an activity, but it is not a process without content. Rather, theorizing must be understood as a discursive practice that involves knowing not only the previous contributions but also how to make new ones.

Above all, what distinguishes teaching theorizing from simply teaching theory is the assumption that classes should be places where theory is done, not merely absorbed. In integrating theory into the curricula of English and other language departments, we must avoid imitating the discipline of philosophy, which typically teaches the ideas of its "fathers" as a series of formulations that must be more or less memorized, its classes most often given over to helping students understand philosophers' formulations as precisely as possible. These goals force philosophers to lecture and preclude discussion as a major classroom activity, an ironic state of affairs in a discipline that traces its origins to Socrates. To ask students to *do* theory in the classroom is quite different from asking them merely to *learn* theories. When doing theory is the goal, the formulations of theorists should be a springboard for the students' own intellectual work.[2] But such intellectual work cannot be purely original; instead of asking students to invent their own theories, we should ask them to play with the theories of others by both criticizing and extending them.

Poststructuralist theory offers no relief from the fundamental problems of education: that students must learn to read critically and write effectively; that certain knowledge must be learned before other knowledge can be understood; and that understanding much of what is taught in cultural studies requires that students already have broad cultural knowledge. We must admit to ourselves that a poststructuralist curriculum will not fundamentally alter the nature of university teaching or learning. Doing theory in the classroom, or asking students to theorize in writing assignments, does not radically alter the relationship between student and teacher typical in most discussion-centered classes, but it does change the nature of the tasks that college students are asked to perform. The most fundamental of these tasks is to read theoretical material theoretically. Obviously, this means that we need to assign theoretical readings in our classes, but I think it also means that we need to recognize that students must be familiar with certain theories before other theories can be understood.

Thus, even though theorizing requires no particular questions, no founding fathers or mothers, no particular canon, and no single policy, to say that it requires none of these things would be disingenuous without the immediate addition that we cannot theorize, much less teach theorizing, without relying on a body of theoretical work. Theorizing is not the natural activity of unfettered reason; rather, it is a particular kind of discursive practice with its own cultural specificity. Theorizing is a particular kind of critical thinking, and as anthropologist Shirley Bryce Heath has argued, critical thinking is a distinctive product of Western cultures.[3] For example, the ideal of thinking critically assumes a competitive rather than cooperative use of language, and such a use is not typical of many non-Western cultures. Given this, both the form and the content of theorizing must be taught.

But even though the project of integrating theory into the curriculum has much in common with projects being undertaken in rhetoric and composition studies that have fostering critical thinking as their goal, most discussions of critical thinking have assumed that it can be taught absent any particular critical positions. The unstated model for this project is formal logic, and "informal logic" is often used as a synonym for critical thinking. But logic is distinguished by its closure; once we move out of the closed systems of formal logic we are thrown back on particular assumptions and beliefs as the basis of our criticism of other assumptions or beliefs. Theorizing differs from the program of critical thinking by acknowledging this condition, and it provides a platform from which criticism can issue. Critical thinking without a critical position can never become genuinely critical. What I am arguing here is that there is no such thing as critical thinking in the abstract. We can describe the qualities that characterize critical thinking, but we cannot teach it merely on the basis of that description.

Theorists, however, have their own version of this mistake. Developing a critical position is not a matter of simply opposing what is already in place. That is the mistake Ulmer makes in advocating a humanities pedagogy that is defined by its opposition to positivism. The cultural studies disciplines could not survive if they were oppositional merely in this sense, but these disciplines cannot be merely oppositional, for to oppose implies a position, an opposite position. It is true that poststructuralists have made a trope—which I call *reversal*—of taking whatever opposite position a positive statement makes available, but although such a trope often succeeds brilliantly in the writing of someone like Foucault, it will not do as a general strategy for teaching theorizing to undergraduates. Furthermore, no significant theorist employs reversal randomly, but rather in the service of a more or less positive position. That a Foucault or a Derrida may frequently change or disavow these positions does not mitigate their necessity to the arguments in which they were set out.

Thus, although I said before that theorizing can be described in terms of some general characteristics including skepticism, playfulness, focus on implication, and lack of immediate practical application, the theorizing that I propose we teach is based on specific theoretical practices, including not only poststructuralism but also Marxism, psychoanalysis, feminism, and others as well. In "Reading Twentieth-Century Culture," one of three theory courses required in what has been described as the first poststructuralist undergraduate curriculum,

I teach no explicitly poststructuralist theory at all. Rather, the course focuses on what might be called prestructuralist theories of culture: Arnoldian humanism, Marxism, Freudian psychoanalysis, feminism, and several anthropological theories in addition to the structuralism of Lévi-Strauss. Familiarity with these theories is necessary for students to comprehend many poststructuralist arguments. In addition to presenting the theories themselves, this course also illustrates a second important principle in teaching theorizing: the need for comparison. Students are asked to use each theory to criticize the others. This does not mean that I present all the theories as if they were equally valid. I am more critical of humanism in my explanation of it than I am of Marxism. Nevertheless, it is my goal that students understand why one might believe what Arnold believed, rather than to dismiss him as a fool, and also that they see the difficulties with culture defined merely as superstructure or with an eschatological vision of history.

What Marxism, psychoanalysis, feminism, and poststructuralist theories have in common is that they all criticize received assumptions, social arrangements, or cultural practices from a particular perspective. Thus, each includes a position from which criticism is made. This position is not identical to any particular proposals for change that these bodies of theory offer, but those proposals are intimately related to the position; for example, we can distinguish Marxist theory from any particular instantiation of Marxist politics, including Marx's own. By treating feminism or Marxism as theory, we distance ourselves from the particular policy objectives of those movements. This is not to argue against the discussion of those objectives but only to indicate the specific level at which theory operates.

At this point, the objection might be raised that the project of teaching theorizing is yet another version of pluralism. Why not merely teach feminism or Marxism (or even both, if you can make them fit together) and forget about trying to teach theory in general, which I have already as much as admitted does not exist? The first response is that the position I support here is not pluralist. It is not based on the assumption that all theories have some elements of truth, or that all theories are equally worthy to be included in the curriculum. Rather, we ought to teach a plurality of theories because our goal is to give students the ability to reflect on their own positions. Thus, although teaching theory means teaching Marxism, feminism, and other politically motivated discourses, it also means teaching students not to accept uncritically what their teachers tell them. This paradox explains both the political and the strategic need for teaching theorizing rather than just theories. The political need is to create antiauthoritarian beliefs and practices; the strategic consideration is that students who come to college with beliefs and practices already in place are not likely to be persuaded to change these by an instructor who insists on the truth of other beliefs and practices. The best we can do is to create conditions wherein it is possible for students to come to accept the theories we advocate. In spite of our inability to ground or metaphysically support our claims for our theories, we must assume that they will be persuasive to those whose interests they serve. Indeed, our theories hold that they will not be persuasive to anyone else.

Another objection to "Reading Twentieth-Century Culture" might be that it violates one of my own principles by treating theory as a discipline with its own canon. But the course does not include only texts that explicitly offer theories of culture. There are also novels, poems, and films, which are presented not mainly as material to be interpreted from a Marxist, Freudian, or humanist perspective but as other forms of theorizing that embody some of the content of Marxism or psychoanalysis but work with it in very different ways. Thus, Buñuel's *Discreet Charm of the Bourgeoisie* is presented as working out some of the implications of psychoanalysis, whereas *A Portrait of the Artist as a Young Man* is read as a meditation on humanism. Several other fictional texts, Faulkner's *The Bear,* Margaret Atwood's *Handmaid's Tale,* and Denise Giardiana's *Storming Heaven,* provide theories of particular social and economic conditions. One point of including these works is to blur the line between theory and fiction, but this blurring is not a major issue of the course, just as hermeneutics is not a focus. To foreground these problems would be to distract students from the problem of culture. Treating explicitly fictional works as forms of theory destabilizes the subordinate relation they have to the explicitly theoretical ones. Thus, whereas the theoretical texts used in this course may be part of a canon, teaching them in relation to very different texts, such as fictional films and books, deprives them of their disciplinary function.

Teaching the practice of theorizing involves more than providing the students with the correct reading list. Curriculum and classroom practice become closely related problems, because no matter what books are taught, our courses must give students the opportunity to theorize. Teaching theorizing thus involves conflicting demands on class and assignment time. Time spent learning particular theories often is not time in which students may theorize themselves.[4] This is not a problem merely of reducing the readings to some manageable amount. We may assume that reading a theoretical text requires the student to do theoretical work, but that is not necessarily the case. My course succeeds in teaching most students who take it to bring theoretical perspectives to bear on important theoretical texts, but this is not to say that they are able to read those texts theoretically, or even with comprehension, the first time through. I am convinced that all students are capable of learning to theorize and of understanding theory, but they must be taught how to learn and understand. More than any other academic ideology, humanism has valued the ease and grace of expression that come from early exposure to a particular discursive practice. Bourdieu and Passeron have shown that in France this valorization has prohibited all but a very few born outside the social elite from certain academic disciplines. We need to break down our prejudice in favor of the "natural" student and tell students how they can learn to learn this stuff.

Teaching students how to learn is not new to education specialists or to those concerned with teaching basic writing, but it is often neglected by teachers in more advanced humanities classes. The assumption is that students in our classes already have learned to read and write and think, so that now they need only to be taught the content of the course and perhaps to refine their previously acquired skills. But few students have learned the skills we assume they have. This becomes particularly clear when one begins to teach theoretical texts. We assume that good readers should be capable of doing something with any nontechnical text written in their native language, yet English majors in a selective institution such as Carnegie Mellon often have trouble reading even traditionally argumentative texts. The problem is that students are typically taught to read in one of two ways, depending on the kind of text they are given. If it is a poetic or fictional work, they know that the teacher will expect them to interpret rather than merely summarize. If it is any other kind of text, however, the students are trained to read it for the facts it presents, because most nonfictional material that students read claims factual content for itself: newspapers, magazine articles, and especially, textbooks. But theoretical texts do more than go beyond facts to arguments; these texts challenge assumptions that students have long taken for granted as common sense and propose ideas that are utterly foreign to many students. Consider psychoanalysis, for example. Although many Freudian ideas and even more Freudian language have become part of popular culture, Freudian theory is not familiar. Not only do students have trouble seriously entertaining the propositions that they are not unified subjects but an amalgam of conflicting components and that sexual desire motivates much human behavior, but they are not even sure about what to do with a text that articulates such propositions. Reading theory is defamiliarizing, which is a major part of its value, but students have no notion of defamiliarization to fall back on, so they may find it merely mystifying. They can comprehend the words and sentences, but they have no context that can render the ideas significant. That context is the project of theory itself, the discussion of the conditions of possibility for various presumed realities.

We theorists want students to do more than *merely* understand an argument; we want them to be able to know its weaknesses, its underlying assumptions, and its unstated implications. But how can this level of analysis be reached if the point of the argument is missed? Some studies of readers suggest that understanding the thesis of an argument may depend on the kinds of analytic skills I have just mentioned, ones normally assumed to be secondary, but this does not relieve us of the necessity to teach these skills. David Kaufer, Christine Neuwirth, and Cheryl Geisler present a new theory of argument that takes as its central trope the metaphor of giving directions. Each argument is thus to be understood as describing a path to the main point the author wants the reader to come to accept but also as warning of faulty paths—conflicting points of view—that might get the reader to the wrong intellectual destination. The theory assumes that students must be taught to summarize the secondary material that they read. Typically, we assume summary to be something students do all too often when we have asked them to do something else, but Kaufer and his associates treat summary as a form of analysis (although they reserve the term *analysis* for reference to the student's exploration of an issue after having read differing positions on it). In summarizing, students are asked to classify the material in the source as being on the main or on a faulty path. Thus, in telling students how to reread and mark an essay so as to label its main and faulty paths, the authors are teaching students to produce a reading or interpretation of it that is motivated by their own interests. The notion that summary is also a form of rereading or interpretation should come as no surprise to poststructuralists, but the notion that we need to teach it for students to be able to read what seem to us to be straightforward arguments may be surprising. In fact, we need to encourage students simply to read complex materials more than once, but we also need to teach them what they are reading for.

My call for teaching theorizing as a particular discursive practice not only requires changes in the material, tasks, and goals of individual courses but also requires changes in the way knowledge is divided, organized, and administered. That is why theory should not be understood as "literary theory" but as a practice that derives from and is relevant to many different disciplines. It is for this reason that I describe teaching theorizing as "postdisciplinary," a word I borrow from Dean and Juliet Flower MacCannell's *The Time of the Sign*. They argue that phenomenology, poststructuralism, and, above all, semiotics form the basis for a new conception of knowledge. The MacCannells do not strongly develop the notion of postdisciplinarity, and their association of it with particular theoretical schools is suspect because it does not take into account the social and technological aspects of disciplinarity. In my view, postdisciplinarity does not assume the disappearence of the disciplines. Rather, it would function in their interstices, forging connections between different disciplines but not seeking to combine them into a new discipline. Postdisciplinarity would abandon territoriality as a principle of survival. Instead of establishing turf to protect, postdisciplinary work would attempt to break down the boundaries of other territories. That means that a postdisciplinary project cannot seek separate institutional status but must exist parasitically within the spaces of the disciplines.

To begin working toward teaching theorizing as a postdisciplinary project, we need to design curricula in English departments that are not restricted to their traditional disciplinary mission. Theory requires that students know philosophy and history, and not just the watered-down versions that creep into traditional literature department courses. Thus, I do not regard teaching theorizing as antithetical to Richard Ohmann's description, elsewhere in this volume, of teaching historically. To include such additional material, however, undergraduate curricula will not be able to include as much literature as many do at present. This is a particular difficulty given the need to expand, rather than narrow, the literary canon. Although I cannot offer a detailed solution to this dilemma here, I believe that the solution must lie in changing the guiding principle of text selection. The goal should no longer be to represent a national literature but rather to provide an understanding of the cultural, social, and historical relations of literature and other texts. Texts should be chosen in terms of the theories and the social and historical relations they may be made to illustrate. This would be a genuinely radical change, for the notion of a national literature is fundamental to the current formation of literary studies. My argument has been that such radical changes are necessary for the insights of contemporary theory to be realized in curriculum design. It is not enough for theory to find its place in the grid of diverse literature department offerings. Rather, theory must transform these offerings, without simply replacing them with its own texts and issues.

NOTES

I would like to thank Maria-Regina Kecht and David Kaufer for their useful suggestions and comments on this essay.

1. Gayatri Spivak's essay "Reading the World" is an exception to this in its cultural studies orientation. For a thorough critique of *Reading and Writing Differently,* see John Schilb's essay "Poststructuralism, Politics, and the Subject of Pedagogy," the second in this volume.
2. Thus, there are pedagogical practices necessary to teaching theorizing. For example, an important classroom practice may be described as student-centered teaching (see Bickman).
3. In a lecture at Carnegie Mellon University, October 20, 1988.
4. For a practical discussion of these kinds of problems, see Bickman.

WORKS CITED

Atkins, G. Douglas, and Michael L. Johnson, eds. *Reading and Writing Differently.* Lawrence: UP of Kansas, 1985.

Bickman, Martin. "The Act of Learning in the University: An Inquiry into Inquiry." *On Teaching.* Ed. Mary Ann Shea. Boulder: Faculty Teaching Excellence Program, 1987. 31–66.

Bourdieu, Pierre, and Jean-Claude Passeron. *Reproduction In Education, Society, and Culture.* London and Beverly Hills: Sage, 1977.

Culler, Jonathan. "Beyond Interpretation." *The Pursuit of Signs: Semiotics, Literature, Deconstruction.* Ithaca: Cornell UP, 1980.

Felman, Shoshana. "Psychoanalysis and Teaching." *Yale French Studies* 63 (1982): 21–44.

Fish, Stanley. *Is There a Text in This Class?* Cambridge: Harvard UP, 1982.

Foucault, Michel. "What Is an Author?" *Language, Counter-Memory, Practice.* Ed. Donald F. Bouchard. Trans. Bouchard and Sherry Simon. Ithaca: Cornell UP, 1977.

Johnson, Barbara. "Teaching Deconstructively." Atkins and Johnson 140–48.

Kaufer, David S., Christine Neuwirth, and Cheryl Geisler. *Arguing from Sources: Exploring Issues through Reading and Writing* New York: Harcourt Brace Jovanovich, 1989.

Knapp, Steven, and Walter Benn Michaels. "Against Theory." *Critical Inquiry* 8 (Summer 1982): 723–42.

MacCannell, Dean, and Juliet Flower MacCannell. *The Time of the Sign: A Semiotic Interpretation of Modern Culture.* Bloomington: Indiana UP, 1982.

Miller, J. Hillis. "The Two Rhetorics: George Eliot's Bestiary." Atkins and Johnson 101–14.

Mohanty, S. P. "Radical Teaching, Radical Theory: The Ambiguous Politics of Meaning." Nelson 148–76.

Nelson, Cary, ed. *Theory in the Classroom.* Urbana: U of Illinois P, 1986.

Penley, Constance. "Teaching in Your Sleep: Feminism and Psychoanalysis." Nelson 129–48.

Rorty, Richard. "Professionalized Philosophy." *Consequences of Pragmatism.* Minneapolis: U of Minnesota P, 1982. 60–71.

Schroeder, William R. "A Teachable Theory." Nelson 9–44.

Spivak, Gayatri. "Reading the World: Literary Studies in the '90s." Atkins and Johnson 27–37.

Treichler, Paula A. "Teaching Feminist Theory." Nelson 57–128.

Ulmer, Gregory L. *Applied Grammatology: Post(e)-Pedagogy from Jacques Derrida to Joseph Beuys.* Baltimore: Johns Hopkins UP, 1985.

Wellek, René, and Austin Warren. *Theory of Literature.* New York: Harcourt, 1949.

5

ALWAYS ALREADY THEORISTS: LITERARY THEORY AND THEORIZING IN THE UNDERGRADUATE CURRICULUM

Kathleen McCormick

> There is just no sense in pondering the function of literature without relating it to the actual society that uses it, to the centers of power within that society, and to the institutions that mediate between literature and people.
>
> Richard Ohmann, *English in America*

Literary theory has become increasingly powerful and prestigious over the last two decades in our profession, and it is now commonplace to hear and read of its making its way in various forms into classroom practice. We are not only quietly arguing in the halls or on the pages of journals about the ontological status of the text, the nature of indeterminacy, or the reification of the individual in bourgeois society; rather, teachers and administrators are also trying to discover ways to move literary theory into pedagogy. Books such as Robert Scholes's *Textual Power,* William Cain's *The Crisis in Criticism,* and Gerald Graff's *Professing Literature* all investigate how literary theory might influence the teaching of English. In addition to such book-length studies, numerous collections of essays and journal articles likewise stress the need for using theory to address issues of pedagogy. Frequent essays in the *ADE Bulletin* show how these ideas are making their way to department administrators.[1]

Paulo Freire's seminal work, *Pedagogy of the Oppressed,* can serve as a continual reminder to us, however, that innovative (or even radical) theory does not necessarily constitute innovative or radical pedagogy.[2] Freire develops an extended critique of what he calls the "banking system of education," in which "education . . . becomes an act of depositing, in which the students are the depositories and the teacher is the depositor. Instead of communicating, the teacher issues communiqués and makes deposits which the students patiently receive, memorize, and repeat" (58). Although one senses from reading the many recent books and articles on connections between theory and pedagogy that certain teachers are indeed working to use theory as a way to provide students with new ways of reading and writing, it would be naive to assume either that the discipline at large necessarily sees a connection between theory and pedagogy or that most people who identify themselves as "theorists" necessarily imagine that their theoretical insights impinge in major ways on classroom practice. As Carl Freedman points out in "Marxist Theory, Radical Pedagogy, and the Reification of Thought," even the (presumably progressive) academic literary left "has been definably split into two principal tendencies, which may be designated the theorists and the pedagogues"; the two show their differences in part by forming "not one but two major affiliated organizations of the Modern Language Association: the (mainly theoretical) Marxist Literary Group and the (mainly pedagogic) Radical Caucus" (70).

In the introduction to their book *Reclaiming Pedagogy,* Patricia Donahue and Ellen Quandahl argue that theory "offers an agenda of radical change that could challenge the foundation of American education." They go on to suggest, understandably, that it is the fault of the American right that this agenda is not being met: "It is thus not surprising that theory is often distorted or neutralized when injected into the pedagogical scene. We are living in a time of stasis when conservatism is revered and diversity, transformation, and analysis are seen as further evidence of the 'closing of the American mind' " (15). Although I am in basic agreement with their point that theory is potentially transformative, it seems that before we place all the blame for our plight on what Henry Louis Gates calls "the killer Bs," that is, Allan Bloom and William Bennett (Begley 26), we should recognize that the very nature of our institution works to neutralize radical thought by the kinds of attitudes toward pedagogy it privileges—in teachers of the left as well as the right.

Given the enormous institutional prestige of "theory" and the still relatively low status of "pedagogy" (despite significant inroads over the last two decades), we must recognize that there is still strong institutional support for falling back into a banking concept of teaching theory, in which the teacher demonstrates that he or she is the mentor with the latest disciplinary insights and the students become disciples, all too willing and eager to follow. As Stanley Fish wrote in *Is There a Text in This Class?* (and stated at Kenyon College):

> The status of the text, the source of interpretive authority, the relationship between subjectivity and objectivity, the limits of interpretation—these are topics that have been discussed again and again; they are basic topics, and anyone who is able to advance the discussion of them will automatically be accorded a hearing and be a candidate for the profession's highest rewards. One incontestable piece of evidence in support of this assertion is the fact that I have been here speaking to you for an entire week, and that you have been listening. (371)

Fish's comments can give us pause for a number of reasons. It is noteworthy that pedagogy is conspicuously absent from Fish's list of high-interest topics, despite his supposed concern in his theory with real (even student) readers. He also suggests that the theoretical interests he has been pursuing in his book are given such status in the profession not because they are new and radical but because they are old and "basic." Fish's comments should be read symptomatically for what they conceal as much as for what they reveal. One of the absences of his text—one of the things that it "did not want to say" but was "*compelled* to say" (Macherey 94)—is that while the profession of English, like any major ideological institution, works to constitute new knowledge, it also functions to appropriate that which might potentially threaten its status and authority. So while we are applauding ourselves for the great inroads we have made in curricular development, we also need to investigate the extent to which the nature of our practice matches the supposed radicalism of our thought. It is crucial to move theory away from the temptation to become an elitist, arcane pastime into the more difficult, but in the long run no less important, area of curriculum and pedagogy. To do so raises a number of questions. Can we choose whether to have theory in the classroom? What are some of the pedagogical implications of "being theoretical"? In what ways might theory be integrated successfully into an undergraduate curriculum? What are some issues raised by theory that are simultaneously accessible and stimulating enough to organize a course or a curriculum? In discussing these last two questions, I will use as an example the developments in the Carnegie Mellon English curriculum between 1983 and 1989, when the English department developed a Literary and Cultural Studies program that attracted a fair degree of attention in educational circles.[3] One guaranteed feature of any curriculum is its continually evolving status, and in 1989 this curriculum began to move into a new phase. Although this six-year period was hardly uniform—our department annually hired new faculty to teach in and build the LCS program—the goals for the program remained relatively constant, and, in its achievements and weaknesses, it constitutes something of a case history for my broader theoretical considerations.

One of the discoveries we made in our curricular development at Carnegie Mellon is that we simply have no choice about whether to have theory in the classroom. Theory is always there—in us and in our undergraduates. We are all always already theorists. We have a choice only of whether we and our students will be self-conscious (that is to say, theoretical) about the theories that guide our perceptions. If, for example, I say, "I know that Stephen Dedalus's poem in James Joyce's *Portrait of the Artist as a Young Man* is meant to be bad poetry," I am not expressing a purely subjective or a purely objective position. Rather, my statement is driven by a variety of theories about what good poetry is, about authorial intention, and about the status of a reader who can truly know what a text means. These theories operate regardless of whether I am sufficiently self-aware to acknowledge their influence on me.

But my discourse will be regarded as *theoretical* only when I stop taking these influences for granted and begin to be reflective about them. Gerald Graff has remarked that theory is a "name for the questions which necessarily arise when principles and concepts once taken for granted have become matters of controversy" (*Criticism* 9). Such a conception of what it is to be theoretical is very much in line with Freire's notion of "problem-posing" education, which he argues is what must replace the banking system of education. "Problem-posing education," Freire writes, "responding to the essence of consciousness—*intentionality*—rejects communiqués and embodies communication. It epitomizes the special characteristic of consciousness: being *conscious of,* not only as intent on objects but as turned in upon itself in a Jasperian 'split'—consciousness as consciousness *of* consciousness" (66–67). Indeed, some would argue that self-consciousness and controversy are what define theory and distinguish it from nontheoretical discourse. Cary Nelson argues that "what probably most distinguishes theoretical from nontheoretical discourse is its tendency toward self-conscious and reflective interpretive, methodological, and rhetorical practices" ("Against English" 1). He further comments that "when a body of theory ceases to be in crisis . . . then it no longer counts as theory" (1).

It is important to underscore at this point that I am not talking so much about teaching theory as teaching *theorizing*. The difference between the two is vital: the first suggests that there is a body of material "out there"; it is known to the teacher and unknown to the student; it can be taught and presumably "mastered." To conceive of theory and the teaching of theory in this way will more often than not result in the banking system of education, a point I will develop in detail later. In contrast, the notion of teaching theorizing requires what Freire calls a "dialogic" classroom situation, in which "[t]he teacher is no longer merely the-one-who-teaches, but one who is himself taught in dialogue with the students" (67).

Although using theory in the classroom in any productive way requires a degree of self-consciousness, can we say that theory does not exist in the absence of that self-consciousness? My contention that we and our students are always already theorists assumes that literary (and more general) ideologies organize our systems of belief, often without our being fully aware of their influence on us. One of the exciting aspects of teaching students to theorize their own positions is helping them (and us) become aware—often for the first time—that they respond to a text or situation in a particular way because they are influenced by some particular theory. This process relates to the wider educational practice of enabling students to begin seeing the general ideological constraints and empowerments within which they live.

A student, for example, may first note that she does not like Gertrude Stein's "As a Wife Has a Cow." With critical investigation, she can be led to discover that her dislike is not random or arbitrary: she does not enjoy other fiction "like that" either, all of which she calls "strange" or "pointless." On further analysis, she can come to realize that her position is informed by a theory of fiction that privileges plot and character development and that she does not like the Stein piece because it does not conform to this theory. The next step is to help this student discover that her theory is called "expressive realism," a concept presupposing assumptions about text and reading strategies that still seem commonsensical, even though they are built on a now largely abandoned nineteenth-century world outlook of an orderly and rational universe. I have discovered that when students realize that their beliefs and positions can be seen as a part of larger cultural movements, they become fascinated with developing, analyzing, and critiquing them. Their confidence in their abilities rises, as does their need to investigate the cultural antecedents of their positions. I have found that students want to become theoretically self-aware once they discover that theories are working in them anyway.

To become theoretically self-aware is to recognize the situated nature of both our critical positions and our interpretations of texts, to acknowledge that they come about as a result of certain beliefs, principles, and broader ideologies—to see that they are *not universally true* but rather historically situated. Recognizing the situated nature of our positions should not cause us to despair over a lost objectivity or subjectivity, for the belief in objectivity or subjectivity is itself situated. This is not to say that our beliefs are any less *real* than we once might have thought they were: it is our very situatedness or interestedness that impels us to take up certain positions in the first place. As Terry Eagleton comments, "There is no possibility of a wholly disinterested discourse. . . . All of our descriptive statements move within an often invisible network of value-categories, and indeed without such categories we would have nothing to say to each other at all. . . . Interests are *constitutive* of our knowledge, not merely prejudices which imperil it" (13–14).

If we agree with Eagleton that interests are constitutive of our knowledge, then it becomes impossible to impart or acquire knowledge without examining both the ways in which it happens to be interested and our own positions in relation to others. Of course, what we as teachers lose when we become theoretically self-aware in the classroom is the illusion of objective authority, which can be maintained as easily from a position on the left as on the right. Yet the potential pedagogical gains of the dialogic theorizing classroom are rich. It can create an environment in which the principles of the production of knowledge itself are interrogated. As Jeffrey Peck argues in talking about such an environment: "The classroom . . . becomes a productive rather than a reproductive environment, one in which not only interpretations, but also standards, expectations, and goals are negotiated by the teacher and student" (51).

Peck's statement hints at another difference in the theoretically oriented classroom, that it recognizes and may study itself as a disciplinary force affecting reading and writing practices in particular ways. Scholes has commented that each of us possesses a "professional unconscious," that is, that each of us is influenced by the "arche-institution of English" (4). Our professional unconscious works to make us think that certain information is tacit rather than produced by a discipline, but one of the very powerful cultural forces influencing the production of knowledge is the educational system. It is only when we and our students become conscious of disciplinary influences on us that we can begin to resist certain ways of thinking and explain our reasons for embracing other modes of thought.

Bringing theorizing into the literature classroom can also help establish greater links between the teaching of composition, rhetoric, and cognition and the teaching of literature. Contemporary rhetoric is centrally interested in pedagogy, so some of the new approaches to teaching in the theorizing classroom might well profit from years of rhetorical research in the area. As Donahue and Quandahl point out, writing teachers have often been among the first in the discipline to develop pedagogical applications of contemporary theory (1–3), and teachers of literature can greatly benefit from a study of these applications. Further, the notion of theorizing I have been talking about is related to the process of critical thinking discussed in much composition research. Most of the research suggests that despite recent emphases on teaching critical thinking, students of all ages still have difficulty doing it. Collaborations between those interested in rhetoric and cognition and those interested in literary theory may help develop more successful ways to teach critical thinking.[4]

I want now to turn the discussion to the practical question of curriculum development and examine three ways in which theory can be introduced into an English program: canonizing it, adding it on, or integrating it. The first two methods, which I do not advocate, are unfortunately the more common ways of getting theory into the curriculum because they are more strongly rooted in particular institutional attitudes that pervade both our "professional unconscious" and our classroom practices.

In the canonizing method of teaching theory, "theory" texts are substituted for "literary" texts, and theory thus constitutes something like a new canon. Like the canon of literary texts it attempts to replace, the canon of theoretical texts too easily may be essentialized. This will almost certainly yield the sort of unfortunate pedagogical consequences of which Freire speaks: students are likely to be encouraged either just to master the theoretical canon rather than to interrogate it or to become a particular kind of theorist rather than, say, to work creatively among a variety of approaches. Just as at one time romanticists or medievalists might have been uncritically "reproduced" by their teachers on the assumption that Wordsworth or Chaucer was a "great" writer, without the historically constructed nature of that "greatness" being examined, now deconstructivists or New Historicists may too readily be made in their mentors' images and likenesses, without detailed examination of the political and intellectual implications of taking such positions. To teach theory by canonizing it may end in teaching theory without theoretical self-consciousness. I am by no means against the teaching of courses whose primary content is theoretical texts, but I am warning against setting up that theory as an objective, transcendent body of knowledge that is assumed not to require cultural and historical interrogation. Tony Bennett argues eloquently against this penchant to universalize and essentialize in Marxist literary theory, suggesting that the only appropriate "response to the discovery that there can be no transcendental guarantees is: who needs them, anyway?" (3). He contends that "it is only by being ongoingly revised that a body of theory retains any validity or purchase as a historical force" (1). Because the essentializing approach may lack an acknowledgment of the situatedness of all theory, it can discourage critical debate—which should, after all, constitute the major practice of the theorist-teacher. Cary Nelson rightly sees our discipline's penchant to make sacred either a literary text or a theory as a move to protect the profession of literary studies from outside influences. In analyzing the American taming of deconstruction, Nelson writes that "the problem arises when a depoliticized version of immanent analysis becomes a transcendent moral value. . . . When Derrida, for example, practices close textual analysis, the status of the text as an object of veneration or doubt is always open to question. . . .

However, under the leadership of what was once the Yale school, deconstruction in America restored the text to a venerated position and militantly dropped any consideration of larger social questions" ("Against English" 2).

In addition to venerating texts and theories, the canonization of literary theory tends to elitism. Geoffrey Hartman's attack on "remedial gymnastics" (12) and the "decorum of accommodation . . . all around us" (13), for example, assumes both that theory is difficult and, as with the traditional study of literature, accessible only to an elite.

The second way of teaching theory is the additive method. It has been a seemingly natural part of the professionalization of our discipline that new areas of study get added to departments in an attempt to establish what Graff terms the "field coverage model" (*Professing Literature* 6–9). Departments feel a need both to "keep up" with changes in the field and yet to maintain "tradition" in some form or other, two seemingly contradictory goals that Graff says are simultaneously met in the additive model: "innovation even of a threatening kind could be welcomed by simply *adding* another unit to the aggregate of fields to be covered" (7). Whereas the canonizing approach tends to elitism, the additive approach is supported by the dominant ideology of pluralism.[5] Since the seventies, it has been most fashionable for English departments to "add on" one or two literary theorists to their ranks, so that theoretical voices could be heard amid all the other voices (Harris 62). But there is a danger that simply "adding on a theorist" will fail to underscore the fundamental ways in which a theoretical approach to texts may differ from or conflict with more traditional approaches. The theorist teaches a few isolated courses, and to undergraduate requirements in "Shakespeare," "American Literature before 1900," and "Romantic Poetry" are added courses such as "Psychoanalysis" and "Deconstruction," without much if any sense that these courses may have anything to say to one another.

In reporting a study by an ADE ad hoc committee investigating the English major in America, Gary Waller comments: "What emerges from our data is that English departments see themselves as uneasily pluralistic, dominated by strong conservative forces residing largely in traditional literature but encompassing various peripheral or marginal forces—women's studies, linguistics, various kinds of writing, for instance" (*Powerful Silence* 31). To this list of marginal forces coexisting in uneasy pluralism we can certainly append literary theory.

A department's failure to integrate the literary theorist causes not only a lack of cohesion among its faculty but also confusion for the students, who become increasingly disoriented as the courses they take appear to have nothing to do with or say to one another. Graff's "conflict model" of organizing teaching is one way of responding to this problem raised by the additive approach (*Professing Literature* 247–62).

The third way of teaching theory, the way I advocate, is to integrate the practice of theorizing into the curriculum as a whole. The first two approaches assume that theory is a body of knowledge that can be taught and mastered. In this third approach, the very nature of what is taught—whether literary, popular, or theoretical texts—is theorized in ways that directly affect how a department's whole program of study is structured. Further, such an approach, I suggest, has as a corollary the adopting of a mode of pedagogy designed to emphasize the historically situated (and therefore inevitably changing) nature of curricula.

If we assume, following Graff and Nelson, that theory is what occurs when concepts that once seemed "natural" become controversial, the theorizing curriculum would be one in which, in addition to reading a body of material called theory (along with canonical and noncanonical literary and related texts), students would be encouraged to interrogate principles of the discipline that they had been taught in the past to take for granted: for example, that literature reflects life; that only texts of high culture constitute literature; that one reads to identify with characters; that the meaning of great texts is universal; or that English classes read only fictive texts. Although theoretical texts would help students develop such questions, these texts themselves would also be interrogated: Does Marxism have an adequate theory of the subject? What is the status of the reader and the text in American reader-response criticism? What can psychoanalysis say to British cultural materialism? Why has theory attained the status it has in the discipline today? To situate theory culturally and historically in a curriculum is not to diminish its significance; rather, it is to enable students to realize that they have a stake in the positions they adopt. No longer can students adopt a position simply because it is presented by the teacher as right (or wrong). The process of increasing the students' capacities to commit themselves to a particular way of thinking requires a dialogic, problem-posing, learning environment.

In recent years, a number of teachers and theorists have advocated such an integrative approach, but most recognize the intellectual as well as institutional difficulties of developing it. Graff and Gibbons comment that although "it is not easy to say how . . . cultural criticism can be translated into courses and programs, the desire for it seems widespread and cuts across the line that divides humanists and post-structuralists" (10). Further, even if one can suggest how to translate theory into courses, as many teacher-theorists have, few departments would be willing to make a change of the magnitude that might be needed to carry out a full-scale curricular revision, rather than simply adding a course or two. Robert Scholes, for example, comments: "Though I am convinced that the entire English curriculum needs drastic revision, I know too well the politics of change in academic institutions to suggest that such revision can be accomplished by fiat. . . . Our best chances . . . will come in those courses now called 'Freshman Comp.' and 'Intro. to Lit.' " (19). Notice that it is in the lower-level courses, in which departments generally feel less invested, that change is most likely to occur.[6]

To integrate theory into the curriculum beyond a single course or even a set of core requirements, all members of a department ideally need to become aware that there are major issues being discussed in the discipline, and they need to bring these issues to bear in their classroom practice.[7] At Carnegie Mellon we were fortunate to have had institutional support for a curriculum revision of the English major from the freshman literature course, through a set of English core courses, to upper-level courses. Many courses, therefore, became theoretically focused, though they certainly did not all employ the same particular theories. What most of these courses had in common was a recognition that every position a student or teacher adopts is theoretically inscribed and that certain issues are of particular interest because they are currently the source of intense theoretical *debate;* that is, an issue is studied in the classroom not because it is of universal or transcendent concern but because it is seen as significant at our current historical conjuncture.

One of the many interesting issues involved in an integrative view of curricular change—and one on which quite different views are argued—is whether departments should return to a structured curriculum or at least to one that is organized by particular issues rather than by chronology or major authors. At Carnegie Mellon we organized our undergraduate curriculum around *language, history,* and *culture.*[8] The freshman literature course, "Reading Texts," integrates these three concepts.[9] Beyond the freshman year, all English majors were required to take three core courses: "Discursive Practices," which focused on language; "Discourse and Historical Change," which focused on history; and "Reading Twentieth Century Culture," which focused on culture. The theory behind the development of this structure was that certain crucial issues, not theories, could be used to focus students' thinking about the ways they read and receive all cultural texts, older as well as contemporary, canonical as well as popular, third world as well as first world.

Language, history, and culture are not themselves theories. They are, rather, opportunities for theorizing—sites of struggle that have generated diverse and often contradictory critical practices in the history of literary theory as well as in contemporary theory. The issues that language, history, and culture engender are interconnected, yet each was designed to be flexible enough to accommodate a variety of theoretical approaches: feminism, psychoanalysis, Marxism, deconstruction, various historicisms, reader-centered criticism, and semiotics. This flexibility meant that throughout the development of the curriculum, the three courses could be and were taught in different ways; these were shaped by the preference of the instructor, by what was felt to be the political situation in the department or the profession at the time, and by the perceived needs and demands of a particular group of students.

In "Discursive Practices," under the rubric of language, for instance, we explored issues of cultural semiotics, looking at the interconnected systems by which subjects simultaneously speak and write and are spoken and written. We studied such issues as the ways in which language preexists its users, why it is always value laden, and the ways in which the meanings of words and texts have changed over time. The course investigated how fundamental systems of language—in the broadest sense, not only in written or spoken discourse—are constitutive of our perceptions, exchanges, and cultural practices. Students might read extracts from such semioticians as Pierce, Barthes, Eco, Sebeok, and Kristeva; they would also analyze literary texts, as well as such nonliterary texts as advertisements, film, journalism, and music.[10]

One of the characteristics we emphasized about history in the second of the core courses, "Discourse and Historical Change," is its perspectival nature—that people necessarily read the past from the present. In "*English in America,* Ten Years Later," Richard Ohmann rightly complains that English studies, "as it has increasingly colonized the experience of literature for American young people, has pretty successfully abstracted it from any but literary history" (13). In our course we attempted to teach students how to read with a historical perspective that goes beyond the simply literary or an exposure to texts from different historical periods. By focusing on the issues of historical thinking, "Discourse and Historical Change," as Peggy Knapp noted in writing about the course, attempted to give students a sense of "the relationship between the historical 'origins' of a text and its modern reception." Those "origins" were presented as constructed, not given. As Knapp recognized, to give students a sense of history one must resist "monolithic general assertions." We tried, therefore to teach students to learn to read for absences, that is, to recognize that texts are often unable to articulate the ideological struggles of their own period but that their language may nonetheless suggest these struggles. Readers from a later period may be able to read texts *symptomatically,* to look for the symptoms of a text's ideological battles and to give language to what the text was struggling to articulate.

One of the trends our department has attempted to reflect is the shift from literary to cultural studies called for by Terry Eagleton and a number of cultural critics. We have tried to see literary texts and literary theory as part of a larger cultural conjunction and to regard as appropriate objects of study not only literary texts but also texts of popular culture. And we sought to explore how and why the ideology of any cultural period is fraught with contradictions. "Reading Twentieth Century Culture," the third of our core courses, helped point up the interrelationships among the issues surrounding language, history, and culture. This course explored major theories of culture in the twentieth century, from humanism to cultural materialism, and attempted to read other cultural texts such as novels, film, and drama against these theories. In a version of the course that I taught we focused much of our time on the political, educational, and esthetic implications of the conflict between humanism and social constructivism, reading such theorists as Arnold, Freud, Althusser, Eagleton, Hirsch, and Graff.

I believe our program was extremely successful in a number of ways that are important for my argument. Within a few years, it produced students who were able to pose questions about their reading experiences, and about literary and other cultural texts, that were sophisticated and self-reflexive to a remarkable degree. A number of my colleagues have observed that the kind of questions posed and the contexts were far beyond what, a few years before, they might have expected of advanced graduate students.[11]

Nevertheless, we had some salutary failures, as we found ourselves inevitably caught up in the current contradictions of the profession. Institutional pressures were such that at times it became impossible for us not to fall into methods of both teaching and curricular organizing that resembled the previously mentioned canonizing and additive approaches. In the six-year period during which this curriculum developed, a central question (never adequately faced, perhaps) was the relation between the theoretically oriented core courses and seminars and the more traditional upper-level courses. The new program introduced seminars on diverse theoretical perspectives such as feminism, psychoanalysis, Marxism, theories of reading, hermeneutics, and the like, and many upper-level "period" courses were taught as "cultural periods," including a strong theoretical orientation and requiring students to read literary and nonliterary texts of the period in addition to various theoretical texts. But we never carried out the wholesale rewriting of the curriculum that at least some of us advocated. A number of upper-level courses remained traditional period courses. In part, this was simply a necessity, given the makeup of the faculty at the time, but in retrospect it seems to me that it was easy for us at times to lapse into an atmosphere of more or less happy pluralism, despite the department's many formal and informal discussions about theory and pedagogy and despite Graff's speaking to us about the conflict model of education and about the ways in which our department was particularly well poised to enact it both with traditional and theoretically trained faculty in literary and cultural studies and with a faculty in rhetoric. That the traditional and more theoretically oriented faculty got along relatively well was perhaps a good and a bad sign. It points, I think, to the power of the residual pluralist model, for it functioned in a positive as well as a negative way. Although it helped ease new faculty—indeed in this case, a whole new program—into a department with an absolutely minimal amount of hostility, it also may have encouraged us not to be as articulate as we might have been about our differences, particularly to our students.

As we sometimes lasped into a pluralist model of English studies, so at times did we treat theory as the new canon, establishing it as a master discourse. Part of the reason for this was perhaps simply the difficulty of many of the theoretical texts to which we were trying to introduce our students. If a text seemed particularly impenetrable, the simplest thing for a teacher to do was often to "explain" it by lecturing. Although lecturing may be necessary from time to time in almost any course, a teacher has to handle such occasions with a fair amount of tact. A lecture, after all, is always received on at least two levels. It may serve the undeniably useful purpose of informing the class about a particular text or theorist, but it also sends the pedagogical message that the banking system is back in operation. The sheer difficulty of many theoretical texts, combined with the rising authority of the teacher when he or she lectures, is a strong enough deterrent to a progressive pedagogy; when combined with a recognition of the wider disciplinary status of theory, the result may too easily be to silence the students whom one wishes to empower. The vocabulary of "ideological situatedness" and "divided subjects" can become just as empty as the language of plot, metaphor, and theme for students who feel themselves to be in a banking rather than a learning situation.

The all too easy relapse into a traditional model of learning that the canonizing approach encourages was perhaps most interestingly demonstrated by some of our graduate students when they taught the freshman course "Reading Texts," which I directed from 1985 to 1990. Several of these students would often rush to teach a theoretical essay such as Eagleton's "What Is Literature?" rather than pose an interesting problem that could enable the class to enact the debate that the essay discusses. It is easy to write this off as lack of teaching experience, but why does that lack of experience manifest itself in a return to authority? I suggest that the canonizing approach to teaching theory is the least threatening to the teacher because it discourages students from putting the teacher's authority into question. It has the potential to grant the teacher the status of an authority that he or she simply cannot maintain in a more dialogic classroom, in which the theory studied is itself historically situated, scrutinized, and theorized. A teacher can be authoritarian in the classroom about many subjects, but to be authoritarian in the current historical moment about theory is to attain a kind of double status in relation to one's students (and perhaps one's colleagues)—that of an authority and that of a theorist.

The banking system of teaching is also tempting because, despite recent arguments to the contrary, it retains broad-sweeping institutional approbation. It presents the subject matter of the discipline as objective and definable, regardless of whether that subject matter is Coleridge or Foucault. Further, most major research institutions in the country value scholarship well above teaching. In *Professing Literature,* Graff provides a detailed account of the ongoing debate in the profession between teaching and research. After the First World War the research model of literary studies achieved great prominence, but Graff notes that even well before the war, in 1902, *PMLA* discontinued its "Pedagogical Section," with William Riley Parker writing that "the MLA had become so absorbed in the advancement of research in its field that it was ready to leave to others all talk about teaching and enrollment" (quoted in Graff 121). Such institutional moves have established an opposition between pedagogy and scholarship rather than seeing them as mutually implicated. This hierarchical opposition lowers the status of pedagogy in the field, which, in turn, may once again promote the banking system of education—which is often seen as the most efficient way for a teacher to teach and as the most appropriate way for a "scholar" to present him- or herself.

This case history of our work at Carnegie Mellon, then, provides examples of significant achievements, disappointments, and contradictions. More important than these particulars, however, is the way they can be read as symptoms of larger disciplinary tensions. We can see aspects of our professional unconscious—the ideology of pluralism, the practice of canonizing our major texts of study, the research/pedagogy dichotomy—operating in this example, and perhaps more interestingly, we can begin to glimpse some of the ways in which they implicate one another. Unless we bring these aspects of our professional unconscious into the open, we will find ourselves repeating the mistakes of the old paradigm of pedagogy. If theory is to be used to change teaching practices, it is not enough just to put theory in the classroom.

What the profession sees as research changes over time, but the research/pedagogy dichotomy has remained fairly entrenched throughout this century. Recognizing that this dichotomy is still at least residually operative in our discipline and that, at the moment, theory is the privileged form of research, we must be alert to the ways in which we move theory into our courses and curriculum. For the conservative force of the institution is working to encourage us to go into the classroom and teach as an expert. This has several results: we may retain the illusion of our status as powerful individuals; the structure of the classroom remains unchanged, so it will easily adapt to a new area of research a few years down the line; and perhaps most significantly, our students will remain disempowered.

The discipline does seem poised at a unique moment in that it is attempting, as Donahue and Quandahl put it, to "reclaim pedagogy," that is, to "examine pedagogy as a theoretical field or investigate the pedagogical subtensions of a specific theory" (1). But if the moment is necessarily a contradictory one, it is nonetheless stimulating and hopeful. What we need to learn is that theorizing, not just theory, is what our curricula need, that pedagogy needs the institutional and professional prestige accorded to "theory," and that the intellectual paradigm shift we are attempting to effect will occur only in the material details of the classroom, the reading and writing practices of our students and ourselves. As Freire notes, "since it is in a concrete situation that the oppressor-oppressed contradiction is established, the resolution of this contradiction must be *objectively* verifiable. Hence, the radical requirement—both for the man who discovers himself to be an oppressor and for the oppressed—that the concrete situation which begets oppression must be transformed" (35).

NOTES

1. The essays collected in Gerald Graff and Reginald Gibbons's *Criticism in the University* are a particularly powerful and practical expression of the desire to translate theory, particularly cultural criticism, into courses and programs. Other collections of essays on theory and pedagogy include Cary Nelson's *Theory in the Classroom;* Douglas Atkins and Michael Johnson's *Writing and Reading Differently;* and Patricia Donahue and Ellen Quandahl's *Reclaiming Pedagogy: The Rhetoric of the Classroom.* In addition, articles in *College English* have increasingly been devoted to developing pedagogical applications of literary theory; in particular, the April 1990 issue, guest edited by Elizabeth Meese, addresses feminist and pedagogical concerns and the October and November 1987 issues, edited by Robert Con Davis, were

devoted specifically to psychoanalysis and pedagogy. Gerald Prince's "Literary Theory and the Undergraduate Curriculum," Jeffrey Peck's "Advanced Literary Study as Cultural Study: A Redefinition of the Discipline," and Gary Waller's "Working within the Paradigm Shift: Poststructuralism and the College Curriculum" also explore ways in which theory can be used for curricular development. Jonathan Arac, Christian Messenger, and Gerald Sorensen's "The Place of Literary Theory in the Freshman Literature Classroom," my "Theory in the Reader: Bleich, Holland, and Beyond," and some work in the GRIP project discuss how literary theory can change specific classroom practices. Finally, in the area of textbooks, Gary Waller, Kathleen McCormick, and Lois Fowler's *Lexington Introduction to Literature* and Kathleen McCormick, Gary Waller, and Linda Flower's *Reading Texts: Reading, Responding, Writing* employ literary theory to develop a reader- and culture-centered approach to the teaching of literature, nonfiction, and media texts.

2. Many have noted the obvious problems with uncritically adapting a pedagogical approach created for the dispossessed in Latin America to members of an economically developed first-world country—see, for example, Michael Holtzman's "A Post-Freirean Model for Adult Literacy Education" and Ann Bertoff's " 'Reading the world . . . reading the word': Paulo Freire's Pedagogy of Knowing." Nonetheless, Freire's model has been compelling in this country, at least in part because our dominant educational practices tend to oppress students very much by a "banking system." Further, we can argue that even though many students, particularly on the university level, are members of a middle class that is closer to an "oppressor" than an "oppressed" class, in a capitalist society, as subjects for ideology, the middle class occupies a much more contradictory subject position, functioning simultaneously as both oppressor and oppressed.

3. See e.g. Heller's article in *The Chronicle of Higher Education,* Aug. 3, 1988.

4. See McCormick's "The Cultural Imperatives Underlying Cognitive Acts" and "Task Representations in Writing About Literature" for further discussions of the complementarities between cultural and cognitive analysis.

5. See Rooney's *Seductive Reasoning: Pluralism as the Problematic of Contemporary Literary Theory.*

6. Developing a new freshman sequence is the kind of change that Arac, Messenger, and Sorensen describe as having taken place at the University of Illinois Chicago campus in their innovative three-part freshman course entitled "Reading Literature." Jeffrey Peck, somewhat more ambitiously, proposes curriculum revision at the level of three core courses (52), although he does not report that those changes have been approved. Perhaps most significantly, the report of the English Coalition Conference in 1987 called

for "an increase in the rate of change, with respect to curricula" in English departments throughout the country (Lloyd-Jones and Lunsford 33). The coalition argued that the English major should be reconceived to include, among other areas of study, "several methodologies of reading and interpretation . . . something of the critical and historical principles behind the construction of literary and cultural histories . . . [and] something of the study of language and discursive practices" (35).

7. See Gary Waller's discussion on the Carnegie Mellon curriculum in "Working within the Paradigm Shift: Poststructuralism and the College Curriculum."

8. Language, history, and culture are hardly the only issues that could be used to organize a curriculum theoretically. Various teacher-theorists have suggested a number of possible organizing concepts. Scholes wants the object of study to be *textuality* (20); Arac, Messenger, and Sorenson want to concentrate on hermeneutics, poetics, and criticism (23); Cary Nelson wants to emphasize textuality and culture (AE, 6). Although each theorist suggests somewhat different focuses for teaching, what they all have in common is the recognition that new methods for teaching must be developed if we are to teach with theoretical perspective.

9. The course is discussed in detail in my articles "Using Cultural Theory to Critique and Reconceptualize the Research Paper" and "Theory in the Reader: Bleich, Holland, and Beyond" and provided the basis for the development of *The Lexington Introduction to Literature.*

10. For a detailed discussion of the three core courses, see Waller's, "Writing, Reading, Language, History, Culture."

11. A visiting committee chaired by Gerald Graff said our undergraduate core was the best conceived in the country, one that ought to be a model for other departments.

WORKS CITED

Arac, Jonathan, Christian Messenger, and Gerald Sorenson. "The Place of Literary Theory in the Freshman Literature Classroom." *ADE Bulletin* 82 (1985):22–26.

Atkins, Douglas, and Michael Johnson, eds. *Writing and Reading Differently: Deconstruction and the Teaching of Composition and Literature.* Lawrence: UP of Kansas, 1985.

Bate, Walter Jackson. "The Crisis in English Studies." *Harvard Magazine* 85 (Sept.–Oct. 1982):46–53.

Begley, Adam. "Black Studies' New Star." *The New York Times Magazine* 1 April 1990:24–26; 48–50.

Bennett, Tony. "Texts in History." *Journal of the Midwest Modern Language Association* 18 (1985):1–16.

Bertoff, Ann. " 'Reading the world . . . reading the word': Paulo Freire's Pedagogy of Knowing." *Only Connect: Uniting Reading and Writing.* Ed. Thomas Newkirk. Upper Montclair: Boynton/Cook, 1986.

Cain, William E. *The Crisis in Criticism.* Baltimore: Johns Hopkins UP, 1984.

Con Davis, Robert, ed. *Psychoanalysis and Pedagogy. College English* 49. 6, 7 (1987).

Culler, Jonathan. "Beyond Interpretation." *The Pursuit of Signs: Semiotics, Literature, Deconstruction.* Ithaca: Cornell UP, 1981. 3–17.

Donahue, Patricia, and Ellen Quandahl, eds. *Reclaiming Pedagogy: The Rhetoric of the Classroom.* Carbondale: Southern Illinois UP, 1989.

Eagleton, Terry. *Literary Theory: An Introduction.* Minneapolis: U of Minnesota P, 1983.

Fish, Stanley. *Is There a Text in This Class?* Cambridge: Harvard UP, 1980.

Freedman, Carl. "Marxist Theory, Radical Pedagogy, and the Reification of Thought." *College English* 49 (1987):70–82.

Freire, Paulo. *Pedagogy of the Oppressed.* New York: Continuum, 1989.

Graff, Gerald. *Professing Literature.* Chicago: U of Chicago P, 1987.

Graff, Gerald, and Reginald Gibbons, eds. *Criticism in the University.* Evanston: Northwestern UP, 1985.

GRIP Report. 7 vols. N.p.:n.p., n.d.

Harris, Charles. "The ADE Ad Hoc Committee on the English Curriculum: A Progress Report." *Profession* (1987): 60–65.

Hartman, Geoffrey H. "The Advanced Study of Literature: Elementary Considerations. *ADE Bulletin* 80 (1985): 11–14.

Heller, Scott. "Some English Departments Are Giving Undergraduates Grounding in New Literary and Critical Theory." *Chronicle of Higher Education* 3 August 1988. A15–A17.

Holtzman, Michael. "A Post-Freirean Model for Adult Literacy Education." *College English* 50 (1988): 177–89.

Knapp, Peggy A. "Literary History in an Age of Theory." *GRIP Report* 6 (1985): n.p.

Lloyd-Jones, Richard, and Andrea Lunsford, eds. *The English Coalition Conference: Democracy through Language.* Urbana: NCTE, 1989.

Macherey, Pierre. *A Theory of Literary Production.* Trans. Geoffrey Wall. Boston: Routledge and Kegan Paul, 1978.

McCormick, Kathleen. "Task Representations in Writing About Literature." *Poetics* 16 (1987): 131–54.

———. "The Cultural Imperatives Underlying Cognitive Acts." *Reading to Write: Expanding the Context.* Ed. Linda Flower, Victoria Stein, John

Ackerman, Margaret Kantz, Kathleen McCormick, and Wayne Peck. Oxford: Oxford UP, 1990. 194–218.

———. "Theory in the Reader: Bleich, Holland, and Beyond." *College English* 47 (1985): 836–50.

McCormick, Kathleen, Gary Waller, and Linda Flower. *Reading Texts.* Lexington: D.C. Heath, 1987.

———. "Using Cultural Theory to Critique and Reconceptualize the Research Paper." *Cultural Studies and English Studies.* Ed. James Berlin and Michael Vivion. Portsmouth, N.H.: Boynton/Cook, in press.

Meese, Elizabeth, ed. *College English* 52.4 (1990).

Nelson, Cary. "Against English: Theory and the Limits of the Discipline." *ADE Bulletin* 85 (1986): 1–6.

———, ed. *Theory in the Classroom.* Urbana: U of Illinois P, 1986.

Ohmann, Richard. *English in America: A Radical View of the Profession.* New York: Oxford UP, 1976.

Ohmann, Richard. "*English in America,* Ten Years Later." *ADE Bulletin* 82 (1985): 11–17.

Peck, Jeffrey. "Advanced Literary Study as Cultural Study: A Redefinition of the Discipline." *Profession 85.* New York: MLA, 1985. 48–54.

Prince, Gerald. "Literary Theory and the Undergraduate Curriculum." *Profession 84.* New York: MLA, 1984. 37–40.

Rooney, Ellen. *Seductive Reasoning: Pluralism as the Problematic of Contemporary Literary Theory.* Ithaca: Cornell UP, 1989.

Scholes, Robert. *Textual Power: Literacy Theory and the Teaching of English.* New Haven: Yale UP, 1985.

Waller, Gary. "A Powerful Silence: 'Theory' in the English Major." *ADE Bulletin* 85 (1986): 31–35.

———. "Working within the Paradigm Shift: Poststructuralism and the College Curriculum." *ADE Bulletin* 81 (1985): 6–12.

———. "Writing, Reading, Language, History, Culture." *GRIP Report* 6 (1985): n.p.

Waller, Gary, Kathleen McCormick, and Lois Fowler. *The Lexington Introduction to Literature.* Lexington: D.C. Heath, 1986.

6

LET'S GET "LITERATE": ENGLISH DEPARTMENT POLITICS AND A PROPOSAL FOR A PH.D. IN LITERACY

Susan R. Horton

> Man is, for himself and for others, a signifying being, since one can never understand the slightest of his gestures without going beyond the pure present and explaining it by the future. Furthermore, he is a creator of signs to the degree that—always ahead of himself—he employs certain objects to designate other absent or future objects. But both operations are reduced to a pure and simple surpassing. To surpass present conditions toward their later change and to surpass the present object toward an absence are one and the same thing. Man constructs signs because in his very reality he is signifying; and he is signifying because he is a dialectical surpassing of all that is simply given. What we call freedom is the irreducibility of the cultural order to the natural order.
>
> Jean-Paul Sartre, *Search for a Method*

The "surpassing" Sartre describes is probably the best—because most capacious—way of defining literacy. That will be one of my subjects. At the same time, struggling and sometimes lurching toward some consensus in my department about what a Ph.D. we might offer would look like—with some of us arguing for a Ph.D. in literacy—is the story of another kind of collegial, communal "surpassing." I want to interweave these two stories of surpassing to help produce the concept of another kind of literacy: an ability to read better one aspect of our own institutional practice.

In the English Department at the University of Massachusetts at

Boston our quest to design a Ph.D. that serves our clientele (urban, working class, and older, with every fifth face something other than white), that reflects the intellectual and political interests of a committed and productive faculty, and that at the same time flows from our individual convictions about what is best for "our kind of student" has generated a vigorous and sometimes painful debate. This essay is in part a plea for the particular kind of Ph.D. program we have been deliberating and in part a contribution to what is at this point in our collective professional discourse only a fledgling analysis: an analysis of how our intramural, departmental discourse works; of how the language we use with one another does or does not generate collaborative effort; of how the tropes we fall into when we talk about pedagogy turn out to be exclusionary or inclusionary and to encourage or impede change within English departments; of how the tropes we use when we refer to our students might reveal more than we think about how we conceive our relation to them; of how the common assumption of many of us that our major business is simply to teach students to read closely and to write clearly, insofar as we do those things without some ongoing auto-critique, perpetuates a certain vision of what literary studies is and of what we ought to be doing with those particular cultural productions we call novels and poems.

What prompts this essay above all is the belief that *any* pedagogy that aspires to be a substantial intervention in our students' lives needs also to be an intervention in our colleagues'. If we do not talk with and listen to one another—in colloquia, faculty seminars, and departmental meetings over curriculum—at least as much as we talk with students, we can never do more than create islands of cultural critique and self-reflectiveness that are quite literally surrounded by other rooms, courses, and classes where the status quo prevails undisturbed. Many of us—the sometimes-token Marxists, feminists, and deconstructionists in our departments—have the uneasy feeling we are half-obligingly, half-grudgingly, and half-consciously serving as visible evidence of our departments' virtuous support for diverse opinions and radical pedagogies. To put it bluntly, we are tolerated for so long as we point that vocabulary of ours and its attendant ways of seeing literacy and literary works at our students but not at our colleagues, who ask of us only that we *not* use words like *cultural production* around *them.* We can aim our discourse at the profession, where I am told the same 2,500 of us continue to produce and consume "theory" in places like this collection of essays, or we can aim it at our students. It is the *intermediate*-range weapons that are the focus of our disciplinary arms limitation agreements. The fact that we feel comfortable talking out into the profession or at our students but not at our colleagues ought to inspire some questions: like why we focus so much on teacher-student situations, where our interventions have our relative power behind them, rather than on our colleagues, where the power relations are more equal, older attitudes toward literary study more entrenched, and successful intervention less certain.

What follows is a version of a talk offered to my colleagues: call it a kind of intermediate-range weapon lobbed into a department feeling itself radically split about the substance, emphasis, aims, and even the title of a Ph.D. But it would be wrong to see these perceived "splits" as being produced by our discussions of what a Ph.D. should look like (though that was at times the charge). Rather, as I suspect is often the case, the opening up of a frank departmental discussion about our separate pedagogical assumptions and the aims of a literary education released from repression splits already operating below the surface for some years and periodically surfacing in skirmishes over curriculum ("Should we require a course in African-American literature of all our majors?") or over recruitment ("This candidate talks too much of that theory jargon."). We are not at all cursed as a department by major philosophical rifts or ill will; we are in fact a gracious and tolerant group, embarrassingly and healthily normal. It is this "normal state of affairs" I want to bring to consciousness and then crisis as a prelude to change, because whatever political interventions we might make and wherever else we make them, the unglamorous, mostly invisible local interventions that take place in the cement-block corridors of state universities, colleague to colleague, will probably continue to matter most.

In my department, then, some of us argued that we might consider offering a Ph.D. in literacy rather than one in English (as some of my colleagues argued) or in composition (as some others argued). Either of the other two names, we said, would start us off on the wrong foot by requiring teacher and learner at the outset to engage in a deconstruction of "English" or "composition" before anything useful or interesting could begin to happen. If we take the word *literacy* to refer to the *relation* between an individual and a signifying practice,[1] even using the word signals a deliberate attempt to enlarge the province of literature to include more kinds of cultural significations, to make it possible to explore the consequences of acquiring any kind of literacy, and to highlight the fact that "composition"—both teaching and learning it—is not a kind of drudgery or necessary duty but just one among the many kinds (including literary) of work with words that produces texts and readers. This latter move has the paradoxical advantage of raising composition studies to the status it deserves by dissolving it into the larger context in which it belongs. Finally, construing literacy in the broadest way prompts a questioning of the disciplinary divisions on which our conception of knowledge has depended and repackages what we in English departments already do, making that work appear both more visible and more important.

Wally Martin points out that one of the pieces of this project—questioning disciplinary boundaries—has philosophy as its obvious starting point, philosophy being the place where the distinctions putting figuration, pretense, play, and fiction outside the pale of truth were first born. Crossing from philosophy to literature, he says, produces a chiasmus in which the "referential-nonreferential" and "fictional-nonfictional" oppositions get shuffled, and the terrain of literature, where certain questions about truth-value arise, is either not accurately mapped or simply set off limits for philosophic purposes. Simultaneously, philosophy and the sciences continue to rely on analogies, metaphors, structural models, hypothetical examples, and paradigms—all of which are by definition "fiction"—to discover the truth.[2] Carrying out research under the rubric of *literacy* is one way to subvert that system of distinctions. Once that is done, literary scholars can train their skills in analysis and close reading not only on literature as it has been traditionally construed but on the language and other signifying practices of scientists, administrators, teachers, and institutions, and a new field—one that at its heart challenges the *notion* of "field," not to mention the *episteme,* or ways of thinking of individual "fields,"—is born. A Ph.D. in literacy could open up a space in which we could invite literature students who are well-trained in close reading to use their skills on, say, institutional discourse, in a practical course that could combine readings of Foucault, Benjamin, Nietzsche, and Vico—all people who have written about the hidden tropes of discourse and how those produce, in Nietzsche's words, the first best discourse—with a reading of, say, the language of university memoranda and college course syllabi.[3]

The object of such study is "signifying practices," in part because the phrase comfortably refers simultaneously to literature and to the ways we read and write about it, which in turn become major objects of study. The phrase also has the advantage of comfortably referring to cultural forms of all kinds, including the ways in which we dress, dance, decorate our houses, write our memos, present ourselves as teachers in the classroom, and behave in post-office lines. Sealing the literary scholar skilled at reading one kind of cultural signifying practice off from reading *other* kinds of cultural signifying practices, including those that do not exist in written form, keeps us harmlessly occupied in our playpens and guarantees we will one day be obsolete.

Recognition of this reality has resulted in the new constellation of intellectuals—many but by no means all literary scholars—concerned with questions like how do individuals constitute themselves out of the signifying practices of their culture(s)? How do institutions form themselves? How do language and literacy operate to institutionalize certain ways of seeing and to exclude others? How do knowledge-constituting interests come to be? How does an academic institution perpetuate certain concerns through and as a consequence of the language it uses?[4]

No one is advocating that we stop reading, teaching, and analyzing literature. But at the present moment it makes sense to face the fact that important signifying goes on in a host of other forms that are changing us, and much of that is produced by people who seem to prefer *not* to commit anything to writing. Increasingly, the most authoritative texts tend to be anonymous, like bibles or laws or committee reports: "Refusing to reveal their origins, they distribute their authority to the highest bidder, the institutions that use them."[5] So I take a Ph.D. program in literacy first of all to be one that studies the production and reception of cultural texts, whether written or otherwise, and, necessarily and at the same time, studies and evaluates the methods for studying cultural productions.

The study of literacy broadly construed has a substantial psychological as well as a sociopolitical dimension. To say the word *literacy* describes a *relation* between an individual and a signifying practice is to assume a *gap* between the individual and any particular signifying practice or cultural form: the two are never identical. Were human beings and their signifying practices identical, we could never refer to such a thing as illiteracy. A baby comes into the world with some repertoire of signifying—it can communicate by crying and smiling. But once beyond those basic signifiers, people can be—and are—pronounced illiterate all the time.

Allan Bloom and William Bennett, whom Henry Louis Gates, Jr., calls "the killer Bs," recommend that schools ensure a cultural literacy they claim too many students lack. This is reasonable and desirable. But literary theory and the dialectic it proposes can help us foster that literacy from a self-reflective perspective, so that we do not unwittingly perpetuate certain kinds of misperceptions about cultures and their signifying practices. Pierre Bourdieu, both in *Distinction* and in *Reproduction in Education,* provides ample demonstration of how a dominant class's or culture's power comes to be partly as a result of its ability to declare certain objects self-evidently more valuable than certain others.[6] More to the point, those certain other cultural productions tend to be anything not originating from a rather small corner of Western Europe.

Common practice assumes achieving literacy is one of two things: the acquiring of a neutral skill enabling fuller access to jobs and status or the correcting of some lack to create either more "fully human" humans or, at the least, more fully articulate humans. But by defining literacy as a gap between an individual and a signifying practice, we acknowledge that the achieving of literacy is never simply enabling people to "get in touch" with language or cultural forms that will allow them to articulate an innermost being that has been inarticulate, inchoate, or "illiterate" before. Rather, the achievement of literacy of any kind *produces* the self it articulates; put more generally, culture produces those who produce it. Vološinov says "a word is not an expression of inner personality; rather, inner personality is an expressed or inwardly impelled word"[7] or an inwardly impelled cultural form of any kind.

If nothing else does, my own experience tells me this. In making part of a Christmas present for my parents I haunted all the used record shops in Boston, hunted down the fine old swing music they used to listen to as they courted, and then taped it for them: Bunny Berrigan, Bix Beiderbecke, Duke Ellington, and Johnny Hartman's buttery voice singing "You Are Too Beautiful." But when I sat down to listen seriatim to the tapes I had made I discovered the *product* of my efforts had become a cultural portrait of my mother's self so intimate I was not sure I could send her the tapes. They made me think, too, of all those women who grew up on those romantic movies of the forties, the ones where the girl kisses her returning soldier boy with her leg crooked out behind her at that 90-degree angle. Those images of the kiss produced a whole generation of women who were or are literate in—not only "read," but worked to become—those productions.

In *Search for a Method* Sartre says man defines himself by his project. And man's project involves his using the material available to him to "perpetually [go] beyond the condition which is made for him; he reveals and determines his situation by transcending it in order to objectify himself—by work, action, or gesture. . . . This immediate relation with the Other than oneself, beyond the given and constituted elements, this perpetual production of oneself by work and *praxis,* is," he says, "our peculiar structure."[8] None of us, then, is either literate or illiterate in the absolute. We work to achieve various kinds of literacies to transcend our selves by internalizing culture into the very stuff of our being.

I am *not* taking the position we in composition studies took just a few years ago, which I now see as the idealist position, that the subject "makes" the world as a consequence of his or her concepts. Although we see the world through the concepts we make, as Adorno suggests in his *Negative Dialectics,* those concepts do not cover the world. Neither does the world exist to be discovered, as the positivist assumes. What the study of literacy promotes is a reading and self-reflectiveness that allow people to devise various strategies for moving back and forth between their postulations or concepts—which might be seen as their particular integrations of cultural productions—and what Sartre calls the "brute objectivity of the world." This project resembles the Heideggerian one: what we call "meaning" is always historical. First we know, and then in naming what we know we come into contact with the "irreducible givenness" of experience, or the *Dasein.* If Sartre sees what he calls our "surpassing" as a feature of our humanness, Heidegger sees a similar "throwing ourselves forward of where we are" as constitutive of the human. "We" are never identical with ourselves. "We" are always a fresh possibility, so that human existence itself might be defined as that which is made up of time, history, and language.

What follows from all this is that if we were to teach literary texts in the context of a Ph.D. in literacy we would move with our students between our readings and experiences of the particular literary works to the objectivity of the literary object; from there we would step aside to critique the kinds of humans we are making of ourselves in our specific historical moment through the readings we are producing. From there, we would step aside yet again to look at the ways in which earlier eras produced their own cultural moments as a consequence of their own readings. In so doing, we would learn something not only about earlier historical times but also about how cultural formation works in time and over time.

Paul Bové's chapter on I. A. Richards's teaching in *Intellectuals in Power* is both a powerful demonstration of how our teaching of critical literacy, in the terms just described, produces particular kinds of readers (and people) and an explanation of how and why as a consequence our classrooms need to be seen as texts.[9] Thus, a Ph.D. student in this kind of critical literacy program will study lots more than just a body of written texts on literacy; indeed, the major "texts" for study will be not only the entire literary tradition, as well as the newer tradition of composition studies, but also the classrooms in which students and instructors enact the methods dictated by those disciplines. Despite what we might want to be true, all evidence seems to suggest that ninety percent of what students learn in school is promptly forgotten. This seems to me a strong argument *against* attempts at "coverage" in any discipline and *for* moving toward an education in which competence is defined not as successful transmission of facts but as coming to problematize and examine assumptions about what our discipline is about and to study how language and history combine to produce human beings of particular kinds.[10] In the process, what constitutes "knowledge" is redefined, and traditional disciplinary divisions become far more permeable as students and teachers study history, psychology, anthropology, and a host of adjacent disciplines to answer the questions this new constellationary "discipline" provokes.

Just as the teacher of literature continually produces particular kinds of people by teaching particular kinds of readings of literary works, the teacher of writing always teaches much more than simple facility with a particular kind of discourse. The instructor never teaches only a "skill," or "good writing," or "good close-reading strategies," but always simultaneously teaches particular ways of seeing, selecting, and organizing experience, determining, for instance, what is appropriate for discursive elaboration and analysis and what is not. Also, because each person steps into a class already part of one or more fully formed cultures, we are never in the business of replacing illiteracy with literacy, or bad writing with good, so much as we are pushing students to generate alternative versions of the self.

That being the case, I am surprised at how very little attention has been paid to coming to understand the kinds of literacy already present in students when they enter our classrooms. When they fail to produce the kinds of essays we deem acceptable academic discourse, for instance, what exactly *is* it they are producing instead? My hunch is what we are getting is not illogic, or inchoate responses to questions, but various kinds of logic, culturally produced but by cultures other than the academic, struggling to approximate the *one* kind recognized in the academy. A study of the different kinds of logics and literacies at work in students, carried out in part by those students themselves as part of their classroom work, would be at the very least a valuable addition to the study of literacy teaching and at the very best a contribution to our own enrichment, giving *us* other ways of seeing the world and of understanding the other cultures in the middle of which we inevitably and increasingly live.

As so often these days, Jürgen Habermas gives us a point of departure here. For Habermas, transmission of knowledge can never be seen as only one-directional; it is inevitably—or maybe I should say "*should* be," for Habermas has always a utopian edge—an exchanging of equivalent "knowledges." All forms of human communication, however asymmetrical the social or intellectual relations between participants may be, Habermas sees as always a dialogue between active human subjects. This means the character of relations established between the communicators, and the message that relation implies about the nature of social relations in general, is as much a topic for inquiry as the *content* of that dialogue.[11]

The notion here is that what a particular group takes to be "knowledge" is culturally produced (by *knowledge* I mean not just a body of facts or information but also a whole way of knowing and its attendant ways of focusing attention and determining as discussible some things and not others). This notion has been variously traced and discussed. In their *Dialectic of Enlightenment*, for instance, Adorno and Horkheimer say we fully realized what they call our "fully administered world" only in this century. "Epistemologically, it began when man separated mind from the material world. Once radically parted from the object, man reduced it to his own measure, the subject swallows the object, forgetting how much it is an object itself."[12] This domination of the object by the subject is evident in both positivism and idealism. In the first, a subjectivity stands coolly apart from its object to manipulate it. Seeing him- or herself as passive, the positivistic subject really has an instrumental relationship to the world on which he or she unreflexively projects the scientifically ascertainable traits he or she claims merely to discover. In the second, a more frankly constitutive subjectivity assumes the world as the product of a consciousness that recognizes itself in its objective creations. Behind this assumption is a rage against the otherness of the natural world, which the allegedly sovereign mind tries to devour. In contrast to both positivism and idealism, a genuinely negative dialectics acknowledges what Adorno calls "the preponderance of the object, irreducible to—although also mediated by—an active subjectivity."[13]

The work of the literature and composition teacher in this context, then, is the same as that of a cultural critic of any kind: it becomes "neither to celebrate the separation of mind from matter, art from administration, culture from civilization, nor to paper over the splits (that is, between mind and matter) as if they had not occurred." Rather, it is to "insist on the radical ambiguity of a high culture whose objective content, its promise of happiness, could only be realized with its generalization to culture in the larger sense, while at the same time, its dependence on the material conditions of this and past societies helped thwart that very realization."[14] Adorno claims that the only way to rescue the emancipatory potential in the fractured cultural reality of our day lies in two approaches he calls "immanent" and "transcendent" critique. The first requires us to recognize that we are firmly ensconced in the culture we want to critique and, as much as possible, to understand the contradictions between what we believe and seek to do and what our actions in fact do: we must face the fact that, by and large, cultural practices are destined to be "unmediated reproductions of the status quo."[15] Further, Bové's recommendation is apt to this issue when he suggests that we study the kinds of palliatives popular culture offers so as to tap the desires those artifacts were trying to sate and to discover better ways to satisfy them.

The second kind of critique lies in part of what we can make of art—what Walter Benjamin and others have called its "compensatory function." Like Benjamin, Habermas believes art expresses more than just the suffering of humankind, but unlike vulgar Marxists he does not recommend reading to uncover evidence of class struggle or market forces everywhere. Rather, art taps the sensuous sources of language, referring inevitably to the nature humans have so harshly dominated, including of course most notably their own. Works of art are objects—objective—in that they are irreducible to their merely constructive subjective origins. Their mimetic moment, as Martin Jay suggests, is "intrinsically utopian because it preserves a memory of man's prehistoric oneness with nature and is thus a prefiguration of a possible restoration of that condition in the future. Aesthetic mimesis also contains a utopian moment in affirmation of sensuous appearance, which philosophers ever since Plato have tended to demean as inferior to ideal essences."[16]

But my own utopian assertions here need to be brought back to the possibilities of everyday practice. Our department offers monthly colloquia wherein faculty present some of their ongoing research to colleagues and master's-level students. In a recent colloquium, my colleague Robert Crossley gave a wonderful reading-in-progress of the function of scenes in science fiction novels featuring the museum. His specific text was H. G. Wells's *Time Machine,* and he talked about how the scene in which the Time Traveller wanders through a museum reveals characteristic attitudes toward the past. He noted that the Morlocks, a breed of small, semi-human creatures, had broken up fossil bones in the museum to make jewelry for themselves, and he strongly implied that this fact, together with descriptions of charred remains along the wall (which may have once been books) and other mishandled museum pieces, strongly signals a decline of civilization and a lack of respect for the past. There is nothing "wrong" with such a reading, which could be called "conservative" in the most literal and generous sense; that is, it assumes that a major role of the individual in society rests at its most admirable in preservation of past civilizations. It also presumes that preservation of the past takes precedence over creative activity in the present: preserving yesterday's fossils is more important than producing today's jewelry from those fossils. To the extent that this is true, then, it effectively disenables, or at the very least makes less visible or possible, a reading that would allow for people in the present to regard the cultural productions of the past as raw materials, subject to use and change. In that sense, his reading is what Adorno, Althusser, and others would call a "state-sponsored" one. I am not interested here in running around with a flashlight hunting down "ideological" readings or in trying to distinguish "ideological" from "nonideological" readings. As does Terry Eagleton, I believe academic scholarship is most interesting where it most obviously is *not* revealing ideological interests. What we consider most disinterested is in fact the purest lens through which interests may be focused, untainted by more instantly recognizable modes of subjectivity.[17]

I am also at the moment not so much interested in what Wells really intended so much as I am in what his intentions might reveal about how his age saw both itself and its responsibility to the past and, what may be even more interesting, about how we in our *own* historical moment reveal in our readings our *own* cultural presuppositions, which we reproduce in our classrooms when we teach. There is nothing wrong in a desire to preserve the past. I share the same goal, else I would not be devoting my life to teaching and writing about nineteenth-century literature. At the same time, certain readings reveal traces of what might be seen as a "Fall narrative." The message conveyed by what I have called the conservative reading is clear. We have fallen from a better time; nothing we can produce now could possibly be as good as what has already been produced, and the proper role of the educated person lies not so much in producing art as it does in preserving it. The political and social implications of such a reading, especially as we impart it to students, remain largely unexamined because the mechanisms for making them visible have only recently come to exist.

These two opposed attitudes toward the cultural productions of the past that I think Bob and I—and perhaps all of us—share might stand in synechdochically for a widespread ambivalence about cultural production in general, one I most recently felt at the Museum of Modern Art in New York when looking at Anselm Kiefer's artistic attempts to come to terms with Germany's past. Not a small number of his works contained the charred remains of books. They evoke *Kristallnacht*, of course, but at the same time they are overdetermined figures, ambivalent and highly charged. Books and the literacies that produced them produce particular kinds of selves, the consequences of which we have barely begun to study.

If, as Adorno suggests, the cultural productions we call "art" are intrinsically utopian, hauntingly evoking a past in which we were at one with ourselves and with the rest of nature, a unity that eventuated in the art we made of the materials of the world, then the readings we produce in particular classes with particular groups of students might further a genuine utopian project if we remain conscious at all times of the ways in which our readings do or do not further such a dream.

Applied to the study of literature, then, "literacy" prompts analyses of how the signifying practices of the age—in which a particular work was written, in which later critics like us interpret those works—generate or perpetuate certain ways of seeing the self and its possibilities in the world. It also demands a rigorous study of the *methods* we use and have used to make sense of literature: what methods produce what readings; what values our readings generate and perpetuate; what interpersonal relations they encourage; what mechanisms for testing methods we have; and what kind of self-reflectiveness on those methods is available and how we generate that kind of self-reflectiveness. The *object* (*or subject*—and that itself indicates a philosophical issue at the heart of the study) becomes not "literature," "literacy," "pedagogy," "philosophy," "history," "readers," "psychology," "politics," or "culture," but the intersection of all those things that occurs at the gap between individuals and individual and communal acts of signification, cultural production, or reception. As I suggested at the outset, a realignment of traditionally constituted fields or disciplines occurs at that intersection, bringing with it a new set of questions and, ultimately, a reconstitution of what we mean by knowledge itself. By looking in our classrooms not just at what a poem or novel means but at the different ways in which earlier eras produced their readings, and at how those cultural productions have been read in each subsequent era, we learn something not only about how to interpret a literary work as its immediate producer intended (which is the narrowest construction of literary study, that recommended by people like E. D. Hirsch) or about earlier historical times (a somewhat broader but still narrow construction of literary study) but also about how cultural formation works in time and over time.

At the very least, we will find ourselves defamiliarizing what we may have come to take as natural and normative in literary studies, taking the time to explore, for instance, *how* and *why*, especially since Kant and Hegel, literary study and teaching writing have developed in the particular and particularly complex relations to the structure of official (state- and institutionally sponsored) discourse that they have. One central question to be asked is why we have acquired the rage to *explain* and *interpret* poems and novels rather than to do any of the other things we might be doing with them, including studying them as instances of cultural production reproducing particular cultural values. Sartre suggests that humanity has a certain drive to reduce praxis, creation, and invention to the simple reproduction of the elementary "givens" of life. We tend to want to explain the work, the act, or the attitude by the factors that condition it, and Sartre takes our desire for explanation to be a disguise for the wish to assimilate the complex to the simple, to deny the specificity of structures, and to reduce change to identity.[18]

If we spend more time reading our readings, we will also spend more time reading the scene in which our readings take place, the institutional setting that enables and sponsors the reading of texts in the first place. At this point, finally, comes my contribution to what I called the fledgling analysis of the tropes of institutional practice: the ways in which we talk among ourselves about our students and our work. Here, a reading of our departmental discussions surrounding the institution of a new Ph.D. program in literacy are most interesting. In the assertion that the kind of philosophical thinking it would require is "too hard" for "our kind of students" lurks a fully operative set of mechanisms whose function can be described only as a kind of containment. "This is too hard" is the trope of difficulty, which manifests itself in various ways and raises a host of questions: Anything difficult is not worth studying? "Our kind" of student cannot handle difficulty? Anything complex cannot be of any use?[19] Anything that takes time to master is not worth the effort? It is painfully evident here that we are the *product* of our own cultural productions—"fast-food selves" with no patience for difficulty.

The assumption that anything multi- or interdisciplinary must necessarily be "watered down" is a trope one can recognize operating in the service of those disciplinary divisions that have kept us all playing in our separate playgrounds in the academy since the nineteenth century generated the whole notion of specialization and professionalization. Knowledge is hardly ever specific to any one discipline, and surely *modes* of inquiry cross disciplinary boundaries every day. As Terry Eagleton points out, the *classical* intellectual has always been defined as that person who works at the frontiers between the traditionally differentiated academic subject areas, drawing on more than one such specialty for his or her work; the intellectual then deploys such knowledge acquired as a way of "reading" the cultural situation. The academic scholar largely fails to qualify as an intellectual on both these counts, the scholar's work being neither rigorous nor broad enough.[20]

The assumption that students are "too young" to handle what we are teaching, or are "unprepared" and have "insufficient background," is a trope masking the fact that once learners have sufficiently "mastered" (the term itself is telling) the existing ways of doing, saying, and seeing, they have been, in turn, thoroughly mastered by them. Ultimately, the reason Bloom, Hirsch, and Bennett argue for a canon, a set of shared cultural facts, is not only because what have made it into the canon are unarguably the greatest of our cultural works but that those *particular* canonical works enshrine particular ways of experiencing the world. Once those have been thoroughly inculcated, we can ensure that all other cultural productions will remain marginal, because once inside a particular way of experiencing the world, all other ways *will* be perceived as "marginal." Learning not only the canon, or canonized academic discourse, but also canonized ways of reading canonized texts is very much like entering a secret society. In learning the secret codes, we *become* them. Once inside, we cause no harm to the institutional ways of seeing and experiencing and articulating into which we have been allowed entry.

Other tropes in our own institutional responses to such a proposed way of teaching literature and writing under the rubric of literacy need to be unpacked as well. One is that "only a few care about this esoteric stuff." This trope of the majoritarian has its functions, too: it makes it impossible to critique either the ways in which the majoritarian came to be majoritarian or what values the majoritarian may perpetuate, or to analyze the normative, pressuring power of majoritarian discourse. That the Ph.D. we propose is "elitist"—by which is meant that it is highly intellectual—is also a trope to explore if certain colleagues announce that their voices, work, and research are being masked, muted, or marginalized precisely by such majoritarian discourse.

If Adorno in *Minima Moralia* can analyze zoos, divorce patterns, jogging, IQ tests, and insomnia, and Barthes, wrestling, strip joints, and laundry powder, I believe exploring the rhetoric of departmental interchanges has become a respectable—and maybe even necessary—

enterprise. Inscribed in our exchanges is a politics of learning and a politics of cultural transmission, a set of assumptions about the direction in which authority flows, about the *source*—not to mention the generation and possession—of knowledge as a commodity that profoundly affects how and what we teach and learn.

I could not say in advance how such a course or such an exploration would be done, partly because I take this Ph.D. to be about the production of new knowledge rather than the transmission of existing knowledge. But I can point to a body of philosophical work that would provide a place from which to launch such an inquiry. Jürgen Habermas provides one, for instance, in all his analyses of the possibilities for a third or public sphere existing somewhere between the private (family) and the state, a sphere where there is the possibility for consensus and shared, communal endeavor. At one point he uses the phrase "the scientization of politics" in his distinction between two types of action. The first, "purposive-rational" action, involves the manipulation of nature and human beings to produce material means of subsistence. The second, "communicative action," is the kind we take to produce frameworks of reciprocal expectation that make it possible for us to live as members of collective social institutions. These concepts come in part from Aristotle's distinction between *techne* ("the skillful production of artifacts and the expert mastery of objectified tasks") and *praxis* ("action directed toward human education and the realization of human potential").[21] According to Habermas, in late twentieth-century society (including, I think, the academic one) the "purposive-rational" has developed to an intense degree and, perhaps as a consequence, has tended to universalize and regard as normative that form of action and those standards of discourse that correspond to it, simultaneously tending to render all others "deviant." All questions come to be framed as essentially technical or strategic questions, questions about the most effective means by which a given end can be attained. (Thus, discussion about the *content* or *aims* of such a Ph.D. rarely took place in our department. Instead, such discussion as there was centered on strictly technical issues: "Can these Ph.D.s get jobs?" "What is the market like?") As a result, society—and the academy—is unable to develop a capacity for the communicative action through which it could resolve practical questions, those that have to do not only with *means* (generating "clear prose," passing proficiency exams in writing, learning the canon, or getting a job) but also with *ends:* What does this kind of logic get you, and what does it cut you off from? What does this kind of prose teach as a way of experiencing the world, and what ways of experiencing does it render invisible? What kind of literacy generates what kind of "illiteracy," and with what consequences?

All of what I am saying here—about students feeling the imposition of one kind of literacy as a threat to one they already possess; about students coming to us with alternative literacies; about students' ambivalence about and resistance to the overheated, overanalytic kinds of discourse we teach; about the valid reasons for their suspicion of our discourse—is apparent to me in what I think of as my daily empirical audit. For example, why is it that students in writing courses so often dangle their papers away from their bodies—metaphorically if not actually—saying "help me fix this paper" while implying "but don't mess with *me*"? They know that to change their articulation is to change the self that produces the articulation, and many are not sure they want that change. (The equivalent is true of their teachers. *They* know that a new curriculum with a new emphasis will change *them*. So, as often as not, many resist.) This is as true in a literature class as in a composition class. When I found myself *thinking,* as I wrote my dissertation, that Charles Dickens did not like to say he was uncertain, and *writing* "Charles Dickens had a constitutional indisposition to expressions of incertitude" I recognized the extent to which reformulations of an idea—from one level of discourse to another, just as much as from one language to another—bring with them changes in the self doing the articulating that have not yet, psychologically, socially, politically, rhetorically, or historically been fully explored.

The reciprocal relation between the student, the "literacy learner," and the teacher has also hardly begun to be explored; the student by and large remains the unarticulated, or at least poorly articulated, Other in our disciplinary discourse. If what we are teaching is "academic discourse," that post-Kantian form that splits mind from matter and valorizes the former over the latter, then students, insofar as they have not yet been fully "initiated" into the fraternity of that discourse, retain access to realms we have to some extent forfeited. This, I think, explains the so often great extent to which teachers teach by giving with one hand and taking away with the other. We *need* the "illiteracy" students possess; namely, the access to a more immediate and visceral relation to the world.

If we work out our selves by choosing and fitting ourselves into the existing procrustean beds of culturally available signifying practices, we also produce our shared cultural identities in the same way. We can see that happening in a recent exchange in the pages of *New Literary History* between an African-American woman scholar, Joyce A. Joyce, on the one hand, and Houston Baker and Skip Gates, two other prominent African-American scholars and theorists, on the other.[22] Joyce had attacked the others' use of the rhetoric of literary theory. How can you talk that language, she asked, when it will not be understood by the majority of our people and our primary task is to lead our people to freedom? They responded in the language of the literary establishment she was challenging. She in her turn responded in a way that left them almost speechless, from a place that the terms of their "literacy" failed to make available to them. *They* were ready to launch an intellectual defense of their position. *She* said they had violated the first of the codes black people should share: you do not attack a sister in public, and most certainly not in the white press. Gates and Baker had allowed themselves to become so immersed in the critical language of the academy that they *became* that adversarial language. I believe that Joyce misconstrues Gates and Baker, but the point here is that there are not only canonical literary works, or canonical literary interpretations, but also "canonized" literary attitudes embodied in our critical approaches, one of which is the belief in the "neutral," "value-free" pursuit of "knowledge" at any cost, even at the cost of civility. Or at least so was Joyce's point.

None of us is either literate or illiterate in the absolute. We work to achieve various kinds of literacies to do what Sartre describes: transcend our selves by internalizing various cultural forms—various forms of literacy—into the very stuff of our being. Gates's and Baker's reaching toward one kind of literacy produces one kind of self; Joyce's, a different one. And each of these competing kinds of critical literacies generates a different way of being in the world.

The advantage of constellating our discipline around the issue of literacy construed as broadly as this is that it forces the focus of our work to shift from techniques for writing and analyzing, or recipe-sharings of how to teach writing and analyzing, to an exploration of standards of human conduct and ways of world-making.

NOTES

1. One place where this assertion is made is in Jeffrey Kittay and Wlad Godzich, *The Emergence of Prose: An Essay in Prosaics* (Minneapolis: U of Minnesota P, 1987) 112.

2. Wallace Martin, Introduction, *The Yale Critics: Deconstruction in America,* ed. Jonathan Arac, Wlad Godzich, and Wallace Martin, Theory and History of Literature 6 (Minneapolis: U of Minnesota P, 1983) xxxi.

3. I have in mind here students and teacher reading together things like Benjamin's *One-Way Street and Other Writings,* Vico's *The New Science,* Nietzsche's writings on figuration and troping, and instances of close reading of institutional and public discourse like the exemplary piece by the Cardiff (England) Text Analysis Group on the nuclear discourse of Reagan/Gorbachev at the Intermediate Nuclear Forces Treaty in Washington in December of 1987; see "Disarming Voices (A Nuclear Exchange)," *Textual Practice* 2.3 (Winter 1988): 381–93.

4. This is the work of Jean Baudrillard, Pierre Bourdieu and Jean-Claude Passeron, Jean-François Lyotard, Roland Barthes (of course), Michel Foucault, Jacques Derrida, Paul Bové, G. C. Spivak, Edward Said, Frank Lentricchia, Sam Weber, and a host of others.

5. See Lawrence Lipking, "Life, Death, and Other Theories," *Historical Studies and Literary Criticism,* ed. Jerome McGann (Madison: U of Wisconsin P, 1985) 181–82.

6. Pierre Bourdieu and Jean-Claude Passeron, *Reproduction in Education, Society, and Culture,* trans. Richard Nice, foreward Tom Bottomore (London and Beverly Hills: SAGE [Studies in Social and Educational Change] 5, 1977), and Pierre Bourdieu, *Distinction: A Social Critique of the Judgment of Taste,* trans. Richard Nice (Cambridge: Harvard UP, 1984).

7. Vološinov, *Marxism and the Philosophy of Language* (New York: Seminar Press, 1973).

8. Jean-Paul Sartre, *Search for a Method,* trans. Hazel E. Barnes (New York: Vintage, 1968) 150–51.

9. Paul Bové, "A Free, Varied, and Unwasteful Life: I. A. Richards' Speculative Instruments," *Intellectuals in Power* (New York: Columbia UP, 1987) 39–77.

10. The same model for education was recently explored in a NOVA television special on medical education at Harvard. Given the revelation that 90 percent of the factual information learned in medical school is promptly forgotten, and that more important than possession of specific bodies of facts was a particular understanding of what *doing* medicine involves and a particular understanding of the practitioner's place in the profession, Harvard has introduced actual patient contact in the first year of medical school,

along with seminars in which students are enabled to think critically about what engaging in medicine involves.

11. Daniel C. Hallin, "The American News Media: A Critical Theory Perspective," in *Critical Theory and Public Life,* ed. John Forester (Cambridge: MIT P, 1985) 123.

12. Martin Jay, *Adorno* (Cambridge: Harvard UP, 1984) 62, quoting Theodor Adorno, "Subject/Object."

13. Adorno, quoted in Jay 62–63.

14. Ibid. 115

15. Ibid. 117.

16. Ibid. 156.

17. Terry Eagleton, "Ideology and Scholarship," *Historical Studies and Literary Criticism,* ed. Jerome McGann (Madison: U of Wisconsin P, 1985) 121.

18. Jean-Paul Sartre 151.

19. See Colin McCabe's introduction to Gayatri Spivak's *In Other Worlds* (New York: Methuen, 1987) xvii–xviii for a passing reference to the function of the trope of the "too difficult" as well, but his discussion has to do with the rationale people in the profession offer for not reading theory.

20. Eagleton 124.

21. I am grateful to Hallin ("American News Media" 122) for this distinction. See also Jürgen Habermas, *The Theory of Communicative Action,* 2 vols., trans. Thomas McCarthy (Boston: Beacon P, 1984) and see especially the useful analyses of Habermas's work in Hallin. I should also add that I am not unaware of criticisms of Habermas's "utopian" vision and that many people prefer a Marxist or Foucauldian analysis. Nanette Frank, for instance, in a recent issue of *Social Text,* argues that Habermas's failure is that he cannot show, "at least in a derivative way, that solidarity and community would have a place in his vision of an emancipated society" ("Habermas and the Social Goods," *Social Text* 18 [Winter 1987/88]: 24). I should say that I am still struggling with the question, but I am inclined to prefer a model that does not require that people "transcend" their differences to arrive at "solidarity," partly because I believe that to be truly impossible, and partly because I would prefer differences to be celebrated and highlighted rather than "transcended." See also Nancy Fraser's introductory chapter in her *Unruly Practices: Power, Discourse, and Gender in Contemporary Social Theory* (Minneapolis: U of Minnesota P, 1989) for a shrewd comparison of the merits of a Habermasian versus a Foucauldian view of the workings of discourse.

22. Joyce Ann Joyce, " 'Who the Cap Fit': Unconsciousness and Unconscionableness in the Criticism of Houston Baker and Henry Louis Gates, Jr.," *New Literary History* 18.2 (Winter 1987): 371–84. In the same volume, see

Henry Louis Gates, Jr., "What's Love Got to Do With It: Critical Theory, Integrity, and the Black Idiom," 345–62, and Houston Baker, "In Dubious Battle," 363–69.

7

BLUES AND THE ART OF CRITICAL TEACHING

Jim Merod

(in memory of Raymond Williams)

If the first resistance any teacher confronts is the student's defense against the threat of change—intellectual, personal, or professional—the second resistance is already at work in the collective nature of defense structures. Opposition to the teacher's art resides at every point in the cultural and ideological matrix that frames social action. Such resistance rests within habitual values we call by various names in various contexts. In academic and other long-standing institutions, we call this resistance *tradition*. Across the spectrum of professional habits and identities, we call the collective defense *protocol*. Professional protocols, of course, create the condition for another form of defense against change that is too great or too rapid. That defense is called *prestige*, the intertwined seduction and privilege of personal differentiation reinforcing prevailing norms. In immature classrooms, the collective defense is called peer pressure. In more mature learning environments, the typical dispersed resistance teachers encounter is more self-conscious but no less disabling. This defense appears in a number of forms: fear of failure, desire to conform, and any of hundreds of ways to reduce, literalize, misinterpret, or merely deflect a strong teacher's invitation to activate the vulnerable energy of creative curiosity.

If we follow Freud, whose central analytic concept is repression, we not only discover the huge array of defense mechanisms that individuals (and collectives, institutions, and cultures) employ to *not know* and thereby absolve obligations, but we find that defenses of all sorts protect by ignoring both real and imagined antagonists. The crucial element of this for a teacher is to see that defenses work as much in deflecting *representations* of antagonistic or uncomfortable energy, aims, ideals, and the like as they work to cope with potentially traumatic face-to-face encounters. The strongest, most useful defense in the face of an alien or troublesome situation is not a turning away or falling asleep, not the massive denial of obliteration. Defenses that successfully defer or waylay antagonism absorb some component of the antagonist the way a skillful wrestler counters a hold, the way a tactical boxer rolls with a punch. The irony of defense structures is their ability to deny what they assert. Defenses, when most effective, appear to ignore what they acknowledge by erasure.

The covert public life of defense structures seems to construct one of those clever paradoxical knots that critical theory learned to enjoy as compensation over the last two decades, as academic life grew more insulated or more desperate for cultural well-being. Just as culture, in the late twentieth century in North America, Europe, Japan, and elsewhere, cannot be posed as an organic and unitary structure—a structure with a "dominant" core of practices and beliefs—so intellectual discourse in classrooms inevitably reflects a potentially unassimilable variety of personal and cultural outlooks. At an advanced stage of intellectual give and take, the concept of discursive ideology (the combative, sometimes stratified, but nonetheless truly heterogeneous competition among discursive ideologies) offers a useful framework for the interpretive rivalry of well-developed readers. At an earlier, more rudimentary stage of classroom dynamics, the battle for conceptual clarity and ideological differentiation is impeded in several ways, not the least by the competing modes of misunderstanding operative when people begin to discuss texts and ideas without a fairly clear sense of the shared assumptions that both enable and confuse debate.

The "art" of teaching I have in mind is called to life by those unsettled assemblages of uncertainty that mark so many conversations where common intellectual (for that matter, common cultural) terms are absent or undefined. I have in mind particularly the kinds of survey courses in colleges and universities that lump together a wide range of abilities and outlooks, students with diverse preparations, where common terms of some kind are needed. Such circumstances demand the tacit force of an available cultural "text" appealing enough and immediate enough to serve as a heuristic intermediary in the triangulated reckonings of classroom debate.[1] "Uncertainty" in this setting is a euphemism for the clash of interests, attitudes, values, and vocabularies within the great majority of school environments, where the first stirrings of analytic insight are supposed to begin. The art I allude to is in part a blind fumbling among thematic and interrogative goads. One gets intellectual debate started any way one can. This has less to do with psychoanalytic awareness than with the ability to provoke sustained, intelligent, if sometimes fitful and abandoned, responses between members of a conversation.

When I allude to an art of teaching I do not intend to map out a well-worked scene of classroom interactions. Anyone who has spent years in universities, attempting to tease light from the obscurities of silence and opinion, knows the fragility of the teacher's enterprise. I am thinking only of the fact that teaching is, mostly, conversation of one kind or another—that it is, among other things, questioning and naming. And questioning and naming are in some real sense both alike and opposed, because questions well posed and explored patiently often lead to better names (more naming, imaginative and frequently bizarre), just as questions sometimes undermine names that are in place or accepted readily. Questions quite often undo the demand for rigid definitions; they undermine categories and fixed boundaries. This accretion of names and the emptying or aborting of the act of naming work together. In its double exploration of possibilities within and surrounding concepts, statements, texts, images, laws, appeals, and so on, the teacher's act of questioning and naming may usefully be thought to provoke the student's questions and names. This simple complex field of conversational interaction is the terrain where the teacher's "art," an art of teaching, takes place.

I do not want to assert here that teaching, especially in textual and verbally enriched areas of investigation, is only or essentially the conjoined act of naming and questioning. There is much more involved. Teachers usually take positions of this or that variety. It is virtually impossible, it seems to me, to teach from a relentlessly skeptical position. If that were possible, the act of undermining each item of attention would become a position: a ceaselessly depositioned or repositioned stance. My point is simply that teachers assert points of view and carry values and outlooks of their own. Such a "stabilizing" of the pedagogical outlook not only creates a kind of consistency within a teacher's practice, it is a component of the teacher's authority.

One of the most chastized yet least debated elements of teaching—one that is always in a tense relation to any "art" that teaching can construct—is the ideological substructure of the teacher's authority. Teachers have a relatively direct access to the privilege of insinuating values, outlooks, attitudes, and cognitive points of view. Much of the subtext of classroom interactions is written in terms of fairly unexamined agreements that teachers impose or extract from students. In successful situations, which as I understand the notion of the teacher's "success" means that students have taken on the act of naming and questioning as their own, the subtext of traditionally unstated pedagogical outlooks becomes a central and undismissed text for ongoing analytic discussion. In sum, both the teacher's place and the student's place are examined as parts of specific hierarchical structures. In addition, they are looked at as having representative status no less than they have a concrete, embodied position within language, institutions, and behaviors. This "representative" value of the student's and the teacher's involvement with structures of language and authority broadens any examination of the force (the persuasive and coercive power) of naming and evaluating. The representative value of each is uniquely connected to the institutionalized possibilities, existing and still to be achieved, for uninhibited questioning and naming.

No doubt a great deal rides with such possibilities. One of them is the improbability of summarizing or assessing in any global form what, precisely, effective teaching can be thought to be. If I am right in thinking that effective teaching, however it *is* effective, is an art that is irreducible to formulation, then the value (perhaps this is an attitude, distinctly pedagogical) at stake in that art is an art of listening. I am aware that tenure committees and school evaluation boards often assume that subject matter covered in a somewhat clear style of declarative insistence, coupled with a determined amount of time put into office hours and preparations, constitutes an unflinching baseline for the sober transfer of information. But teaching of the kind I have in mind is not information exchange, essentially or provisionally; it is a much more fragile inducement to semiconfident reflection on the student's private mental ground. No one I have ever known has yet described how that inducement takes root, what intimate transfer of will and hope, of tenacious self-scrutiny, takes place within the energies of instruction that turn out to be less "instructive" than constructive. The construction that follows whatever art teaching upholds is the somewhat confident but not too bold production of an interrogative skill. A student who comes to such a need and capacity has been, perhaps, goaded there by one or two teachers (or parents or friends) who listened intelligently—which usually means a listening direct enough to ask for more than was offered, a listening that hears enough to nudge, modify, and affirm what is offered. Such affirmation may very well be a sort of testing of the other's position that opens up problematic areas to the mixed anxiety and excitement of dialogue. Is there any teacher, committed to such ambitions, who does not realize the difficulty of lifting intellectual debate above (or dropping it below) the invested alienation of classroom interactions?

I take it, therefore, that many fields of force are at work when we walk into our classrooms. One of them is the practiced inattention of academic professions to the structure of desire and the structure of defense-making by students trained in our culture to read television images and popular song lyrics with an unproblematized exuberance. The result of repeated ritualistic television viewing may be a characteristic apathy or boredom that appears most graphically in the stupefied bliss of inarticulate glib suspicion, a rampant distrust of claims to authority. It is likely, as Michel de Certeau insists, that such reactive suspicion operates within a large-scale logic of resistance to power and to widespread technologies of accountability and surveillance. In a world in which technocratic rationality owns considerable privilege, where the power of naming is used in the service of controlling or manipulating behavior and quantification and information retrieval give increased access to the means of control, the tactics of resistance and subversion in the activities of everyday life are practical ways to preserve a space for individual creativity. "What can be written about what everybody does?" de Certeau asks.[2]

The answer to that question is up for grabs, but silence is often a tactic of survival in the classroom. In the presence of expertise invested with evaluative authority, anyone may well imitate the silence of students who do not find their own experiences taken into account. One of the desires that shape student responses is self-preservation. The "self" to be maintained is often a precritical identity that desires the means of educational success without sacrificing modes of feeling and habits of speech or thought that are both comfortable and individually affirming. Part of my concern in pointing to a malleable yet highly contentious notion of the teacher's *art* is to counter, on one side, the persistent belief that teaching is a form of expert instruction and, on another side, a more recent image of pedagogical empowerment that serves to relativize the making of intellectual identities among students who have good reasons to resist taking on a fully self-conscious intellectual ambition.

Susan R. Horton has written a provocative critique of the lamentable persistence of strategies that uphold pedagogical authority without a sufficiently dialectical appreciation for the tactics of resistance expert authority always breeds.[3] To foreground the student's own texts, culture, hesitant curiosity, and resistance is not to convert the "scene of instruction" (which in fact is a scene of interpretive exchange) into an open agenda. My sense is that no teacher can teach very well without sustaining the student's attention. And one of the most permanently unsettling ways of maintaining critical dialogue is to lead students into the intimate yet wholly foreign world of their own desires. That world is constructed of ideals and motives that defend against unwanted intrusions, one of them quite frequently the teacher's.

One goal of critical teaching is to allow the affiliation between desires and defense structures to emerge. This may seem an obscure target of pedagogical interest given the fact that most teachers are masters of a specific body of learning. A great majority of teachers are accountable for imparting a supposedly quantifiable amount of information across the breadth of a course. Such quantification and the bureaucracy of accountability are more tenacious for high school teachers than for college and university instructors, though we find a dulling continuation of bureaucratic schooling among state and community colleges (among the second and third tiers of the public university system).[4]

My aim here is directed toward the live, erotic exchange of ideas, opinions, responses, readings, impressions, and fragmentary "starts" that make up the interpretive give and take in classrooms. I call attention to the eros of classroom intellectual combat because, when the classroom does in fact become an arena of conceptual and imaginative energy, the shared staging of respect and aggression is literally a controlled tug of heightened awareness. It is neither sentimental nor hyperbolic to refer to the most splendid moments of sustained classroom dialogue as erotic very much in the sense suggested by Socrates' perverse playfulness in *The Symposium*. Eros, it turns out, is a lack or absence seeking its own completion. The Socratic eros is not like the Freudian eros. The older, Greek notion sees eros as a need aligned with an essentially cosmological order, so that seductive love (eros) desires both organic and spiritual perfection. It is appropriate to think that the eruption of curiosity, the hesitant or more cogent conversation among teachers and students, enacts the sublimated libidinal aggression of Freud's notion of eros working toward the cooperative rational emotion at work in Socrates' erotic idealization.

We can unpack these terms, Freud's dialectical libido (both biological and mental) and Socrates' or Plato's sublime erotic self-abnegation that achieves an improbable self-fulfillment. The act of decoding each in terms of the other, however, and both in yet more vigilant terms of critical inspection, would likely overlook the fact that most classrooms do not achieve the heightened awareness and conceptual combat implied in the notion of intellectual eros. We risk dissolving the actual conditions of teaching if we imagine unattainable intellectual goals. When it is not a holding pen for unemployable, self-defeating ambitions, the classroom, whether urban or suburban, is too often the site of surveillance, information control, information clutter, and a gaggle of mind-numbing habits that defend schools and teachers from the daily pressures of lives mystified if not (more reactively) corrupted, made cynical or hostile, by our culture. The blockage from the open exchange of imagination that marks supportive learning environments is not a blockage on one side only, a product of student defenses against intellect. Teachers frequently carry deformed notions of their intellectual tasks into schoolrooms. Those defenses are no less disabling to both students and teachers than other, apparently institutionalized antiintellectual attitudes.

I am concerned here with the imagery and the drama of "opposition" that has run aground within the academy. I have attempted in the past to encourage a mediated, highly differential form of opposition to cultural and political banality and to a number of professional, antitheoretical motivations.[5] Any project of critical insurgency within theoretical work, within schools and professions, needs constant vigilance about its own authority and, therefore, about its responsibilities, liabilities, and limits in confronting what Gayatri Spivak has called "legitimate cultural explanations."[6] At the same time, the critical teacher needs to acknowledge ways in which the class structure enables and actually founds theoretical questioning. Theory is always related to ideas and ideals of legality, sufficiency, truthfulness, and rationality. Among the many elements that a politically committed form of intellectual responsibility must continually clarify are questions that seek more knowledge about the normalizing function of critical consciousness, intellectual identity, and pedagogical alertness—in short, about the competent witness and instructor, the stable teacher and critical authority. Some questions to be asked are: Whose law governs adequate practices? What notion of truth regulates writing or teaching? Whose rationality is in play when we speak or converse, and for what declared and covert purposes?

Critical intervention within schools and professions and within the area called theory cannot be undertaken singly or heroically. It needs to be a collective and cooperative act, the cooperation of antagonists. As it collides with the world of critical teaching, such intervention is intended to encourage among students a felt sense of self-worth, because resistances and defenses of many sorts deserve to be given room to exert their own pride and their own logic. When I suggest that the affiliation between desire and defenses is a necessary area for critical interrogation, a foreground of conceptual and textual analysis, I have in view the sense that a student's themes and texts need to be brought alongside those that teachers propose if the otherwise foreign language of critical analysis is to gain intimate entanglement with the student's life. One of the dangers of this endeavor is the very real possibility that a "dialogue" between two kinds of texts will be subverted by an overt or unconscious elevation of an official or canonical text. If the de-idealizing suspicion of the critical project is incomplete, incompletely turned on itself and its privileged terms, the massively defended student will not get lost in the enterprise but find confirmation of the project's uselessness. A more vulnerably skeptical student, one who tries to employ critical "moves," may well flounder in the reigning mood of smug common sense.

The resistances I point to, including our own as teachers, situate a critically oriented teacher with many more questions than there are sure responses. I am concerned that, like the knowledgeable theorist who knows what to say but not quite what its effects may be, many teachers unknowingly participate in the creation of subjectivities, identities, and modes of conscious and less conscious introspection without taking into account the overdetermined and invisibly colonized subject positions that shape the way each of us enters into critical discourse. One of the signs of this oversight appears in the language of frustrated commitment that teachers sometimes use to name their inability to engage well-defended students. But defenses operate on both sides of the podium. When the culture at large or the neighborhood that has powerfully informed the precritical intellect becomes an opponent for the somewhat stumped teacher, such opposition constitutes a defense that dampens the possibilities of bringing distrustful students to the threshold of critical imagination.

I do not know how to address this sometimes unknowingly polarized opposition except to argue for both the strategic as well as the absolute value of admitting into conversation the sub- or extrahumanistic (the noncanonical) margin that holds, in many forms of unvoiced witnessing, the heterogeneous logic of gender, race, and class exclusions. In this activity I think of the notion—doubtless an ideal demanding caution—of "responsibility" as involving, in some flawed but undismissable way, the giving of an account. It is also the staking of claims. As I imagine it, however, if such responsibility is both a personal acceptance of obligation and a politically engaged summoning of others to act or think, it begins and continues by inspecting everything within the lines we write as critics and teachers. It continues further by inspecting, with the help of others, everything "between" and "beneath" those lines. The vigilance of the critic's and the teacher's responsibility is not to establish an exemplary career, despite the fact that the academic system is contrived to create the reductive singularity of professional exemplification. The vigilance I allude to is "for the sake of" expanding the possibility of public questioning that can transfer or translate critical interrogation wherever it may be useful. Let me note, in passing, my assertion of a phrase as loaded with pathos as this one: "for the sake of." I accept responsibility for handing it on, for holding it to myself and holding it out, as if the concept of professional and personal critical accountability to human goodwill, to the uncoercive force of a meddlesome idea of justice, were of permanent interest.

In the wary, if also urgent, spirit of that all-too-cryptic phrase, "for the sake of," I want to look at the Blues. I want to look at the Blues as a cultural given, as a native African-American discourse reared on suffering (on the economics of slavery), perfected in the lyrical woodshed of the vernacular, and open to the piracy of insurrectionary thought—which the Blues support and disarm all at once. I want to look at the Blues because Blues music, Blues lyrics, Blues culture, and what you can call the Blues feeling stand opposed to smug stabilities of intellectual reason. The Blues are not against intelligence and reason. They do, however, oppose a good many instances of self-legitimacy, disengaged understanding, and repeated social deformations produced by long-standing habits of social inequality.

Blues, as Houston Baker has pointed out, "defy narrow definition" because they "exist, not as a function of formal inscription, but as a forceful condition of Afro-American inscription itself."[7] This is a fancy but accurate way of saying that the Blues are fundamentally "placeless." They arrive the way a song arrives. The deep history of a song cannot be historicized with much confidence. A song, or the singing of a song, delivers an excess force and knowledge irreducible to its composer or conditions of its creation (recording, duplication, and the rest). Blues singing and playing "stand in" for another person's burdened awareness. The Blues, in short, carry immediate significance and felt utterance the way that well-spoken poems carry a verbal charge that stretches semantic clarity. The poem, read or heard, always demands more readings. So, too, Blues playing and singing. Each is lyrical in ways that critical readers recognize in well-rehearsed canonical works: at once "presenting" and derealizing the world and human relations in the world.

To present the Blues to students as a critical text within a critical venture is to invoke several discontinuities that estrange the familiar sound and feel of the music. One of those discontinuities is the rupture between a singing voice (a lyrical surface) and the fiction of a wholly unified soul, a fully discoverable self within or behind the performance. Another "break" takes place in the textual structure of the Blues. To read the Blues critically is to come on a disconnection at work in the represented immediacy of a word, a sound, or a voice that seems to hold the revealed meaning of a once-secret sense, even as the allegorical duplicity of language and of sound structures unfolds wholly ambiguous possibilities of meaning. If we add to these formalistic difficulties of "reading" the Blues the almost universal incapacity of musical texts to specify the range of performative interpretation, we begin to see that the Blues can be looked at as artistic events that both defy formal inscription and succumb without reduction to the ambivalence of textual structures.

Opening up the Blues for a class in textual relationships, which is to say, for a study of the relations between intertextual and interinstitutional operations, adds a problem to other troubles that critical teaching encounters. The discontinuity between the representational (or the notational) and the allegorical poses one dilemma for relatively unsophisticated readers. In the mode of the Blues that discontinuity actually serves critical purposes, because it creates an "opening" that acts as an invitation to interpretive speculation. Precisely this speculation allows all the particularity of racial, cultural, class, and gender conflicts to begin to assume weight and urgency. This "invitation" to interpret gains energy, no doubt, from the passionate force of the music. The persuasive sensuality of the Blues is an appeal prepared in almost every crevice of a ubiquitous and dominant commercial culture. One of the initial moments in approaching the Blues as a text for critical understanding must be scrupulously self-conscious in marking out the allegorical "placelessness" of the Blues as a discrete set of musical events and as a tradition. This placelessness is not a lack of historical and social grounding. To the contrary, it is the image of human activities and social places removed from official cultural awareness. Such a lack of publicly acknowledged space has relegated the Blues to a unique and somewhat awkward status. The Blues have become, by the magisterial force of artistic tenacity, both a living tradition and a cultural archive—a tradition and an archive that attest to the emergence of an entire race from exploitation, domination, perpetual injustice, and cultural erasure. To be blunt, the Blues tradition and its accompanying jazz heritage have provided North American culture an unrivaled and continuous artistic energy that has yet to be fully recognized, honored, and supported by schools, colleges, intellectuals, journalists, media executives, and foundations.

Unique in its legacy, unmatched as an unbroken organic cultural ensemble across a century and a half of North American social upheaval, the Blues carry a moral as well as an esthetic power. In a society that continues to separate whites from blacks, separating the characteristic economic hopes each might expect and overlooking educational deprivations (despite court mandates) in every American city, the Blues speak with a weight of experience that crosses racial and economic lines. The Blues speak from an African-American awareness to the shared partnership of any unmystified consciousness. The many voices and themes of the Blues enact a history, as Stanley

Crouch has noted, in which "the Afro-American experience provides the appropriately corkscrewing path through the spiritual and intellectual thickets of our time, exposing us all to ourselves as often through art as politics."[8]

This sense that the African-American experience provides critical mediation through the turmoil of contemporary North American culture needs a continually revived awareness of profound institutionalized resistance to the emergence of collective black cultural energy. For that reason, the notion of historical self-discovery as an event experienced "as often through art as [through] politics" threatens to miscast both the political consequences of art and the artful manipulation of political spectacles. To read the Blues demands a never-ceasing cultural clarification in which the African-American heritage comes to appear as a cultural and a political force no less ambivalent, fractured, and snagged by self-contradictions than other social or historical ensembles.[9] But anyone working to give the Blues tradition a pedagogical and critical dignity long overdue will soon encounter both the hostility and the cultural denial that Blues artists have had to surmount.

A many-sided debate has gone on for some time among high-ranking North American critics regarding the costs of theory. The most incisive challenge from an antitheoretical position views theory as hegemonic, part of the dominant culture and its domineering attitudes and practices. Barbara Christian has written a powerful polemic concerning "the monolithic, monotheistic" tendency of what she calls "the race for theory."[10] I think Christian has made an argument that artists like Billie Holiday and Big Bill Broonzy would find more appealing than arguments more deeply engaged with Antonio Gramsci and Walter Benjamin. At least that is provisionally so, because nothing rules out writing about (or with the aid of) Gramsci and Benjamin with a feeling for "the complexity of life," as Christian honors it. If the Blues as a long and still-gestating tradition uphold a repeated insight, it may well be "an affirmation that sensuality is intelligence." That phrase, assigned by Christian to appreciate the informed force of Toni Morrison's writing, applies just as well to lyrics and music born on plantation fields and transformed by thousands of revisions across one hundred plus years of increasingly complex rhythms, harmonies, and instrumentation.

Two explicit worries or objections drive Barbara Christian's disavowal of theory as it stands. One is the abstractness of theoretical debate, "the sheer ugliness of the language, its lack of clarity, its unnecessarily complicated sentence constructions, its lack of pleasurableness, its alienating quality."[11] The other is the distortion that dominant (white) critical language imposes on writers who are not male or white, a distortion that "mystifies rather than clarifies our condition, making it possible for a few people who know that particular language to control the critical scene—that language surfaced, interestingly enough, just when the literature of peoples of color, of black women, of Latin Americans, of Africans began to move to 'the center.' "[12]

I situate any use of the Blues by academic intellectuals, especially white intellectuals, within Barbara Christian's concerns because, even though the popular audience for both Blues and mainstream (blues-driven) jazz is largely white, the appropriation of this heritage within reigning intellectual and pedagogical structures of authority and value charts a tangled course. What, for example, does it mean to grow up in essentially white, middle-class circumstances, through the years of rock music's first emergence, with a singular devotion to Louis Armstrong, Sidney Bechet, Bessie Smith, and their heirs? Is it credible to imagine, as I do, that a young white man or woman, listening continuously and obsessively to what can only be thought of as the canonical works of black culture, develops structures of feeling as deeply antipathetic to supremacist thinking as are those represented in that unrepressed legacy of songful feeling? But more is at stake in foregrounding the main lines of North America's black musical heritage than structures of feeling. The relationship between an extraordinarily diverse and rich cultural heritage denied its proper acknowledgment and a "postmodern" commercial reality glutted with cultural stereotypes needs far more precise inspection. During the fifties, for example, when Louis Armstrong was sent to the Soviet Union in the midst of Cold War tensions, what characteristic exploitations allowed the State Department to dub his "ambassadorship" a goodwill tour under the banner of "America's" most original art form?

Despite laudable changes in literary studies, such as an expanded inclusiveness in many university curricula, as well as intellectual and pedagogical openings that challenge the privileged status of white professional male authority, the persuasive power of that most emblematic of all African-American art forms, the Blues tradition and its jazz frameworks, still stands outside the circle of literary interest. This exclusion is neither inadvertent nor likely to be transformed by resolutely non- or antitheoretical forays into African-American cultural life. Henry Louis Gates, Jr., is moved by a just subversive energy when he insists that "the challenge facing the critic of black literature" today is

> not to shy away from white power—that is, literary theory; rather, [it is] to translate it into the black idiom, *renaming* principles of criticism where appropriate, but especially *naming* indigenous black principles of criticism and applying these to explicate our own texts. . . . And what do I mean by "appropriate"? Simply this: any tool that enables the critic to explain the complex workings of the language of a text is an "appropriate" tool.[13]

One hears in this a remarkable translation of R. P. Blackmur's no less subversive call for an antidoctrinal critical flexibility in his well-known but seldom heeded essay of 1935, "A Critic's Job of Work." Blackmur's opening sentence carries a stunning provocation. "Criticism, I take it, is the formal discourse of an amateur." Rarely has a professional critic so arrestingly pursued the intricate evasions of knowledge marked by the erotic attraction of all that knowledge animates. That the critic in Blackmur's sense is a lover, in the root concept of an amateur's ambition, is an identity not foreign to Barbara Christian's plea for the dense substance of expression unburdened by abstractions. It is an ideal made more bold by Henry Louis Gates, Jr.: "How can the use of literary analysis to explicate the racist social text in which we still find ourselves be anything *but* political?" Therefore, Gates continues,

> my task—as I see it—is to help to guarantee that black and so-called Third World literature is taught to black and Third World (and white) students by black and Third World (and white) professors in heretofore white mainstream departments of literature and to train university graduate and undergraduate students to think, to read, and even to *write* clearly, helping them to expose false usages of language, fraudulent claims and muddled arguments, propaganda and vicious lies, from all of which our people have suffered just as surely as we have from an

> economic order in which we were zeroes and a metaphysical order in which we were absences. These are the "values" that should be transmitted through black critical theory.[14]

This remarkable passion is directed toward advancing critical theory as an agent of teaching, the professional art of the critical amateur. A small step takes it to Blackmur's subtle ideal that criticism, like teaching, is itself an art—"a self-sufficient but by no means an isolated art [that] witnesses constantly in its own life its interdependence with the other arts."[15] Blackmur is ahead of most critics and theorists in understanding that intellectual and artistic constructions are affiliated in unavoidable networks of prejudice and belief that congeal as doctrinal frameworks. In each society such frameworks enable and limit ideological combat. But Blackmur's criticism stands committed to point out, repeatedly, how the tenuous yet combative "interdependence" among the critical and expressive arts keeps room available (within otherwise turbulent or closed cultural areas) for challenging the moment's reigning doctrines.

There has been a pervasive sense of separation or exclusion, nearly doctrinal in its unspoken tenacity, by which "things intellectual," things related to theory and critical practices, have been detached from things seen and heard passionately. I mean not so much that intellectuals in our era have not written about the arts; they have. I mean that the force of music and film and painting and dance has seldom been allowed to collide and intersect surprisingly with conceptual and critical activity. If the unstated resonance I find between Gates's words and Blackmur's has a common source and aim, it may be in their deep awareness of an energy in language—a propulsive, musical heartbeat—that makes language memorable and helps to make memorable language persuasive.

When I propose the Blues as a body of texts, songs, and narratives to animate conversational urgency in classrooms, I neither mean to privilege the Blues as a scene of soulful purity nor to designate which "texts," songs, and narratives should make up the Blues canon. My ambition is to put students and teachers more often in touch with music and its interdependent connectedness to interpretive arts that gain as much grounding (as much specific cultural placement) from the extraverbal and nonverbal artistic world as well-executed criticism lends to music and all other creative experiments. And yet, beyond the give and take of pedagogical innovation, the deconstructive urge that Gates acknowledges is at stake, albeit in a more profoundly historicized form of critical attention than academic writing usually promotes. The "deconstruction" Gates has in view predates contemporary French theory:

> If only for the record, let me state clearly here that only a black person alienated from black language-use could fail to understand that we have been deconstructing white people's languages and discourses since that dreadful day in 1619 when we were marched off the boat in Virginia. Derrida did not invent deconstruction, *we* did! That is what the blues and signifying are all about. Ours must be a signifying, vernacular criticism, related to other critical theories, yet indelibly black, a critical theory of our own.[16]

Precisely this deconstructing "black language-use" that Gates names as a long-standing undoing of the master's commanding voice is at work in the art of the Blues in each of its instances. That language, the language of the Blues, is not reducible to verbal dialectics and spoken or written statements that signify, trope, and undo or assert authority. Black language use carries a historically overdetermined relationship to musical structures, to prayerful hymns and field chants, to a single lyrical voice as well as to the hypnotic movement of calls and reverberating responses. To recognize a reworked musicality in black language use is not to essentialize black rhetorical energy, but that recognition does direct a critic, aware of the alienation of a good many classrooms (an alienation endemic to the white academy), to accept and further explore the range of thought and feeling at the heart of the Blues tradition.

Teaching, it seems to me, is most often artful in its moments of lucid abandon, those moments when language reveals its own complexity, which is the complexity of everything worth savoring. Such moments are shared between participants lured by the enchantment of the clarity and obscurity linked in the conversation's chain. The clarity one seems to find gives courage to continue. It is bright and high, if also momentary, but it goads inquiry to push inside what is not so clear. When teaching gathers such momentum or such courage, things seen and said and "known" may be no more illusory than the slur of a horn that seems to "speak." But they are no less illusory. And listening to what is said becomes at the same time a listening to what one heard, attention collecting pieces, words, phrases, images, ideas, and scattered moments in the effort to reclaim an elusive awareness of what this single notion, that situated event, may mean.

The Blues are no doubt only one set of countless invocations to such shared concentration. That heritage, widened to include jazz as an improvisational ensemble, an art of making the moment come alive by reviving and extending the intelligent passion of one's ancestors, carries both a pedagogical and a cultural importance not easily dismissed. Much of the sobriety that constricts the pedagogical interaction derives from the perverse identity—molded by British and American analytic self-possession—of desperate intellectual solitude. Precisely that mournful inwardness, elevated to an almost unchallenged ideal, is what the Blues contend. Kenneth Burke, thinking of the way that art makes a public reconciliation of personal torments, once noted the capacity of art to soothe what ails the soul. By such strength, poets and singers employ the wisdom of an unperturbable hypochondriasis. With such wisdom, the Blues tradition forged a collective ethos. That tradition has become an infinitely displaced apothecary, the funky agent of relief for morbid self-containment.

The uses to which art and intellect, and the art of the Blues intellect, are put prepare the critical teacher's early morning amusement. The use of the Blues in a bloodless commercial market is no less precarious than are the uses of courage and passion and preemptive cunning. But one use, less troubling for the teacher's critical art, can be found in the erosion of monumentalist curricular logics. If the Blues help create an "indelibly black" critical theory, they are also much more than an instance of postcolonial deconstructions. The Blues carry knowledge of suffering inflicted by the tyranny of systematic oppression. They also enact tactics of protest, resistance, and complaint that draw from the common ancestry of human feeling. For students in the late twentieth century in North America to find that black songs and black history are embedded in their inherited culture—for white students in particular to find that black artists, black men and women, are their rightful cultural ancestors—is to move beyond the polemics of theory.

NOTES

This essay was first given as the keynote talk for a three-day conference on "The Political Responsibilities of the Critic and Teacher" at Carnegie Mellon University, May 1988.

1. Mary Louise Pratt has written a lucid account of the now well-mythologized Stanford University debate of 1988 concerning canonical humanities offerings. Several points under consideration here are reflected in Pratt's discussion of the somewhat retrograde interest to preserve "a common intellectual experience" among Stanford undergraduates by way of a great books core reading list.

My inclination in this essay is to offer the Blues as a cultural ensemble, a "text" only in a broad yet historically layered sense: a cultural text that holds a number of problems and intellectual areas to be explored. The notion of such a "cultural text," then, is not technically overloaded. Because a leisurely and attentive reading of the Blues undermines traditional emphases on high cultural literary and philosophical monuments, the mediating force of the Blues tradition does not replace autonomous texts with texts only slightly less fixed by interpretive conventions. The Blues offer one step toward an intercultural and nonhierarchical investigation of historical, social, political, and institutional relationships that have both troubled and expanded the idea of "Western culture" and civilization. See Mary Louise Pratt, "Humanities for the Future: Reflections on the Western Culture Debate at Stanford," *The South Atlantic Quarterly* 89.1 (Winter 1990): 7–25.

2. Michel de Certeau, "On the Oppositional Practices of Everyday Life," *Social Text* 3 (Fall 1980): 10.

3. Susan R. Horton, "Let's Get 'Literate': English Department Politics and a Proposal for a Ph.D. in Literacy," the previous essay in this volume.

4. Stuart Hall delivered an unpublished lecture at McGill University in April, 1988, in which he outlined a desultory scene of catch-22 financing now squeezing each tier of the British university system. In brief, the greater centralization passed into law with a new education bill, sponsored by the Thatcher government, has taken much greater control over academic appointments and curricular financing. The effect is a potential for permanent government and bureaucratic intervention within the entire range of universities in Great Britain (Stuart Hall, "The Crisis in English Universities, and its Political and Economic Context").

5. See Jim Merod, *The Political Responsibility of the Critic* (Ithaca, N.Y.: Cornell UP, 1987).

6. Gayatri Chakravorty Spivak, *In Other Worlds: Essays in Cultural Politics* (New York: Methuen 1987) 117.

7. Houston A. Baker, Jr., *Blues, Ideology, and Afro-American Literature* (Chicago: U of Chicago P, 1984) 4. Baker employs a provocative but problematic image to characterize African-American culture. That culture "is a complex, reflexive enterprise which finds its proper figuration in blues conceived as a matrix. A matrix is a womb, a network, a fossil-bearing rock, a rocky trace of a gemstone's removal, a principal metal in an alloy, a mat or plate for reproducing print or phonograph records. The matrix is a point of ceaseless input and output, a web of intersecting, crisscrossing impulses always in productive transit" (3). It is possible to admire the ambition for capturing the rich and evolving overdetermination of Blues forms and their significance without overloading the comparative image that suggests an almost unnameable cultural excess. More specifically, Baker holds the Blues to be "a synthesis (albeit one always synthesizing rather than one already hypostatized). Combining work songs, group seculars, field hollers, sacred harmonies, proverbial wisdom, folk philosophy, political commentary, ribald humor, elegiac lament, and much more, they constitute an amalgam that seems always to have been in motion in America—always becoming, shaping, transforming, displacing the peculiar experiences of Africans in the New World" (5).

It is to Baker's credit that he has brought the Blues forward as a cultural ensemble worthy of serious and sustained critical investigation. Anyone interested in his treatment of the Blues tradition should look also at his *Long Black Song: Essays in Black American Literature and Culture* (Charlottesville: U of Virginia P, 1972).

8. Stanley Crouch, *Notes of a Hanging Judge* (New York: Oxford UP, 1990) xiv.

9. I am not invoking an ageless manichean allegory to surreptitiously blur the power of Blues or of the Blues within their African-American lineage. The self-contestations I point toward are at work in any cultural network, the African-American cultural setting no less than any. How could any culture so surrounded by racial suspicions and hostilities through the majority of its most powerful years of creativity avoid the contradictions of such contestation? See Abdul JanMohamed, "The Economy of Manichean Allegory: The Function of Racial Difference in Colonialist Literature," *Critical Inquiry* 12.1 (Autumn 1985): 59–87.

10. Barbara Christian, "The Race for Theory," *Cultural Critique* 6 (Spring 1987): 58.

11. Ibid. 56.

12. Ibid. 55.

13. Henry Louis Gates, Jr., "Authority, (White) Power and the (Black) Critic; It's All Greek To Me," *Cultural Critique* 7 (Fall 1987): 33.

14. Ibid. 34.

15. R. P. Blackmur, *Language As Gesture* (New York: Columbia UP, 1981) 372.
16. Gates 34.

8

TEACHING HISTORICALLY

Richard Ohmann

When I think about the great, blank space in our national consciousness that in part justifies historical teaching, I often think of an exemplary memory. One night in 1979, shortly after the Iranian takeover of the U.S. embassy, I was watching television coverage of a spontaneous demonstration on a Washington, D.C., street. A man repeatedly shouted "We're *tired* of other countries telling us what to do" and then led the people around him in a scraggly rendition of "God Bless America." In his frustration, the man spoke for millions of citizens. I doubt he knew what almost all had forgotten, that in 1953 our secret government had shanghaied a nascent democracy in Iran and put the shah in its place.

That would have been pertinent knowledge. It would not have freed the hostages, and it would have come too late to change the dismal course taken by the Iranian revolution. But it would have suggested two crude lessons. First, when people are trying to push the United States around, their actions may be the long-muted reflex of a push in the other direction. Second, if you steal a society's right of self-determination, you may not like what it does when it takes back that right. Applying those crude lessons to Central America in 1979 might have led people who could remember what the Monroe Doctrine had concretely meant for those countries to demand a posture toward Nicaragua, Guatemala, and El Salvador different from the one adopted by our leaders—who are incapable of learning such lessons except in those few occasions when citizens raise the issue of what is quaintly called the "political cost" of killing peasants, as did the movement against the Vietnam War.

These are and will be matters of life and death, in which the sense of history plays a role. Of course, more than one sense of history is at play on this stage. The historical vision given currency by our leaders and their complaisant friends in the media sees an endless struggle between two great forces, one for good and one for evil, with freedom or slavery as the stakes. Here, in the bastion of freedom, a smiling, progressive evolution was set going by the American War of Independence and the U.S. Constitution, by the Puritans and the pioneers, and that history keeps delivering the fruits of democracy and hard work so long as we do not betray it or let the Evil Empire terminate it. Within that historical vision, the overthrow of a Mossadegh, or Arbenz, or Bosch, or Allende, or Bishop takes its place as a minor act of altruism, or at worst, an unfortunate necessity, and is easily forgotten—except that these forgotten bits of history sometimes snap up to bark our shins later on.

So *a* historical sense is not enough. Official history is apologetics; maybe its salience is one reason so many students write off history in general as bunk. Maybe they get the idea that history supports a crackpot reality they can do nothing to change. Obviously, I think that a sane historical sense has to define itself as *critical* of both official history and the power relations that sustain it and are sustained by it.

My subject is teaching historically about cultural texts, not teaching about American adventures abroad, but I frame it in this way to indicate the urgency I feel about the project. That urgency does not entail a particular vision of history, or a particular way of teaching about it, and the ways I will sketch here raise theoretical problems that I will acknowledge at the end of the essay. Also, the dangerous historical void in our public life is not the only reason for teaching historically about texts. We should do so because, in addition, we and our students cannot understand texts very satisfactorily without making them part of some historical narrative. With those premises out, I will try to suggest through two examples how a critical historical sense might come into play in our classrooms.

The first example concerns teaching about mass culture, in particular, about advertising. Consider the series of ads that probably gets into as many classrooms where advertising is taught as Shakespeare sonnets get into classrooms where poetry is taught: those for Virginia Slims cigarettes. You know the genre: an "old" brownish photo, usually in the upper background, evokes the bad time before women were free. Perhaps it shows a turn-of-the-century woman sitting demure and alone at one end of a dinner table, while three or four men at the other end exclude her from their talk, brandy, and cigar smoke; perhaps it just shows a group of Klondike miners with a subservient woman or two off to one side.

In the foreground of the ad, striding forth in brilliant color and bold, idiosyncratic fashion, is the Virginia Slims lady, confidently, even defiantly flourishing her cigarette, yet gorgeous and still somehow quintessentially feminine. The familiar slogan, "You've come a long way, baby," annotates the contrasting images with the correct historical reading of their juxtaposition.

Everyone who has thought for five minutes about these ads understands how they mean to turn critical history into good marketplace behavior—how they swallow up ninety percent of what is creatively critical in the women's movement of the last twenty years, convert it into freedom of self-presentation in public, and hand it back to women as inseparable from commodified glamor. And of course they subsume the women's movement within official history: just part of the long forward march of progress, a natural outcome of our social and economic system, rather than a battle against persistent inequalities of that system. So the Virginia Slims ads, like all others, but more openly than most, do not just ignore history, they enter into a contest over its meanings and direction. Awareness of that contest is essential to the critical sense one needs to keep one's bearings in mass culture and in the politics of our lives.

What might historical teaching contribute here, beyond rescuing the development and ideas of contemporary feminism from the ad agency's cynical assault and extending the reach of an eighteen-year-old's memory? I suggest contextualizing the Virginia Slims ads more deeply in the commodification of desire and in mass culture's characteristic attempt at sanitizing and incorporating whatever threatening tendencies arise outside its sphere. One might, for instance, look with students at commercial and ideological uses of the flapper image in 1920s advertising. Or one could trace this strategy farther back, to an ad like that for Rubifoam, reproduced here. "The New Woman" was the term that designated the feminist of the 1890s. Like Virginia Slims today, Rubifoam appropriated its positive force, made a little fun of it via the woman's mannish pose, neutralized the politics of dress reform by calling her clothes a "costume" and by recuperating them within the familiar dynamic of "fashion," and mobilized this reading of history to sell not cigarettes but a dentifrice.

Advertisement run in a number of magazines around 1896.

While enlisting a social movement in the promotion of a humble commodity, the Rubifoam ad did a number of other things that are common in advertising today, of which I will mention just three.

1. It connected meanings in a way that was semantically (though not politically) arbitrary: a tooth cleanser signifies women's liberation. Such links were constituting a *language* of advertising, an essentially magic system of meanings.
2. The ad hinted at the possibility of raising oneself socially, of attaining distinction, of standing out from the crowd, not by actually gaining in wealth or status but by using a product that cost twenty-five cents. It promoted the "democracy of goods" that was feeding on and supplanting the old Horatio Alger dream of success.
3. It addressed the reader as valuing *modernity,* indexed here as advanced dress, "the New Woman," "fashion," "fashionable," and "up-to-date." It hailed her as one hoping to ride the wave of historical progress, *and* it invited her to take that historical part by a private act of consumption.

In short, the ad mystified human relations and the social process in ways extremely familiar to us today, displacing needs that are intrinsically social into that arena of individual choice, the marketplace.

Finding such antecedents does not in itself do much to nurture a historical sense, though it is a beginning. A danger is that by stressing likenesses between this ad of 1896 and many ads of the 1980s, one may seem to imply that the more things change, the more they remain the same—that advertising is advertising. Not so. You could search the ad pages of national magazines just fifteen years earlier and find nothing like the Rubifoam ad in appearance or technique of signification. In fact, in 1881 publications, you can find few ads of any sort for nationally sold, brand-name commodities. Those you can find are small, without sophisticated graphics, and printed in tiny type, more or less like classifieds today. Their texts all read like this one for a baking powder: "Absolutely pure, grape cream tarter and bicarb of soda; contains nothing else. . . . All other kinds have filling, as starch, flour, . . ." This might well have been false, but my point is that earlier ads gave information and made offers instead of magically linking products to social ideals and personal dreams of glory.

Why? What happened between 1880 and 1900? Very many related things, including the birth of both the national mass circulation magazine (*The Cosmopolitan*, not then a women's magazine, was one of the leaders) and the modern advertising industry (led by ad agencies, specialists in consciousness): linchpins of the national, mass, commercial culture that surrounds us today. Behind those new cultural institutions was the sudden development of the large, integrated corporation, drawing together the entire productive process, from raw materials to sales, in strategic response to the instability and repeated crises of entrepreneurial capitalism. Through the new arrangements, businessmen sought to organize markets rather than just get out the goods and hope for the best. Advertising as we know it was a byproduct of that need; in turn, national mass culture was (I exaggerate only a bit) a byproduct of national advertising and the circulation of brand-name commodities like Rubifoam, Ivory Soap, the Gillette safety razor, Cream of Wheat, and dozens of others—including cigarettes, transformed from a rare luxury into a common necessity by the wonderful new Bonsack machines and the promotional genius that James Buchanan Duke employed to market their output. The magical language of advertising was and is both specific to our social formation and responsive to the needs of powerful actors within it.

In teaching critically about mass culture, I find it essential to explore this network of economic and social relations. Otherwise, the critique stays on the surface and tends to promote a shallow cynicism and a false, conspiratorial understanding of cultural production, the notion that media corporations are intentionally brainwashing audiences into zombielike acceptance of the status quo. That is better than the *non*critical understanding, that we have a cultural democracy in which audiences get just what they want, but it misses the depth, the rootedness, of cultural relations and renders the critical attitude ineffectual, leaving us with the feeling that "we" sophisticated college people can see through these crude deceptions, whereas the masses remain forever victims. And that points to a second way in which the historical sense can be empowering, if sobering. By dissipating the solipsism of the present moment in which many students live, owing partly to mass culture itself, it lets them and us see that things could be different because things *have been* different—and very recently. Social formations are temporary. Something worse or better will supplant this one. We who are living will, by action and inaction, give it shape. Historical teaching can awaken a sense of agency outside the sphere of the personal.

My second example, which moves away from my individual teaching practices, concerns not the historical contextualizing of recent texts but the approach to texts from other societies and other times. I refer to a course in the historical study of literature that my department at Wesleyan has been teaching for about five years. It is the second semester of a year-long sequence for sophomores considering an English major. There are usually about 100 students in that category, and the course usually has around five sections. About half the members of our twenty-person department now have the course in their repertories.[1]

First, I need to say a word about the course's genesis. Like anything that an eclectic department agrees on, it is the product of a compromise, and one that interestingly embodies some of the divisions in literary study today. Eight or ten years ago it became clear that most of my colleagues wanted to reconsider the no-requirements free-for-all that had been our response to the late sixties. In the curricular discussions that followed, however, we were naturally up against a range of disagreements about the premises of literary education, indeed, of literary study. What might we all agree to say through a required sophomore course about the kinds of reading we thought essential? Nothing, obviously. But we could and finally did agree to suppress our differences beneath two platitudes: every student should know how to read a text with careful and subtle attention to its language, and every student should be able to read a text with some appreciation of its historicity.

From this plain credo we developed two semesters of study with a chasm between them. In English 201 the students read mainly lyric poems in the way that became traditional after World War II. One poem per fifty minutes; no intentional fallacy, no context, little intertextuality; key in on voice, register, metaphor, syntax, dramatic situation, prosody, and so on. In English 202, suddenly, the texts are fat novels surrounded by journals, memoirs, documents, historical arguments, criticism, and so on, all somehow to be grasped as participating in the historical process. It is as if the English Department were kidnapped and taken en masse to a reeducation camp over winter break. The schizophrenia makes for quite a pedagogical jolt that I will not attempt to rationalize; I am speaking of what one disparate and overworked group of people actually does, not about a utopian scheme.

To suggest some implications of the pedagogical shift, and to give an idea of what we try to do in the course, I will focus for a while on issues we engage in a unit on Jane Austen's *Emma.* A characteristic passage of exposition in the novel begins this way: "The Coles had been settled some years in Highbury, and were a very good sort of people—friendly, liberal, and unpretending; but, on the other hand, they were of low origin, in trade, and only moderately genteel."[2] Well! This sort of judgment, fundamental to Austen's narrative, troubles most of my students. It expresses an outlook that puts the novel at a considerable distance from them, temporal, cultural, and indeed moral, as if one were to say, "She is a wonderful person but, on the other hand, a dental technician." (Never mind that few of my students are likely to marry dental technicians and mechanics, or even drink beer with them; the *sentiment* is old-fashioned, snobbish, and offensive.) How do we bridge, historically, the gap between this twentieth-century American response and the early nineteenth-century English context? One way would be to grant that, yes, by our standards Austen was a snob, and go on to praise the counterbalancing virtues of her work. But this is to endorse a dismissal of it as simply outmoded, a dismissal that not only could be extended to most older literature but also denies our own connectedness to history.

A more common strategy among critics is to save the work from the scrap heap of outmoded values by claiming it as universal, or modern, or at least in advance of its time. Nonhistorical techniques of reading in service to this strategy are readily available. For instance, a New Critical close reader, after noting the tidy opposition of triplets ("friendly . . . of low origin"), might look for internal evidence to determine whether the opposition is ironic. And such evidence is abundant. After explaining that the Coles have experienced a rapid increase in prosperity, the narrator continues: "Their love of society, and their new dining-room, prepared every body for their keeping dinner-company; and a few parties, chiefly among the single men, had already taken place. The regular and best families Emma could hardly suppose they would presume to invite—neither Donwell, nor Hartfield, nor Randalls." Until that last sentence, no distance seems to separate the narrator from Emma; but here, surely, is the tipoff. Emma will be proven wrong in her expectation; furthermore, once others from "the regular and best families" accept the Coles' invitation, Emma will swallow her pride and do likewise. Thus, the Coles gain admission to the inner circle on at least probationary terms, and Emma learns yet another lesson about rank, social mobility, and true gentility of conduct.

The close reader may now confidently label as ironic the narrator's balancing of "friendly, liberal, and unpretending" against "of low origin, in trade, and only moderately genteel." Here, one may conclude, the narrator voices the inhumane class feeling of Emma (and of "every body") only to discredit it and to establish a higher moral community between the narrator and the democratic reader, to which Emma will be fully admitted only at the end of the novel. In such ways, I believe, teachers and students often enlist close reading in tacit defenses of writers, aligning their values with ours and claiming them as advocates of universal values, or at least of the "modern" ones that inhabit the American classroom. Lionel Trilling is one of many who have claimed Austen for modernity. In English 202 we ask students to read his well-known essay "*Emma* and the Legend of Jane Austen," in which he credits Austen, "conservative and even conventional as she was," with having "perceived the nature of the deep psychological change which accompanied the establishment of democratic society." And he argues that the novel shows Emma's initial snobbery to be "a mistake of nothing less than national import," a "contravention of the best—and safest—tendency of English social life," in that it would have excluded not only rising tradespeople like the Coles but also members of "the yeoman class" like Robert Martin.[3] This is indeed to make Emma's moral education an education in democratic sensibility and conduct, as well as to naturalize the novel for young readers in this society.

But in calling Robert Martin a member of the yeoman class Trilling makes an interesting error that perhaps is nonetheless understandable: he took his lead from Emma, who, in her famous put-down of Martin to Harriet Smith, says, "The yeomanry are precisely the order of people with whom I feel that I can have nothing to do." Although she knows well enough that Martin is a tenant farmer, already prosperous and likely to become rich, she chooses to place him in an older social structure that by the beginning of the nineteenth century was in an advanced state of disintegration. Some families, like the Martins from the old yeomanry, had made it in capitalist agriculture, forming a new class adjacent to, and in partnership with, the great landlords. Most yeomen and peasants, done in by the enclosures of the eighteenth century and by the new rules of the game, had slid off the edge of respectability and disappeared into the great mass of agricultural laborers, by far the most numerous class in the time and place of Emma's story. Students in English 202 read about the three rural classes and the new exploitative basis of agriculture in a chapter from *Captain Swing*, by E. J. Hobsbawm and George Rude.[4] In Hobsbawm's *Industry and Empire*[5] they also read more broadly about the industrial capitalist transformation of English society—the proletarianization of labor, the polarization of city and country, the assimilation of successful merchants like the Coles into the class of "gentlemen," and so on: the entire, dynamic, world-transforming process from which Austen abstracted her "little bit (two inches wide) of ivory."

Such a reading does more than merely ground the questions of the Martins' and Coles' proper social rank in a historically specific process of class formation and assimilation, one that Austen understood very well and in which she chose to give Emma a moral education. It also prompts the following question, an odd one for literary study: where are the rural masses in Austen's world? And that leads us to scrutinize their very few appearances in *Emma:* the "poor sick family" of cottagers to whom Emma and Harriet pay a charitable visit, resulting in the brief ennoblement of their sensibilities; the gypsies whose rude assault on Harriet faintly indexes a challenge to the social order administered by magistrates like Knightley; and, similarly, the anonymous poultry thieves whose depredations hasten the happy end of the story by reconciling Mr. Woodhouse to the treachery of his daughter's marriage. I will not recapitulate here the sorts of discussion that ensue. What I want to emphasize are two premises of our course that emerge from such inquiries.

First, we unabashedly encourage mimetic questions often thought to be illegitimate, like the one about the rural poor. Whom did Austen virtually delete from the social milieu of farmers like Robert Martin, and how does Austen's novel represent that condition? To ask this is to commit what Trilling called the "notable error" of believing that "the world of Jane Austen really did exist," though "any serious history will make it sufficiently clear that the England of her novels was not the real England, except as it gave her the license to imagine the England which we call hers."[6] But what *kind* of "license" was that? What authority issued it? What did it mean for Austen to give only the rarest glimpses of rural laborers, and those only through stereotyped images of the deserving poor and the dangerous poor? "Where only one class is seen, no classes are seen"; so says Raymond Williams in a section of *The Country and the City,*[7] which is also part of our packet of readings. We want our students to consider what kind of "seeing" this was.

That brings me to the second premise. Our effort is not to provide a true picture of early nineteenth-century, rural, southern England, by reference to which students may judge Austen's novel to be a faithful or distorted representation of reality. Rather, we assume distortion and conceptualize it as mediation and ideology. Trilling opposes the mimetic premise by insisting that the England of *Emma* was an "idyll." Fair enough, but questioning does not end there. An idyll grounded in whose values, whose interests, whose project of idealization, whose project of social order? Questions like these are central to the course. We encourage their careful articulation through discussion of an essay by David Aers, in which he argues, powerfully if contentiously, that Austen's mediation of her world is governed more by her ideology than by some abstract "imaginative insight" and that we should see her, in company with Edmund Burke and the like, as a "polemical tory ideologist, a most accomplished partisan in a period of open and intense ideological controversy in which novelists played a significant role."[8]

It is our task, of course, to keep such a position from being reductive; we try always to return such claims to the novel—for example, by considering Williams's point that "the paradox of Jane Austen is . . . the achievement of a unity of tone, of a settled and remarkably confident way of seeing and judging, in the chronicle of confusion and change."[9] This idea takes us back to passages like the one about the Coles and to the precise mobilization of values entailed by balancing "personal" qualities like friendliness against social givens like birth and the sources of one's money, education, and manners. With luck, this movement brings ideology into focus as permeating every line of the novel and inseparable from its esthetic texture, so that history takes shape *in* the text, not just as an external standard by which to measure it.

I hope that this example has provided at least a rough idea of how we conceptualize the task of reading literary works as they participate in the historical process. I have been ruthlessly selective, of course. Our unit on *Emma* devotes little time to the rural poor, more to the intricate matter of gentility and class accommodation, and more still to marriage, sexuality, and gender. In addition, we raise questions of biography and reception, dealing with gentle Janeism through several sources: the Austen Leigh memoir of his aunt, selections from Austen's letters, and Harding's article on "regulated hatred" in Austen's works—in particular, his well-known statement that "her books are, as she meant them to be, read and enjoyed by precisely the sort of people whom she disliked."[10] The "historical process" is more than the class struggle, in English 202 as in life.

Now let me quickly sketch in the rest of the course. It has four units, each lasting three or three and a half weeks and centered on a major fiction. Each year we replace one unit to keep us fresh and to allow us to keep rethinking the aims and methods of the course. Last year *Moll Flanders* was the first main text, buttressed by Ian Watt's *The Rise of the Novel* and by a brief comparison with *Pilgrim's*

Progress, a text that both provides a sharp contrast to the "economic individualism" Watt finds in early eighteenth-century novels but in some ways presages their concerns. There were also readings on marriage and the condition of women in eighteenth-century England, on crime and prisons, and so on. After the unit on *Emma,* we vaulted the Atlantic and 130 years of history to read Faulkner's *Go Down Moses* against material on slavery and plantation life; readings, including Thoreau's "Walking," that delineate an American relation to nature quite different from that expressed by Emma's rhapsodic thought of "English verdure, English culture, English comfort";[11] and readings from the debate initiated by the agrarians on Southern culture. Race was even more central to the final unit, along with gender, as we concluded with Morrison's *Song of Solomon,* pondering various strategies for black liberation, various relationships of writers to black oral culture, and so on. (The writers included Hurston, Gwendolyn Brooks, Ellison, and several others.) This year, Faulkner gives way to a section on Hemingway's *Farewell to Arms,* contextualized, especially by reference to 1920s writers, to main currents of U.S. culture.

Naturally, this course works less smoothly in the classroom than in my retelling. I want to name some problems that arise in this course and doubtless would arise in any course that attempts a serious engagement with history and literature for first- or second-year college students. First and most obviously, the task is impossible. The students know too little, we know too little, the semester is too short, the leaps from text to text are irreducibly speculative, and so on. To this objection—which is not just theoretical, but which makes itself felt in our and the students' frustrations at hundreds of loose ends, at lack of closure, at uncertainty—I can only say, yes, it is hard to understand the world, including literature and history, but we have to start somewhere or accept the false reassurance of a narrow, formalist definition of ourselves. I myself am glad my department insists on a course that many students initially find uncongenial, precisely because in doing so we directly confront the blank refusal of history endemic in this society.

Second, there is a constant risk of privileging the nonliterary texts in the course as unchallengeable reports on how things really were, in a neat reversal of the way English departments usually privilege the literary—as if Hobsbawm did not have his own ideological project; as if Bennet Barrow's *Plantation Diary* were not itself mediation of slavery, comparable in that way to Faulkner's "Was." We try hard not to sanction two different ways of reading and a simplistic view of direct access to historical truth through "nonfiction," but I know we sometimes fail.

Third, as we enlarge the usual mandate of criticism from interpreting texts to explaining them, we sometimes inadvertently give students the idea that the game is to *see through* literature, for example, either by discovering what dirty business Jane Austen was "really" up to or by casting her as the helpless instrument of historical forces. Our aim is indeed to dissipate some of the aura that surrounds Holy Literature, as we challenge the idea of its autonomy, but we do not want to leave students thinking that literature is only a self-interested scam. Certainly we do not want the challenge of historical thinking simply to dislodge the pleasure of the text.

Finally, there is the closely related danger of actually promoting a kind of ahistorical feeling and thinking to which some students are already inclined, even as we combat the ahistoricism that conceives literature as timeless, universal masterworks. I have in mind the tendency to confront the ideology of an older text as if its writer were an entrant in our own arena of discourse. Jane Austen may not have been the precursor of democracy that Trilling casts her as, but neither is his a totally misguided way to judge her. A difficult relativism is necessary in such matters, but hard to achieve. Most canonical writers were both progressive and reactionary in relation to the possibilities of alignment and feeling available in their own times. English 202 insists that they can be held accountable, just like the mass of human beings who are not writers, but it is another thing, and a bad one, to ride through literary history on an ideological white horse from the left-liberal barn of Wesleyan's political culture. After all, students can censure Austen's class consciousness well enough without taking English 202.

Beyond these pedagogical problems, and related to them, lie vexing theoretical issues that, because they permeate the cultural atmosphere of this discussion and of any attempt to teach historically, claim at least a brief acknowledgment on my part. As noted, English 202 tends to privilege a version of what really happened in history and use it to explain and interpret the literary texts at hand; my strategy for teaching about advertisements certainly does so. It is easy to see in such pedagogies the specter of a master narrative, subject to attack as both an illusory metaphysical presence and an instrument of coercion. To the second charge I reply that everyone—even a poststructuralist—is willy-nilly involved in a contest over the understanding of history. There is no way for teachers of literature not to be. One can *limit* the intrinsic risk of coercion by promoting generative historical thinking and an awareness that any master narrative is controverted and provisional, but that is hardly more than an ethical given in the liberal academy. I myself insist in addition that to counter the official master narrative with more liberatory ones is an act that empowers. The coercive power of even dogmatic feminist and historical materialist teaching is, in our present situation, no more than disruptive or subversive.

The other charge is more difficult. A story like that of capitalist crisis and transformation, which I often use to situate and explain texts, is itself a distillation of other texts, read in a certain way. It can have no epistemological priority over, say, *Emma;* indeed, its coherence dissolves along with its explanatory power when submitted to poststructuralist scrutiny. Thinkers in that mode tend to reconstitute history as a parity and interaction of infinitely many structures, with no center except language—and at that, a language diminished in its capacity for reference, expression, and action. Small consolation that on this view language itself is historical, for this is history without causes and without agents. To the extent that it admits change at all, it attributes change to something like the collision of molecules. The "randomization of history," to use Perry Anderson's term,[12] leaves the pedagogies I have recommended hanging over the much-touted abyss.

Of course, that consequence is no argument against the theory, which is notoriously hard to combat on its own ground. I tend to think the theory fails at its origins, inferring from the arbitrariness of the signifier far more than Saussure's observation warrants. I do not think that signifiers are arbitrary in the sense required, which must bypass their social rootedness (and, if Chomsky is right, biological rootedness) or write it off as a delusion. That move led—again, in Anderson's words—to "the exorbitation of language" and "a gradual megalomania of the signifier,"[13] but I am not sufficiently versed in these debates to argue the point, nor are most of us who must choose one way or another to teach about history and culture. For those who want to do and teach explanatory history, I think the apt counsel is Jonathan Culler's suggestion that for the nonce we try to *ignore* deconstruction as irrelevant to our concerns[14]—not kick the stone in useless refutation, like Dr. Johnson, but adopt the double consciousness of Hume when he repaired from his skeptical labors to dinner and backgammon. Ignoring deconstruction will not put its skepticism to rest, but neither will ignoring history stop it from happening, or perhaps from doing us in. We must intervene as if history had causes and we might be agents. History, even without foundations, goes on.

The claim is often made that poststructuralist ideas and methods can ground a truly radical and subversive pedagogy. As S. P. Mohanty writes, if "the mastery of the human subject over its meanings and its consciousness is rendered uncertain and spurious . . . [then] pedagogy, particularly in the realm of culture, needs . . . to face the fundamental challenge to escape both the transmission of coded knowledge and the coded transmission of knowledge."[15] The "archeological examinations performed by deconstructors," says Vincent B. Leitch, "are frequently corrosive insofar as the formations of history are subject to irreverent critiques of founding categories and operations."[16] Does not the "challenge" challenge too much, given our actual circumstances? Does not the "corrosive" reading corrode too much? An early and influential advocate of deconstruction suggested to me, modestly enough, that the method could serve teachers and students as a "crap detector." It surely is that. But when everything smells like crap, we need a more sensitive instrument that will identify the *dangerous* crap. Even if deconstruction should turn out to be "right," a true end to metaphysics rather than one of the innumerable blind alleys of system-building philosophy, that would not entail the rightness of its deployment in our classes—though it *would* enjoin us to remind ourselves and our students that the level of analysis at which we argue for one or another version of history is provisional and vulnerable. But so is every academic discourse.

Mohanty suggests that de Man's position in "The Resistance to Theory" is seductively attractive because it "makes possible a radicalism without the messy implications of *engagement.*"[17] After all the caveats are registered, I favor politically engaged reading and teaching. After all, what is the alternative? Sartre describes it well, I think, in his caricature of "the critic," who contemplates with equal distance the racism of Gobineau and the humanitarianism of Rousseau (between whom he would have had to choose, had they been alive) because both Gobineau and Rousseau are "profoundly and deliciously wrong, and in the same way: they are dead."[18] "Which side are you on?" is a question we should keep in close proximity to our classroom teaching of literature, however much it needs to be complicated by the passage of time. We, the ad man of 1896, and Jane Austen all are part of the same historical process. As we historicize their texts, we should see ourselves and our students as both bearers and creators of history.

NOTES

A few pages of this essay appeared under the title "Teaching for a Critical and Historical Sense" in *The Gallatin Review,* 7 (Winter 1987–88).

1. Since I wrote this essay four years ago, we have regretfully suspended the course because of insuperable staffing shortages and compressed some of its contents into the second half of English 201, the close reading course. We made this decision without much debate; hence I cannot say why in a pinch close reading seemed more basic or elemental than historical reading.

2. *Emma* vol. 2, chap. 7.

3. Lionel Trilling, "Emma and the Legend of Jane Austen," *Beyond Culture* (New York: Harcourt Brace Jovanovich, 1965) 46, 40, 42.

4. Eric J. Hobsbawm and George Rude, *Captain Swing* (New York: Random House, 1969).

5. E. J. Hobsbawm, *Industry and Empire: From 1750 to the Present Day* (Harmondsworth: Penguin, 1969).

6. Trilling 55.

7. Raymond Williams, "Three Around Farnham," *The Country and the City* (New York: Oxford UP, 1973) 117.

8. David Aers, "Community and Morality: Towards Reading Jane Austen," in David Aers, Jonathan Cook, and David Punter, eds., *Romanticism and Ideology: Studies in English Writing 1765–1830* (London: Routledge and Kegan Paul, 1981) 120.

9. Williams 115.

10. D. W. Harding, "Regulated Hatred: An Aspect of the Work of Jane Austen," *Scrutiny* 8 (1940): 347.

11. *Emma* vol. 3, chap. 6.

12. Perry Anderson, *In the Tracks of Historical Materialism* (Chicago: U of Chicago P, 1984) 48.

13. Ibid. 40, 45.

14. Jonathan Culler, *On Deconstruction: Theory and Criticism After Structuralism* (Ithaca: Cornell UP, 1982) 130.

15. S. P. Mohanty, "Radical Teaching, Radical Theory: The Ambiguous

Politics of Meaning," *Theory in the Classroom,* ed. Cary Nelson (Urbana: U of Illinois P, 1986) 155.

16. Vincent B. Leitch, "Deconstruction and Pedagogy," in Nelson 54.

17. Mohanty 156.

18. Jean-Paul Sartre, *What Is Literature?* trans. Bernard Frechtman (New York: Washington Square P, 1966) 20.

POSITIONS

9

ENGLISH DEPARTMENT GEOGRAPHY: INTERPRETING THE *MLA BIBLIOGRAPHY*

Reed Way Dasenbrock

By now, it is no news to anyone that what we do in departments of literary study, especially English departments, is changing rapidly. What we mean by English studies or English has been changing ever since there began to be a field of English, and recently the field has changed at a dizzying pace. Even leaving to one side the development of literary theory, the rebirth of rhetoric, and the emergence of cultural studies and concentrating just on the study of literature, the traditional canon as enshrined in our curriculum and in our anthologies has come under attack as the expression of a white, male, upper-class perspective. The consequent "opening of the canon" to include work by women, minorities, and socially disadvantaged classes is already changing the shape of those curricula and anthologies a good deal.[1] In this situation, the temptation many may feel is to conclude that we have had revolutions enough for one academic generation, that the pressing task now is one of application, figuring out how to teach the new canon and the new literary theory as effectively as the once-new critics taught the old. Even granting this, however, changing our institutions so that they can adequately represent this new-found richness and diversity, particularly of contemporary literature, is going to require rethinking—in ways even the canon revisers have not fully realized—some of our most fundamental concepts about how to map, organize, and categorize the field.

By "map and organize" I mean to refer quite literally to the various compartments into which we divide literature—in our libraries, our departmental and curricular structures, and our professional organizations. These institutions of literary study organize the field of literature according to four hierarchical distinctions, and the same four distinctions run through all our institutional structures. First comes a division between "us" and "them": the nonforeign and the foreign. This pervasive but little-remarked distinction is concretely actualized every year at the Modern Language Association Convention: all the sessions on English language literature are in one hotel, and the sessions on literature in other languages are in another. The two hotels, whatever their official names, are customarily referred to for the duration of the conference as the English hotel and the foreign hotel. This distinction, which is far more than simply an administrative convenience of the MLA, represents the fundamental departmental division on any campus that divides literary study among departments in any way whatsoever.[2] I teach in a Department of English, but my colleagues who teach literature in languages other than English teach in a Department of Foreign Languages. Closely related but far more explicit in all our institutions is a second division according to language, and this division organizes the curricular categories in foreign and modern language departments as well as the departmental structures on those campuses with more than one foreign language department. The third division that follows is according to nationality, but this division only subdivides terrain already divided according to language. The last division is by period.

The same classification system structures our libraries and our professional organizations. Libraries are initially divided according to language; then they are subdivided according to national origin and then according to period, so that anglophone literature is shelved contiguously (as is francophone, hispanophone and lusophone literature), yet it is absolutely divided into national units and subdivided into periods. The divisions that organize much of the program for the MLA annual convention map literatures in the same way: an initial division according to language is then followed by secondary divisions according to nationalities and then tertiary divisions according to periods. These further divisions according to nationality and period are, of course, crucial to the shape of the curriculum as well: in most English departments the curriculum is made up of courses in English literature and courses in American literature, with only an occasional special topics course to bridge the divide, just as Peninsular literature is largely kept separate from Latin American literature in Spanish and Portuguese programs. So we organize our field in four ways. After an initial division between our own and the other comes a second distinction according to language, a third according to nationality, and then a fourth according to period. These four dividing principles are hierarchically structured, each subdividing a terrain already divided by the higher principle.

Though this system of mapping is rarely noticed or discussed, I think it is worth our attention, for if Michel Foucault is right about anything, it is that the shape and categories of discourse are never neutral, never simply "there," but always actively shaping the discourse that emerges. It is true that we are all aware of problems inherent in our systems of categorization, which explains the emergence of certain institutional antidotes to those systems such as work across period and national boundaries and comparative literary study. These allow critics to examine kinds of relations not easily studied given the primacy of linguistic, national, and temporal categories in our mapping system. As any comparatist will tell you, however, comparative work is always against the grain. Most of our discourse comfortably fits within our categories.

But I have a more specific point to make than that. The hierarchical division of literature may have worked once, but it no longer does. Putting historical period at the bottom suggests that it is the most stable and passive of the four categories, but the relation between linguistic and national demarcations differs drastically from period to period. The modern, contemporary period has seen English emerge as an international literary language, and this surely changes the relation between linguistic and national demarcations in a way that makes our current hierarchy untenable. This hierarchy still determines the shape of our institutions, but it no longer adequately represents the literature those institutions are supposed to study and represent.

It should be easy enough to see how this hierarchy has shaped our traditional approach to literature in English. There has always been a powerful tendency among departments of English to represent our role as propagating "our own" literary heritage, but we have never been very precise about what "our own" is. In some cases, this has led to an emphasis on teaching American literature; in others, to a tendency to become almost a department of English studies, sponsoring exchange programs with England and in general being outposts of Anglophilia. This bifurcation perfectly represents our latent sense of literature in English: though at one level we take it as forming a unity, we see it at a more immediate level as a combination of two distinct national literatures, English and American. One of the reasons we tend to leave our defining term, "English," undefined is that we want it to refer to the language (so as to include American literature), but we act as if it refers primarily to the nation, which is our fundamental category.

Because our fundamental category is the nation, yet—as even the most enthusiastic Whitman or Emerson scholar must realize—the major national literature in English is not our own, we present literature in English as if it were simply two fairly distinct national literatures in a common language.[3] This practice can be seen in all our institutions. The major anthologies used in our introductory courses are all anthologies of national literatures: *The Norton Anthology of American Literature* and *The Norton Anthology of English Literature,* each in two volumes, divide up English language literature between them. In case we have any doubt about what is meant by "English" in the anthology's title, volume 2 of the *Anthology of English Literature* has a map of England on the inside front cover and a map of modern London on the inside back cover. Most English departments still organize their curriculum predominately around courses in national literatures: English literature from 1798 to 1832, American literature from 1870 to 1914, and so on. Our libraries, as we have already seen, are organized in precisely the same way. In the dominant Library of Congress system, English literature is PR, American PS, and the field of English is divided between them. Similarly, each period of English and American literature has its own division in the MLA, without a single division dedicated to bridging that gap between them.

However, representing English language literature as a combination of English and American literature, as our professional institutions do, is simply no longer adequate to the world role English now plays. What our institutional structures have not yet come to terms with is that this language is no longer just the language of the English and the Americans but is shared by a vast world community that includes people working out of literary and cultural heritages far different from our own, however broadly we define that. And it is in these new emerging literatures in English that the greatest writing in English is being done today. This leads to the paradoxical situation that departments of English, being really departments of English and American literature and not departments of literature in English, ignore much of the best contemporary writing being done in English. Our line of sight includes everything from John Barth back to *Beowulf,* but it does not include Nadine Gordimer or R. K. Narayan or any of the other great writers in English writing outside England or America.

This English line of sight does work for a good deal of the curriculum. It works well enough until 1800, for until then literature in English and English literature overlap closely enough not to cause insuperable problems. (Perhaps I should say until 1700, as Swift, Goldsmith, Sheridan, Smollett, Burns, and Boswell already make that equation problematic in the eighteenth century.) But in the nineteenth and twentieth centuries that overlap progressively disappeared. First, American literature emerged. Second, the important writers in England were increasingly non-English in origin: of those born in the twenty years after Thomas Hardy, Henry James was a transplanted American, Conrad a Pole, and George Moore, Shaw, and Wilde were Irish. That trend only increased as time passed: literature in English continued to be enriched by exiles from Eastern Europe such as Nabokov and Stoppard, the rich efflorescence of Irish literature between Yeats and Beckett far eclipses anything written by the English in that period, and that part of the literary life of London not created by the Irish was largely created by transplanted North Americans: Eliot, Pound, H.D., Wyndham Lewis, and other "colonials" such as Katharine Mansfield. Finally, the rise and fall of British (and, though less important here, American) imperialism has led to a rich literature in English emerging all over the world in former colonies and dominions, preeminently in Nigeria, South Africa, India, and the West Indies. What would contemporary literature in English be without V. S. Naipaul, R. K. Narayan, Salman Rushdie, Wole Soyinka, Nadine Gordimer, Doris Lessing, Chinua Achebe, and a host of other talented writers from around the world?

Traditionally, critics and scholars of literature in English have approached the diversity of literature in English—when aware of it—in the spirit of Pope Alexander VI in 1494: just as he divided the world between the Spanish and the Portuguese, literature in English has been divided between the English and the Americans. The Irish, the Commonwealth writers, and Conrad traditionally have been awarded to the English; the Americans have scooped up Nabokov; and border skirmishes are still being fought over Henry James and T. S. Eliot.

The most graphic representation of this imperialist appropriation is to be found in our libraries. I am continually amazed by the strange things my library does with new literature in English. The Library of Congress cataloging system provides categories for the new literatures in English—African literature in English, Indian literature in English, and so on—but little of what belongs in those categories makes it there. I will cite just a few examples. The work of the late Shiva Naipaul is found under English literature, but that of his elder brother V. S. is under West Indian literature. Two novels by the superb Somali novelist Nuruddin Farah arrive in the library the very same week: one is classified as English literature, the other as African literature in English. Nadine Gordimer's *Selected Stories* are in the African section, her novels in the English section. Some of the Kenyan writer Ngugi's books are found in English literature, others in African literature in English, and others—though written in English—in the section for literature in African languages. This dismembering of the new literatures in English is not our librarians' fault: they are simply following the Library of Congress call numbers for the books. But the unfortunate impression this gives in libraries all over the country is that the overwhelming majority of literature in English is still being written by English or American writers. Only a handful of books belong in some strange categories placed at the end of the English literature section. And even these categories, including the one for the Philippines (a former American colony) have a Library of Congress PR heading that indicates they are still conceived of as belonging in a loose sense to English literature.

Nor is this combination of appropriation and marginalization unique. It is perfectly mirrored in the structure of the Modern Language Association itself. At the very end of the long line of divisions devoted to American and English literature comes the category for literature in English, the delightfully and revealingly named "English Literature Other than British and American." Again, what falls outside the traditional categories is relegated to the category of the "other," placed at the end of the line, and no positive term can be found to describe it. We can see the same kind of appropriation at work in our curriculum: the course for modern literature is usually called Modern British Literature, not English, so as to get a few Irish writers in, but no real acknowledgment is made of the difference that accounts for that change in name. Though volume 2 of *The Norton Anthology of English Literature* hardly could have excluded Yeats or

Joyce, it includes only one story by Katharine Mansfield and one by Doris Lessing—two white writers who moved to England—to represent literature in English from around the world. Writers such as Narayan and Soyinka from Asia and Africa are included instead in the *Anthology of World Masterpieces,* not in the *Anthology of English Literature.* Like our libraries, the premier anthologies of our profession pretend magnificently—if disturbingly—that English and American literature still divide the known world of literature in English between them.

Thus, our textbooks, our curricular structures, our professional organization, our libraries, and even our sense of appropriate areas of specialization as revealed in our job advertisements all share a resounding silence about the breakdown of the hegemony of English literature in the twentieth century. Everyone who is important can be contained and appropriated within the categories of English and American literature, and no rethinking need take place. Even the Modern Language Association *Bibliography* —which I will argue is far in advance of most of our professional institutions in its responsiveness to the internationalization of English—does its share of such appropriation. Katharine Mansfield, Jean Rhys, and Doris Lessing, born and raised in New Zealand, the West Indies, and Persia and Rhodesia, respectively, are all considered English writers, whereas Malcolm Lowry, Christopher Isherwood, and Aldous Huxley, all of whom left England for North America, are also considered English. Place of birth is all-important if it happens to be England; place of residence all-important if that happens to be England. Heads, England wins; tails, the rest of the world loses. And in case one is born abroad and resides abroad for the bulk of one's life, as in the cases of Norman Douglas, Lawrence Durrell, and Bernard Spencer, then one is English anyway, for one wrote in English, even if one's parentage, as in the cases of Douglas and Durrell, is largely Celtic. So even the *MLA Bibliography* is not entirely free of the Anglocentric cast of mind shown by the institutions of our profession, even though it exceeds our other institutions in its awareness of the global spread of writing in English.

Thus, just as we have realized that our traditional canon privileges work by men over that by women, by Anglos over ethnics, and by the established over the lower classes, so too must we realize that it privileges literature emanating from England and America over that from around the world. In every case, an established tradition presents itself as central and marginalizes everything outside that tradition that it cannot appropriate. Our very reliance on the national categories of English and American literature provides us with a warped representation of literature in English.

How can we move beyond the warping induced by this Anglocentric cast of mind? Here is where we need one more conceptual revolution, for if we open the canon to the new literatures in English without rethinking our conceptual grid, we will continue to inadequately represent contemporary literature in English. In particular, we need to rethink our implicit notion that national literatures form subsets of literatures in a given language, for if we keep that notion we cannot make sense of contemporary literature in English. Literature in English today is something very different from a combination of a number of English language national literatures.

This fact is easy to see in our one institutional attempt to move toward a full representation of literature in English. In its old format, the *MLA Bibliography* was as pure a representation of Anglocentrism as could be found: Irish and Scots writers in English were uniformly classified under English literature, and the new literatures in English were found in a category with the wonderful title, "Australia, Canada, etc.," which came just before the entries on English literature. But this design was radically changed beginning with the *1981 Bibliography*, and the redesign clearly was made with the awareness that imitating Pope Alexander would no longer suffice.

Thus, the redesign of the *Bibliography* is one indication that we have begun to respond to the tension between linguistic and national categories and to rethink—if tentatively—our modes of mapping. And though I have already pointed out a number of instances in which old patterns reassert themselves, the new *Bibliography* should be praised for at least acknowledging that if we stay with the concept of national literatures, then we need many new concepts. It at least recognizes that writers from St. Lucia and India are writing in English. In its new format, the *Bibliography* constitutes our best shot at representing contemporary literature in English as a sum of national literatures. But what that attempt ultimately reveals is that this hierarchy no longer represents contemporary literature in English. I want to show this in some detail so as to suggest the desirability—indeed, the necessity—of moving toward a different system of categorization.

The *MLA International Bibliography of Books and Articles on the Modern Languages and Literatures,* to give it its full title, is currently published in five volumes. When the *Bibliography* was redesigned in 1981 the title on the spine of volume 1 was *Literature,* which implies that the other volumes were devoted to topics other than literature. In keeping with this, volume 3 was titled *Linguistics* and volume 5, *Folklore.* Volume 4 had the odd title of *General Literature,* which in practice turned out to be comparative literature and literary theory. But volume 2 was called *Foreign Literature,* a title that makes us revise our sense of the title of volume 1. If volume 2 is on foreign literature, then 1—despite the title—cannot be on all literature but must instead be on the opposite of foreign literature. Volume 1 therefore needs but significantly lacks an adjective to specify the difference between its contents and those of volume 2. The terms *Literature* and *Foreign Literature* disappeared with the *1986 Bibliography,* but as the contents of each volume remained unchanged, the defining concepts clearly (or perhaps not so clearly) also remained unchanged.

The *MLA Bibliography* is of course an American production, so one's immediate assumption might be that the opposite of foreign would be "native" or "domestic," in this case, American. And so one could assume that volume 1 would be devoted to the study of American literature and volume 2 to everything else. This would certainly be in keeping with the ordinary use of the word *foreign.* But anyone who opens volume 1 finds that "American (U.S.A.) Literature," to use the *Bibliography*'s term, comes last in the volume; further, of the 11,894 entries in the 1988 volume 1, only 38 percent of the entries concern American literature. Pride of place is given to English literature, which takes up almost the entire first half of the volume. This clearly involves a sense of the word *foreign* at variance with ordinary usage—English cars are considered foreign, but English literature is not—but this seeming anomaly is true to the practice of English departments everywhere, in which English literature is indeed given pride of place and considered our own. A volume devoted to English and American literature would in itself say that we consider English literature to be in important senses our own, part of the American literary identity. And the way in which an unexamined—indeed, unstated—concept of "our own" as opposed to foreign literature governs volume 1 is parallel to the way it governs the structure of English departments and the profession in general. Our first categorization is always to separate "us" from "them," even where—as in this case—such a categorization is inherently problematic.

One problem is that English literature accounts for just 48 percent of the entries.[4] The rest are for Irish, Scottish, and Welsh literature, grouped with English literature under the general rubric of "Literatures of the British Isles"; Australian, New Zealand, and Canadian literature, which are placed together under the rubric "British Commonwealth Literature"; and Barbadian, Belizean (added in 1987), Guyanese, Jamaican, St. Lucian, and Trinidad and Tobago literature, all gathered under the rubric "English-Caribbean Literature." This is as the *Bibliography* is presently constituted. Most of these categories have remained stable since the redesign, though New Zealand has strangely migrated over the years. Initially, from 1981 through 1983, Australia was placed with Canada as "British Commonwealth Literature," and New Zealand was given a listing of its own, after English-Caribbean but before the United States. This made absolutely no sense, for geographical considerations suggest putting New Zealand and Australia together, with Canada placed in its own category. So the *1984 Bibliography* moved "New Zealand Literature" to a place between "British Commonwealth" and "English-Caribbean," and then in 1986 "New Zealand Literature" was incorporated as part of "British Commonwealth Literature." This is still far from completely logical, however, for the Caribbean nations grouped under "English-Caribbean Literature" and many other nations not listed are members of the Commonwealth in standing just as good as Australia and Canada.

So what could it be that holds the countries in volume 1 together as "nonforeign" and relegates the rest of the world to the category of foreigner? Is there a coherent criterion of "foreignness" being employed, one compatible with the reliance on national categories as subcategories of the *Bibliography*? The title page itself gives us one answer, presumably that held by the compilers of the bibliography, and this answer is perfectly compatible with the hierarchy of language and nationality I have sketched: "This guide to the classified listings includes headings for literatures in the English language." Hence, foreignness is defined as using a foreign language, and the "foreign literature" of volume 2 is literature in foreign languages. Our own language is English, hence the nonforeign literature of volume 1, our own literature, is that written in the English language.

Adopting this as a criterion would lead to some odd consequences, particularly for a bibliography published in the United States. None of the traditional Native American oral literature, composed in languages indigenous to this land, could be considered nonforeign or our own. The first significant work of American literature written in a language of European origin, Gaspar Perez de Villagra's epic *Historia de la Nueva Mexico,* was written in Spanish in 1610 in New Mexico and hence would be foreign, as would that part of the rich contemporary literature of Spanish-speaking Americans written in Spanish. Ole Rolvaag's *Giants in the Earth,* arguably the greatest depiction of the settling of the Great Plains, would be foreign because written in Norwegian; the fiction of Isaac Bashevis Singer, our third most recent Nobel Laureate, though composed in New York by an American citizen, would be foreign because written in Yiddish; the work of our penultimate Nobel Laureate, the American citizen Czeslaw Milosz, would belong to a foreign literature because he writes primarily in Polish, even though he has written in English and, like Singer and Nabokov, has cotranslated his own work into English; and the work of our most recent Nobel Laureate, the American citizen Joseph Brodsky, would belong to a foreign literature because he writes primarily in Russian, though he has also written in English and translated his work into English. All these essential contributions to American literature would be foreign, whereas the literature of New Zealand and Australia would not be.

In fact, the *MLA Bibliography* does not follow its own criterion, or at least not consistently. Native American oral literature is not considered American literature, chronological listings for which begin with 1500–1599, nor is it really considered literature at all, as it is relegated to volume 5, *Folklore.* However, Rolvaag and Singer make it into the American literature section, though Milosz does not. Chicano literature, whether written in English, Spanish, or both, is considered American literature, though Puerto Rican literature is given a section of its own in *Foreign Literature* (volume 2) as part of Spanish-American literature. Clearly, the linguistic criterion for nonforeignness is violated so as to allow for the multilingual character of American literature, though it is neither violated nor followed in anything like a consistent manner. In the case of American literature, at any rate, the categories of national literature (American) and literature in a given language (English) do not seem to combine so well, and the *Bibliography* wavers between them in its attempt to combine the two under the overall category of "nonforeign."

Other areas produce the same confusing picture, in which the stated criterion of language is only sometimes followed. The Irish literature section ignores the criterion of language completely, as work in Gaelic from both past and present is freely intermingled with English language literature by Irish writers. But Canadian writing in French is "foreign," included as part of French literature in volume 2 and put between Breton literature (a good deal of which is not in French) and French-Caribbean literature. Nonetheless, though these francophone literatures from outside France are included in French literature, francophone literature from Africa is not.

Moreover, as the mention of African literature should remind us, the English language literatures of the world are far from exhausted by the list of countries included in volume 1. Significant creative writing in English is being done all over the world: in the Pacific islands, particularly Samoa; in the Southeast Asian countries such as the Philippines, Singapore, and Malaysia; in South Asia, particularly in India; all over Africa, particularly in Nigeria, South Africa, Ghana, and Kenya, but also in Somalia, Ethiopia, Botswana, and elsewhere; in Malta; and in various other parts of the world. All these literatures are placed in *Foreign Literature,* volume 2, though it is not immediately obvious to me what makes a Guyanese or Australian novel in English less foreign than an Indian or Maltese or South African novel. (Moreover, many of these countries have just as much right to be placed under the "British Commonwealth" rubric as do Canada and Australia.) When we turn to volume 2 to see how the entries of those countries are organized, the Irish model prevails, not the Canadian, as the literature of each country is listed together, not separated according to language of composition.

Hence, no clear sense of a workable definition for *nonforeign* emerges from a scrutiny of the organization of the *MLA Bibliography.* Nonforeign literature is not American literature. It is not literature written in English, for a good deal of non-English language material is included and a good deal of English language writing excluded. Nor is it the entirety of the literature produced by English-speaking countries, as certain countries seem to make it into the magic circle and others are cast out as foreign. That process of separation is also mysterious, as it is hard to grasp the criterion by which this division was made.

Though most of the countries in volume 1 are predominantly Anglo-Saxon, and most of the countries with English language literatures in volume 2 are not, a racial criterion is not being employed, as the predominately black and Asian Caribbean countries are included in volume 1. Nor can the criterion be that of having English as a or the official language: English is the official language of Nigeria and an official language in India, but it has no official status in Ireland. Further, the criterion cannot be that a significant percentage of the population speak English, for in Singapore, Malta, and South Africa (all classed as "foreign literatures") a majority of the population speak English and a sizable minority consider it their first language. The only remaining possibility is that a majority of the present population must have English as their mother tongue, for only this criterion will include Canada and Ireland but exclude Singapore and South Africa.

Though this does not explain every inconsistency, it seems to be the primary criterion for dividing foreign from nonforeign literature in the *Bibliography.* But it is far from clear to me why this should be important. If our categories of foreign and nonforeign are not to depend on the normal strict nationalist conceptions, why should they depend not on the language in which the writer chooses to write, or even on the mother tongue of that writer, but on the mother tongue of the majority of his or her compatriots according to contemporary demography? In what sense can a medieval Irish writer using Gaelic be considered our own, part of our imaginative inheritance, in a way a native speaker of English who happens to have been born in Bombay or Durban is not? And if Stefan Heym writing in East Germany or Manuel Puig writing in Argentina or Sahle Selassie writing in Ethopia chooses to write in English, should that literature be considered foreign in the same sense that literature in German, Spanish, or Amharic coming from the same countries should be? Conversely, if Czeslaw Milosz chooses to live in this country and yet write in Polish, should his work be considered more foreign to us than that of Conrad, as foreign as that of Adam Mickiewicz?

I do not think this series of questions will be answered in a perfectly consistent way. I ask them precisely to make this point: the traditional hierarchical categorization of literature as foreign or nonforeign, as belonging to a certain language, and as belonging to a certain national literature can no longer function hierarchically, as the confusions and inconsistencies detailed in the *MLA Bibliography* should show. First, a good deal of our imaginative inheritance is in languages other than English, so any use of the value-laden term *foreign* (together with its implied opposite, *nonforeign*) makes trouble right away. Second, given the multilingualism of so many national literatures, including American literature, and the internationalism of so many major languages, including English, one can no longer assume that the categories of national literature and literature in a given language are at all compatible.

We need to realize that there are at least two ways of mapping literature. We can map it according to language, the language in which the work of literature is written, or we can map it according to nationality, the national literature of which the work seems to be a member. Neither approach is without its problems or problematic examples, many of which have already been mentioned. But the mistake we have fallen into is to try to use both simultaneously. The traditional approach has simply conflated the two, arbitrarily and unrealistically regarding literature in English as the product of two national literatures. The newer approach, as represented in the *MLA Bibliography,* has tried to use a system based on national literatures as a way to map literature in English. But systems of projection cannot be combined in that way, as I hope my discussion of the inconsistencies and problems in the *Bibliography* has shown. The familiar Mercator projection does a good job of mapping countries near the equator, but it makes Greenland look quite bizarre. A polar projection that represents Greenland and Baffin Island quite well cannot even show half the world. Most of the time, we stick with the Mercator projection because Greenland does not loom that large in most people's scheme of things, but we always need to be aware of the distortions that a system of mapping can cause. It is in the very nature of things that each mapping system will have its problems, and this means that no matter what solution we choose, we must also keep our critical distance from that solution, aware of the extent to which it can distort and misrepresent what it purports to represent.

Given all this, where are we? If we need to rethink our institutions, on what lines do we rethink them? What this extremely telescoped account should suggest is that the perspective that views English literature as a sum of national literatures is now in crisis, a crisis perfectly represented by the *MLA Bibliography.* And this is why, though the new *Bibliography* is conceptually a vast improvement over the old, I have made it my prime exhibit. If one gives the emerging literatures in English their proper importance, as the *MLA Bibliography* does intermittently and inconsistently, then English literature becomes an utterly unwieldy concept. By my count, the *1988 Bibliography* disperses English language literature among fourteen categories in volume 1 and sixteen more in volume 2. In addition, there are a number of other countries in which interesting writing in English is being done, including Samoa, Fiji, New Guinea, Pakistan, and St. Kitts and other Caribbean islands, none of which was given a separate category in the *1988 Bibliography.* And most of these *have* had separate categories in other years, which means that to research contemporary literature in English in the *MLA Bibliography* requires looking in over thirty places.[5]

The understandable response of most people to such complexity is to try to find a way to reduce the number of those categories drastically. Yet is there a way to give us some manageable, unfragmented categories without simply collapsing into Anglocentrism, into the false simplicity of Pope Alexander VI? Combining nationalistic and linguistic categories does not work so well, so it seems as if we must choose between them. This choice is made easier by realizing both how unmanageably numerous national categories would have to be and, more importantly, how much these categories will miss or misrepresent. As some of my examples should already suggest, too many of our important writers fall between the cracks of these national categories. What is one to do, for example, with V. S. Naipaul, resident in England since 1950 but born in Trinidad of Brahmin Hindu parentage? The *MLA Bibliography* puts him in Trinidad and Tobago Literature, which is a marked improvement on the critical studies that, ignoring his complex origins, treat him as an English novelist. But he would despise the category: he once returned to his old publisher because a prospective publisher referred to him in print as a West Indian writer. In important respects, his Indian ancestry lines him up with Indian writers in English such as R. K. Narayan rather than with black West Indian writers, but his two books about India are called *An Area of Darkness* and *India: A Wounded Civilization,* so we may presume the label *Indian* would be even less welcome than the label *West Indian.* To move to another example, what is one to do with Doris Lessing? The *MLA Bibliography* puts her in English literature, but she was born in Persia and grew up in Rhodesia. Though she has lived in England as long as Naipaul (or rather, used it as a base much as he does), she certainly has not abandoned Rhodesia, which provides the setting of many of her novels, or Persia, which is the source of much of the landscape and symbolism of her current series of science fiction novels. Yet to call her a Zimbabwean writer when she left the country long before it was Zimbabwe seems misleading as well; indeed, to put either Naipaul or Lessing in any national category seems absurd. To cite one final example, many more people than just literary critics have recently been exercised by the problem of how to categorize Salman Rushdie. He was born in India and lived there until he was sixteen, so he is put in the *Foreign* volume of the *MLA Bibliography*, under Indian literature. But he has lived in England ever since, though his parents live in Pakistan and he has spent extended stays there. The *MLA Bibliography* insists that he is an Indian writer; the police affording him protection in Britain do so because he is a British citizen, and the question about his national identity is central to the furor over *The Satanic Verses* for both those who attack and those who defend the book.

I cite these three examples because Naipaul, Lessing, and Rushdie would be on anyone's list of major contemporary English writers. They show more than just how un-English that English literature is, however. They also show how difficult it is to put these writers (and many more we could cite) in any national categories whatsoever. And the sheer difficulty of placing any of these writers in adequate national categories suggests both what is wrong with the effort of the *MLA Bibliography* and the direction in which we need to take our categories and structures for English literature. The *Bibliography* is, as I have suggested, to be commended for at least being aware of the problem, but its solution strikes me as moving in the wrong direction.

What I suggest is that we need to make a conscious move away from organizing our institutions around national and nationalistic categories. If we base our institutions on nationalities, as the *MLA Bibliography* does, then most of the best writing in English today will be relegated to strange corners of the curriculum just as it is to strange corners of the bibliography. What I urge instead is a recommitment to the full world of the English language today, to studying the full range of literature produced by English-speaking peoples, including those hundreds of millions for whom English is a working language but not their mother tongue. A reconstructed English curriculum that has escaped the prison of English and American literature and has moved toward a global awareness of literature in English will be able to introduce students to the cultures of much of the entire world in the form of a course on contemporary literature in English. Rather than choosing to narrow our focus to American and English studies, we can choose instead to become aware of the richness of contemporary world literature in English, and the English department can then become the logical place (or one of the logical places) to introduce students to the diversity of the world's cultures. One cannot represent every culture through literature in English, but one can cover an astonishing range. English is a world language and a world literary language; English departments can therefore introduce students to the world.

Our scholarship and our teaching need to embrace the full global range of literature in English rather than the parochial narrowness of English and American literature. The best writing today is not coming from England or America; it is coming from Asia, Africa, the Pacific, and the West Indies. We study only a restricted and impoverished body of contemporary literature as long as we focus on English and American literature alone. Restricting our focus is also to ignore the very dynamic of English and American history and literary history, which has been a great move outward all over the world. The political control of the English has receded, but the cultural empire of English has never been greater, and the dynamic expansion of those two domains has been an important theme of English literature at least since the Elizabethan era. A greater awareness of the contemporary world role of English would, therefore, make us rethink a good deal of our literary history before the modern period, making it less focused on narrowly domestic English literature and more aware of the way in which English literature has always been involved in the dynamics of empire and power.[6] Raleigh, Spenser, Defoe, Swift, Smollett, Scott, Cooper, Melville, and Conrad are only some of the writers whose lives and works were intimately bound up with the expansion of English through conquest and trade, and a broader conception of English literary history would represent their work more accurately than an Anglocentric literary history. And of course, such a history would enable us to make far better sense of a Naipaul or a Rushdie, rescuing them from the limbo of the "other" into which our institutions have cast them.

Thus, the contortions of an attempt like that of the *MLA Bibliography* to represent contemporary literature in English as a sum of national literatures force us to an awareness that literature in English can no longer be represented in this way. Literature in English forms part of at least thirty national literatures, but it cannot be identified with any one of them. To make sense of the plethora of literatures in English emerging around the world today, we need to rethink our categories and see our central category as the category of literature in English. Naipaul, Lessing, and Rushdie are above all writers in English and can be usefully compared and contrasted as writers who are part of the worldwide spread of English. This is not to restrict our focus to a formalistic concern with language alone; it is to become newly aware of the social and political role of language and of the worldwide social and political role of English today. Our disciplinary coherence should be provided not by geographical categories but by the equally social and political category of language. English then would denote the language alone, not the country, and we would see a concern with that language as the abiding focus and continuous thread of all of the various discourses that constitute our discipline today.

The preceding paragraph has a concluding sound to it; indeed, its final sentence ended the original version of this essay. It is almost too easy to criticize the current state of affairs as unsatisfactory, however; the harder but necessary task is to suggest (or implement) an improvement. Anyone anxious to move away from a curriculum dominated by nationalism needs to attempt a fuller picture than I have of what we think we should move toward. This does not mean that an alternative as concrete as the present curriculum needs to be articulated, for it was surely not the product of one person, one intellectual movement, or one moment, and it will not be undone so singularly either. Nor is a complete undoing of the present curriculum desirable. Nations exist, after all: I need a passport if I wish to fly from Chicago to London. And units of geography remain important organizing principles, even if the nation-state is not the only such geographic unit useful for categorizing literature. It is a little more problematic to say that periods exist, for surely terms like English literature after 1660 or from 1798 to 1832 are constructions after the fact rather than objectively given units of study. Chronology nonetheless exists, however: 1660 came before 1798, and chronological ordering remains an important principle of coherence. So the critique of the present order provided here is not based on a utopian hope of overthrowing it; there is to my mind far too much such essentially idle talk in academia today. Neither am I suggesting that organizing courses (and other units of study) around periods in the life of nations is always inappropriate; what I am suggesting is that other kinds of organization should be encouraged and might well prove more helpful than the current use of nation-states as our primary organizational categories. In any case, curricula everywhere are based not simply on conscious reflection or unconscious ideology but also on a variety of contingent local factors incapable of systematization. Nonetheless, I think it is possible to be more precise about the kind of institutional change toward which we might move, and I have three central recommendations in this regard.

First, given a choice between a system of mapping literature based on the nation-state and one based on the language in which the literature is written, we should choose the language-based map (and remember that this is not the same as a nation-based map). This is, after all, a choice true to the literary traditions we hold valuable, which did not ask whether St. Augustine was Roman or whether the authors of the New Testament were Greek; comparably, no one need ask whether Kafka was German or whether Naipaul and Rushdie are English. Moreover, this is a choice true to the dynamic of the modern world, in which the nation-state is increasingly giving way to a world of economic integration and partially and complexly overlapping sovereignties. Anyone who wants to resist this emerging international world is not likely to be enthusiastic about curricular units that cross frontiers, but the real source of resistance to the emerging international order is not the nation-state as much as the region, the pockets of local color and individuality resisting the change involved in internationalization. Breaking free of our overreliance on nationalistic categories would allow a richer recognition of the regional as well as of the international.

This leads directly to my second point, which is that though we inevitably must rely on some system of mapping to structure aspects of our curriculum, we need somehow to maintain an (admittedly elusive) awareness of what that system does not cover so well. To choose literature in English over American literature means that a number of the multilingual aspects of American literature will not be well represented in the curricula of English departments (unless a conscious antidote for this neglect is adopted)—but those aspects are already poorly represented under the current system, with its unreflective choice of unilingual nationalistic concepts. The choice of a system can simultaneously lead to an awareness of what that choice excludes only if the choice is a conscious and reflective one.

My final recommendation, or plea, is to increase the number of antidotes. Every curriculum is going to cover some things badly, which means that we need escape hatches, handy antidotes, ways of reincorporating what we know we do not cover well enough. To organize is inevitably to divide a subject into categories, but we need to encourage the category of "category crosser." In a curriculum built around national literatures, we need courses in international literature; in a curriculum built around literature in a given language, we need courses in bilingual writers. We need to show our students the ways in which any system of categories disables as well as enables, and this means that we need to make a more prominent place in the study of literature for the closest thing we have to a discipline of category crossing, comparative literature. The discipline of comparative literature has not always lived up to its promise; it has to a large extent succumbed to an essentialism of its own, privileging literature emanating from the "major" languages of Europe over that of the rest of Europe and the world. Nonetheless, the ideal of comparative literature seems just right: to study everything worth studying, to compare everything worth comparing, and not to ask writers to show their passports before we let them into our courses. A truly global and international discipline of comparative literature has a great deal to offer those of us teaching in language departments, both those devoted to the language we forget is foreign, English, and those devoted to the other languages we think of as foreign. What it has to offer, most fundamentally, is a way of thinking about courses and curricula based on difference and differences, not identity. I see no reason why departments of English—faced with the challenge and opportunity presented by world writing in English—cannot move in the same direction; I see every reason why we should.

NOTES

1. Perhaps the best sign that canon revision has undergone institutionalization is the appearance of anthologies devoted to the opened-up canon; see, for example, the *Heath Anthology of American Literature.* I have elsewhere expressed doubt about whether the canon can open; see "What to Teach When the Canon Closes Down." Moreover, though the *Health Anthology* impressively rethinks what belongs in the category of American literature, it does not reflect on our reliance on such nationalistic categories in the first place.

2. The MLA provides an endless supply of good examples of this dichotomy, one being the division between the Association of Departments of English and the Association of Departments of Foreign Languages. Another is the *Job Information List,* which is published in two editions, one for English and the other for foreign languages. The *JIL* is particularly revealing, for listings for linguistics and comparative literature are repeated in both lists: they are the disciplines that span the "great divide," but their tenuous position in so doing is revealed by their being placed last in each list.

3. A series of essays by Spengemann, now collected in book form, have already shown the inconsistencies involved in the effort to give American literature its own "exceptionalist" identity.

4. It is interesting to note how stable these percentages are. The equivalent figures for the 10,432 entries in volume 1 of the *1983 Bibliography* are 39 percent for American literature and 47 percent for English literature, with all the rest constituting 14 percent in both years. It is a little sobering to realize that the net quantitative effect of five years of "opening up the canon" was to have a slightly higher percentage of work in the field done on English literature.

5. At this point an earlier draft of this essay said, a little unfairly, that this made the *MLA Bibliography* "utterly unwieldy to use." Eileen M. Mackesy, at that date the director of MLA's Center for Bibliographic Services, responded to a copy of that essay by justly pointing out that I had not mentioned the index to the *Bibliography.* One does not have to second guess the *Bibliography* to find entries on a given writer, so the conceptual confusion I document does not utterly impede the users of the *Bibliography.* She also made the following apposite comment: "One of the concerns of a publisher in the business of collecting and marketing information is packaging and packaging was a major concern that was obviously influenced by the predominant view of the field as being divided into English and Foreign literatures. I see nothing wrong with this as reference sources, such as the *Bibliography,* exist to serve and document a discipline not to define it." Precisely, and it is as a document of the discipline that I am approaching the *MLA Bibliography* here. We need

to rethink our categories, not have the bibliographers straighten them out for us.

6. Martin Green has already begun that process of rethinking, without, however, treating the newer literatures in English today.

WORKS CITED

Dasenbrock, Reed Way. "What to Teach When the Canon Closes Down: Towards a New Essentialism." *Reorientations: Literary Theory, Pedagogy, and Social Change.* Ed. Bruce Henricksen and Thais Morgan. Urbana: U of Illinois P, 1990.

Green, Martin. *Dreams of Adventure, Deeds of Empire.* New York: Basic, 1979.

Lauter, Paul, et al., eds. *Heath Anthology of American Literature.* 2 vols. Lexington: Heath, 1989.

Spengemann, William C. *A Mirror for Americanists: Reflections on the Idea of American Literature.* Hanover: UP of New England, 1989.

10

A BURKEAN CRITIQUE OF COMPOSITION PRAXIS

John Clifford

In *The Political Responsibility of the Critic* James Merod makes a call, first for ideological self-awareness and then for the active transformation of our profession and ultimately our society, that is usually directed at literature teachers, not composition instructors. At least this seems to be the view of the profession in making its primary political focus the reading of texts, not the writing of them. But if language is, as Merod suggests, a material event "embedded with symbolic and ideological mechanisms" (x) then both the production and the consumption of texts need to be interrogated from a political perspective. Antonio Gramsci's contention that "culture elaborates and inserts the role of the state in maintaining order into every sphere" (quoted in Merod 62) reinforces this perception about the pervasiveness of dominant ideas and creates an urgency that should move those concerned with the theory and practice of writing to abandon its lengthy apolitical isolation as a value-neutral skill and think of it instead as one of the apparatuses through which the cultural norms and ideological values of advanced capitalism are reproduced and legitimized. Even more blatantly than literary studies, composition, at least in its most official institutional guise, wants to train writers to move seamlessly from the university to the outside world of business, government, and industry with the proper knowledge of and respect for appropriate rhetorical form and surface decorum. If recent attention to process is characteristic of our more progressive classrooms, unproblematic attention in most of our schools and universities is still relentlessly focused on an allegiance to a priori organizational formats, to the methods and logic of argument, to rigid modes of discourse, and, if there is a writing-across-the-curriculum emphasis, on an elaborate socialization into the habits of mind and rhetorical conventions of various normative discourses. Nowhere in this educational project is there a dialectical critique between the purposes of the disciplinary rhetoric and the goals and values of the writer in the larger culture.

Fifty years ago John Dewey characterized this kind of utilitarian education as concerned with "bodies of information and of skills that have been worked out in the past; therefore, the chief business of the school is to transmit them to the new generation" (17). Dewey reveals the hidden consequences of this strategy by perceptively noting that "since the subject matter as well as standards of proper conduct are handed down from the past, the attitude of pupils must, upon the whole, be one of docility, receptivity, and obedience" (*Experience* 18). Anticipating what could still be said about most standard instruction in reading and writing, Dewey criticizes this traditional view of knowledge as "essentially static. It is taught as a finished product, with little regard either to the ways in which it was originally built up or to changes that will surely occur in the future" (19).

The positivist and conservative implications of this approach are made concrete in composition by teachers who conceive of language as a neutral vehicle for presenting a world that is objectively out there, beyond our confounding subjectivities, somehow disconnected from the class struggle fought daily in other public spheres. Thus, in reading literature they still locate meaning within texts, in the unresolved tensions and ambiguities of syntax, image, and trope, unmediated through the hearts and minds and ideological baggage of readers always socially situated. And in most writing classes, rhetorical structures are thought to exist as apolitical heuristics in a Platonic world of forms, suggesting that form is a neutral container into which one's own meaning can be innocently poured. In this formulation, writing, both one's own disciplinary discourse and the writing of students, is thought to be uncontaminated by the unnerving political contestations swirling "outside" the university's walls.

As politically myopic as all this might appear, Diane Macdonell points out in her study of ideology and discourse that there are always contradictions in the dominant conversation, always opposing voices, redirecting our attention away from hegemonic accommodation. Opposition can be dramatic, but it is often a mundane and tedious struggle over curriculum that must be continually fought for and sustained. There is always a space for voices of resistance, but it is a contest without victory, a struggle always in progress. One of the earliest and most lucid voices is clearly John Dewey's, whose validation of personal and therefore political experience as an instructional resource affirmed diversity while also uncovering, for those who would see, the intimate connection between school and society. His attempt to deconstruct the walls written around the university and its conventions of objectivity has always been an important gesture for educators hoping to make "society a function of education," to produce individuals capable of reflective and critical consciousness. To deepen the notion that one's experiences are intellectually and politically empowering, Dewey also urged the "participation of the learner in the formation of the purposes which direct his activities in the learning process" (67), a collaborative and self-conscious strategy that, because of its ability to move the student's perspective beyond the apolitical subject position constructed by the educational apparatus, has been a linchpin in progressive thinking ever since.

But Dewey went only so far, limiting his reformist vision to a general educational philosophy. Henry Giroux notes that "Dewey's struggle for democracy was primarily pedagogical" (238), whereas Frank Lentricchia, who sees Dewey mainly as a pragmatist with a healthy distrust for repressive structures, finds his underwriting of the "capitalist spirit" troublesome (3). It remained for other thinkers, Kenneth Burke, for example, to deepen Dewey's social perspective by making more explicit the connections among education, discourse, and politics. Ann Berthoff, Richard Ohmann, and others have extended this tradition to writing theory by stressing a Freirean pedagogy of knowing that urges writers to be scrupulously reflexive in understanding our understandings, that privileges context and perspective as interpretive tools, and that sees language not as a mirror or objective instrument but as a rich social heuristic for political awareness. Several generations of such theorists have been directly and indirectly conversing with Dewey's ideas, perhaps arguing with his political timidity here, agreeing with his distrust of custom and authority there, but always incrementally helping us move between the speculative power of abstraction and the instructional specifics of the struggle within schools for an empowering pedagogy that might create a democratic society.

It is often assumed that the current sociopolitical awareness of

English studies had its beginnings in the late sixties and, after four years or so, went into a period of dormancy, to be resuscitated in the eighties as part of the liberal backlash against Reagan's conservative agenda. Now, as Patricia Bizzell notes, "social" is a central concept, "the key word." But for decades there has always been Kenneth Burke, whose work is permeated with a keenly contemporary sociopolitical perspective of how reading and writing are always more than they seem, always reflective of larger ideological purposes. The difficulty the profession has always had with Burke and his politics stems perhaps from the hegemony of our formalist theories of reading, especially our commitment to look for propositions clearly supported with empirical evidence, for textual continuity and coherence, and for unity and lucidity. In composition studies, the problem is deeper. We have always read Burke, but rarely for his insights into ideology. Ross Winterowd, the profession's most consistent explicator of Burke's enigmatic prose, sees in him brilliant examples of an appositional style replete with representative anecdotes, organizational flexibility, foregrounded style, and great presence. He is made to seem interestingly original but, like the rest of the discipline, devoid of political perspective. Consequently, the Burke that survives in our classrooms and rhetorics has been truncated and neutralized beyond recognition, his comprehensive view of understanding reality reduced to the pentad, usually introduced as a heuristic for exploring topics. In retrospect, the burden of responsibility for this political repression should not rest too heavily on the shoulders of writing teachers, for the marginal position of these pioneer composition theorists within English departments guaranteed that only the most utilitarian aspect of Burke's work would enter the mainstream conversation.

Today, it should not seem unusual for those of us interested in a rhetoric with a sociopolitical dimension to see in Burke traces of ideologically focused thinking. His belief in language as a site of political struggle and his emphasis on the social and political context of discourse seem especially compatible with current political and theoretical concerns in composition studies. This is a critical move somewhat different from the usual gambit of claiming that previous commentators misread what is clearly in Burke's texts. With a resurgence of interest in the social context of reading and writing, it is simply that the cultural and intellectual context for rereading Burke has changed; hence, we can now read differently, enabling us to see more clearly the way our "rediscovery" of the radical Burke extends the progressive ideas of John Dewey while also anticipating the political insights of Michel Foucault and Antonio Gramsci.

A recurring theme in contemporary theory is the pervasive force of ideology on our discourse, variously defined as false consciousness, an aggregate of one's beliefs, the unconscious ways we represent our existence to ourselves, or Clifford Geertz's "maps of problematic social reality and matrices for the creation of collective conscience" (64). It is, incidentally, ironic that Fredric Jameson, in a critique of Burke made a decade ago in *Critical Inquiry,* would accuse him of repressing the power of ideology in his writing. In a deeply detailed reply Burke cites numerous references to the term *ideology* and to discussions of its implications, demonstrating not only his awareness of but also his commitment to socialist principles. In his early work and later in his comments on that work, it seems clear that Burke anticipated what is now, after Foucault, a commonplace in our thinking about discourse: that however disinterested and apolitical the form and substance of our language appear on the surface, it is nevertheless thoroughly ideological, that is, imbued with assumptions, biases, constraints, and variable judgments of a specific intellectual community composed of people with their own social and political allegiances. The discourse we write in our disciplines and the discourse we teach our students and expect them to replicate is thereby always ideologically situated in a community already in existence, already value laden.

From this perspective there is no objective academic discourse. Burke knew this as far back as 1931, when, in *Counter-Statement,* he stressed the interrelatedness of form, rhetoric, and power. Rhetoric, for Burke, does not exist in isolation from the larger social world. That is what previous commentators on Burke, and on rhetoric in general, did not and perhaps could not fully confront: the illusion that there is a clear distinction between the inside and outside, between the sociopolitical struggles of the "real" world and the work of university humanists. Anticipating both Foucault and Althusser, Burke knew that discourse tends to underwrite the political and ethical values of the state because, in Burke's terms, behind all writing the mind is ultimately a social product. It is difficult to find any reference to this aspect of Burke's rhetoric in composition studies, perhaps because the usual humanist version of the cultural conversation mainly focuses on the value of uncontextualized ideas. Kenneth Burke did not.

In this regard, Burke's ideas go beyond Dewey's and are more compatible with Frank Lentricchia's notion that this "conversation has been propelled and constrained mainly by collective voices, sociohistorical subjects, not by private ones, not by autonomous intellectuals" (16). Along with many of today's progressive educational critics like Henry Giroux and Michael Apple, Burke believes that as writing teachers within cultural institutions we cannot hold disinterested positions, somehow standing on neutral ground, outside power. Some, like Foucault, view this complicity as dark indeed and see little space for reform. For Foucault, subjects have only a limited ability to resist the unifying, controlling urge of modern institutions and their discursive formations. Although some would agree that our institutions are coercive, with institutional discourse a prison house of ideological hegemony, Burke and those in concert with his ideas are clearly not as pessimistic. Burke is not a messenger of despair or cynical resignation; on the contrary, his political insights allow for, even call for, oppositional thinking, for what Michel Pecheux calls antagonistic behavior, or what some Marxists call disidentification. Burke, who believes with Dewey that the function of education is to reform a limiting, unjust society, is also sanguine about the ability of teachers to intervene in the dominant discourse to alter its direction for the better.

As a first step toward that transformation, Burke wants us to understand that because knowledge is a social construct, "ideas not only have material effects; they have material circumstances as well" (Lentricchia 5). That suggests that we first have to identify ourselves as intellectuals working within an interested web of sociopolitical values. An awareness of how we are culturally situated is crucial if we are to move toward a praxis that conceives of writing, ours and our students, as cultural work with political consequences. According to Lentricchia's meditation on Burke, the most effective site at which to fight against the exclusive socializing implications of traditional writing instruction is where we work, doing what we do—professing reading and writing. This is, in fact, a logical move if the usual oppositions between the classroom and the real world are deconstructed. The profession's resistance to giving up its traditional notion of academic autonomy is, Lentricchia suggests, a double deception, for it encourages students to see themselves as scholarly apprentices, capable of writing as transcendent subjects, unsullied by politics, by exploitation, injustice, and oppression. "Thus," he argues, "do humanists help to fashion the hegemony that will keep us and themselves in the dark" (151).

Recently, Gerald Graff has been supporting the idea that students should be brought into our critical debates. I assume that his attempt to enlighten students would also include this Burkean unmasking of the purposes of traditional writing instruction in our culture. Merod, in his chapter on intellectual identity, suggests that we make the "affiliations between knowledge and power an explicit topic" (131). If we believe that students are unaware of the complex interconnections between their education and social reality, we have a responsibility to confront them with the reasons for our belief that academic discourse appears natural and reasonable but is usually neither, that what happens within the walls of the university both mirrors and perpetuates what happens in the streets.

Burke's goal as a critical rhetor, then, is to shed light on the ways in which we can, through the writing and teaching of discourse, be responsible to the larger social whole. In *A Rhetoric of Motives* he writes that "any specialized activity participates in a larger unit of action. Identification is a word for the autonomous activity's place in this wider context, a place with which the agent may be unconcerned. The shepherd, *qua* shepherd, acts for the good of the sheep, to protect them from discomfiture and harm. But he may be 'identified' with a project that is raising the sheep for market" (27).

It is not hard to interpret this passage as a comment on our service role as writing teachers, training students who might write well technically and are therefore employable but who lack a critical rhetorical perspective and are therefore unlikely to be agents of change. It follows, then, that we need to act on this insight in our writing classes. Basically, after exploring the theme that there is, as Paulo Freire claims, a hidden curriculum of hegemonic assumptions beneath all literacy work, the ultimate goal is to develop instructional strategies that empower students, that enable them to be critical actors. To encourage such persons to develop, Freire, Dewey, and Lentricchia's Burke suggest a pedagogy that is dialogical, explorative, collaborative, and analytically suspicious.

Just such a pedagogy is being urged with more and more frequency, by literary theorists like Frank Lentricchia and Terry Eagleton, composition theorists like Ann Berthoff and James Berlin, and, perhaps most visibly and energetically, by Henry Giroux, an educational theorist with strong interests in the way privileged knowledge gets reproduced in our schools. Giroux, also working from the insights of Foucault, Althusser, and Gramsci, develops the same themes as Lentricchia does, urging the need for a dynamic critical literacy that would help students read the world so they can change it. For Giroux, as well as for Lentricchia and Burke, the agent of this radical education is the teacher as transformational intellectual, a Gramscian term for those who struggle against hegemony. According to Burke, however, this task of resistance can be effective only if we first know who we are, if we first identify our various roles. To raise our political consciousness, then, Burke says we must interrogate our received ideas about rhetoric, problematizing with students such "obvious" notions as form, style, syntax, intention, evidence, and evaluation.

Form, for example, still appears in our rhetorics and handbooks simply as a problem in organizing our thinking. We are still inheritors of the positivist attempt to objectify structure by decontextualizing it, removing it from a historically situated writer and an ideologically interested audience. For Burke, form is far more problematic: it is the embodiment of the writer's attitude toward reality and toward an audience. As such, it helps create a certain relationship between a text and its reception. Form is rhetorical power, a way to shape reality and manipulate audiences. The forms we inherit from our rhetorical past gather an aura of tradition around them, making them seem natural and commonsensical. That, according to Catherine Belsey, is exactly what ideology achieves—making one possibility seem like the only option. But no form can develop in a vacuum. Forms are created to meet and express certain human needs and perceptions. When Burke claims that form was the creation and satisfaction of an appetite in the mind of a reader, he also implies that a particular form might *not* satisfy. Forms can help us see, but they can also obfuscate; they can liberate or they can subjugate. They are never contextually neutral. This linking of form and ideology, for example, is one of the reasons the teaching of writing can never be disinterested. Nonetheless, students are routinely asked to write formulaic essays wherein the organizational scheme of the assignment is given in such detail that even the location of a clearly stated thesis is prescribed. The use of evidence is also highly specified; usually, three examples are required to establish the veracity of the focused assertion. As Richard Ohmann noted some years ago, this obsession with the necessity for concrete, specific details is used instead of a critique of generalizations. What happens is that the concrete becomes reified as adequate for understanding the world. Appearance is thereby privileged over inquiry. In fact, the point of such a mechanistic enterprise often appears to be antiwriting, composing as task, as initiation rite. If the topic, the length, the organizational layout, and the logistics of support and assertion are all specified, what is the writer doing except learning how to accommodate him- or herself to the dominant discourse in superficial ways? The unavoidable lesson is that the novice subject is not supposed to be openly inquiring, to be discovering new knowledge, but rather reinscribing what has already been approved, rehearsing the ideological givens of the discourse.

It is, however, characteristic of discourse to allow space for resistance to these dominant forms. Within disciplines there are always theoretical struggles and contradictions that are reflected at the level of discourse. Burke anticipated this Foucauldian insight by claiming that form is a strategy writers use so that a self can exist in a certain relation to reality. Within the university community there are alternative stances professors can take toward reality other than the dominant one, a discursive struggle for acceptance of variant forms that is ongoing. Students, however, are unlikely to have options. Occupying an inferior subject position, they resist at their peril. Dissenters feel, along with Foucault, that a kind of intellectual tyranny is at work if the self is made to conform to a rigid discursive formation. For example, the conventions of the typical academic, deductive essay as it appears in countless handbooks can be seen from Burke's perspective as ideologically committed: the confident thesis statement and the logical arrangement of concrete evidence is, in fact, a specific way of asserting that the world is best understood in this way, that knowledge can be demonstrated in this unproblematic form, that the self can be authentic within these set confines. If the ideology of oppositional readers and writers is troubled by a particular form, however, their appetites will neither be aroused nor satisfied, only constrained. The secular appetite, for example, is hardly satisfied by fundamentalist rhetoric, and the dominant academic essay is not geared to please those who stand on the margins, those who, like feminists and Marxists, often feel alienated and displaced by the academy's "normal" discourse.

The poststructuralist affirmation of multiplicity and the deconstructive resistance to logocentric thinking, for example, have created a favorable climate for a Burkean critique of what some feminist theorists see as a patriarchal and phallocentric discourse that is repressive to women. Hélène Cixous, for example, along with Luce Irigaray, has repeatedly called into question the objectivity of Western discourse, arguing that it primarily reflects masculine values, such as the need for clarity and certainty, freedom from contradiction and ambiguity, and an assertive commitment to logic and order. Women simply do not find their version of reality mirrored in the dominant discourse. Like Burke, Cixous wants to stress the political seriousness of this exclusion by claiming "that writing is precisely the very possibility of change, the space that can serve as a springboard for subversive thought, the precursory movement of a transformation of social and cultural structures" (879). In her provocative essay "The Laugh of the Medusa," Cixous focuses on what women's writing will do in the world. When she says that women have been driven from their bodies in the same way they have been driven from authentic writing, she clearly implicates the power alignment in the academy and clearly wants women to struggle against this hierarchy by inscribing themselves in history. "Write," she urges, "let no one hold you back" (877). Cixous urges women to invent an "impregnable language" that will break down "class barriers, laws, regulations and rhetorics." She reasons that if woman has always functioned "within" the discourse of man, "it is time for her to dislocate this 'within,' to explode it, turn it around, and seize it; to make it hers . . . to invent for herself a language to get inside of" (886). Stressing the marginality of woman's language, Julia Kristeva and Irigaray also transgress established discourse by advocating tactics that parody, subvert, or disturb patriarchal logic (Moi 139, 163).

Burke would probably agree with this ethic of subversion and applaud the search for a discourse capable of inscribing previously suspect ways of dealing with reality. But a fluid and plural semiotic discourse of creative excess will sound utopian indeed in the context of the American university and will not appeal to most students. Instructors may have some space for discursive resistance, but students are essentially voiceless in disciplinary matters. Burke is, in fact, quite explicit about the need to work within, not outside, established discourse conventions, especially if we hope to change the parameters of discursive possibility. This position was the reason that traditional Marxists in the thirties criticized Burke for recommending that reformers adapt their rhetoric to the values of the American people, that is, to identify with their ideology. As Lentricchia notes, if one is working for a change in consciousness, "one must be careful not to rupture oneself from the historico-rhetorical mainstream of American social and political values" (33). Burke agrees; he does not hope to transcend what some might view as a regimented discourse. Instead, he wants to unmask the neutrality of rhetoric, to alert us and our students to the need to be active, critical rhetors, conscious that the struggle that inheres in academic discourse is not merely over neutral academic conventions but for power, the power to make meaning and interpret experience.

If we follow Burke's advice and confront our complicity in this ideological discursive socialization, there are several options: first, simply to identify with all the values of the dominant discourse; second, to deny its validity and try to begin anew; or third, and this I believe would be Burke's position, to work within the constraints of our discourse, modifying and transforming its limitations. This is, to most writing teachers, almost counterintuitive, for most believe they are simply performing a useful and difficult task, generously introducing students to the academy's ways, not trying to manipulate them. Rhetorics in conflict with their seemingly commonsensical approach will appear eccentric.

But this is a critical notion in ideology, for as Raymond Williams claims, a "lived hegemony is always a process" (112); that is, all our practices in professing writing, from student conferences to our professional conventions, are either gestures in the making of a rhetorical tradition or a move in the ongoing struggle to critique the accepted, to challenge and put into question what seems pellucidly obvious. In this view of how tradition gets reproduced every day, one cannot be unaligned, however distasteful taking an ideological position may seem to some. To choose this textbook over that or even to refuse to choose is still to be a player in the struggle over whose rhetorical definitions of truth, evidence, coherence, and form will prevail. If we teach sentence combining, or use invention techniques that reinforce the autonomy of the self, or urge students to narrow their focus while supporting their assertions with concrete, specific details, then we are helping to sustain a certain view of reality, a certain view of what constitutes proof and authority, a certain ideology. Traditionalists may not want to be part of this power struggle, but in discourse, conflict and struggle are unavoidable.

Armed with an awareness of the multiple and rather arbitrary ways different discourses privilege certain rhetorical strategies, writers beyond the introductory courses might decide more knowingly with which of these conflicting discursive strategies to align themselves. If these writers are younger students, they should be aware that acceptance into various academic discourse communities depends largely on their ability first to conform to the conventions of that discourse. And those conventions are certainly more complex than writing clearly: as David Bartholomae suggests, they are composed of "commonplaces, set phrases, rituals, gestures, habits of mind, tricks of persuasion, obligatory conclusions and necessary connections that determine the 'what might be said' and constitute knowledge 'within the university' " (11). To see academic writing in this way, as a kind of anthropological behavior, is to both demystify and make more accessible our discursive formations. It is a very Burkean notion that as educators our responsibility cannot simply be to prepare students for tasks about which they have no historical or political sophistication. Those students who lack a theoretical consciousness about the power of discourse cannot reread culture; consequently, they risk becoming victims. This ability to see the political and social contextuality of writing is part of Burke's rhetorical equipment for living the examined life.

In the context of the contemporary composition classroom, the Burkean examined life is a radical pedagogical gesture. Not revolutionary in the sense of immediately transforming existing structures on the model of the student militants of the sixties, but still radical in that dominant ideological values are always being called into question, always held up for examination of what we know will always be there in the discourse conventions, however banal they may seem—traces of hegemonic assumptions. Such an interrogation of the work students do in the class can certainly be encouraged by instructors without overtly indoctrinating students within a specific leftist agenda, for students must be allowed the option of aligning themselves with the dominant discourse. Realists will quickly acknowledge that the great majority will do just that, seeing in resistance only frustration and academic risk. Such attitudes are not without foundation, of course, and training students to write the body radical in research papers for conventional history, biology, or economics classes would be counterproductive in the extreme. The Burkean examined life requires more patience, demands more subtly than the grand gesture. Potentially liberating strategies must be incorporated into traditional courses, changing their goals slowly and persuasively.

An intellectual environment that fosters a skeptical and inquiring spirit can easily be blended with various pedagogies geared to enhance the writing abilities of students eager to occupy subject positions within dominant institutions. That is, learning to be a better writer does not preclude learning to be a more self-conscious thinker, a more reflective sociopolitical being. The ethical contradictions many instructors feel can be traced to this problem: can we serve both the university, with its hegemonic tendencies, and our own sense of political responsibility? I think we must. Learning to compose is a thoroughly appropriate time for explorations of how language is a site of class struggle, how all discourses are imbued with interested values, how meanings are constructed in the processes of both reading and writing, and how the subject positions of teacher and student mirror social hierarchies. In keeping reading journals for future writing, for example, students can learn to bring the authority of their own experiences to bear on the texts they encounter and then to dialectically critique their responses next to their comments in a kind of double-entry fashion. This movement between observation and metadiscourse is given as emblematic of strategies that could encourage self-conscious habits of mind that would be likely to oppose hegemony. Students who see the value of knowing their knowledge and interpreting their interpretations and who understand their situatedness as intellectual workers within ideologically inflected institutions hold more promise for creating a just society than those who have merely been urged to be transformational agents. When students begin to see the contradictions between the various discourses they inhabit, they begin to realize that because they have indeed been discursively constructed, they can also be deconstructors and agents of change.

Burke's much quoted and variously interpreted fable of history as a conversation is an interesting representative anecdote for his cogent historico-political vision. A heated discussion is always already in progress when we arrive. We listen for a while, and then, without a full sense of all the previous discursive twists and turns, we begin to take sides, arguing and forming alliances. Eventually, we must leave, with the discussion "still vigorously in progress." As in Foucault's archaeologies, we are here as teachers of reading and writing caught in a particular historical moment, enmeshed in a constraining discourse we did not choose. We are, in part, burdened and belated voices. But against Foucault, in Burke's scenario, we are not helpless. As Lentricchia notes, "history is a masterful, powerful process: it 'makes' us, and yet, at the same time, at any moment in the process, our active willing 'makes' the conversation, gives it the propulsive energy that forces it on" (161).

As Burke's fable suggests, there is no conclusion to this conversation; it is an ongoing struggle, a continuous remaking of rhetorical and literary tradition. This conversation began before our historical moment and will continue with or without us. The oppositional voice of Dewey has been powerfully and dynamically augmented by Burke and many others, but it is only our intervention that can sustain and build on their counterhegemonic themes. Only our active voices can inscribe democratic values on the evolving text of composition studies.

WORKS CITED

Bartholomae, David. "Inventing the University." *Journal of Basic Writing* 51 (1986):4–23.

Belsey, Catherine. *Critical Practice.* London: Methuen, 1980.

Berthoff, Ann E. *The Making of Meaning.* Montclair: Boynton/Cook, 1981.

Bizzell, Patricia. "Foundationalism and Anti-Foundationalism in Composition Studies." *Pre/Text* 7 (1986):37–56.

Burke, Kenneth. *A Grammar of Motives.* Berkeley: U of California P, 1969.

———. *A Rhetoric of Motives.* Berkeley: U of California P, 1963.

———. *Counter-Statement.* 2nd ed. Los Altos: Hermes, 1953.

———. *The Philosophy of Literary Form.* New York: Vintage, 1957.

Cixous, Hélène. "The Laugh of the Medusa." *Signs* 1 (1976):875–93.

Dewey, John. *Education and Democracy.* New York: The Free Press, 1966.

———. *Experience and Education.* 1938. New York: Collier, 1963.

Eagleton, Terry. *Literary Theory.* Minneapolis: U of Minnesota P, 1983.

Geertz, Clifford. "Ideology as a Cultural System." *The Interpretation of Cultures.* New York: Basic Books, 1973.

Giroux, Henry, and Peter McLaren. "Teacher Education and the Politics of

Engagement: The Case for Democratic Schooling." *Harvard Education Review* 56 (1986):213–38.

Graff, Gerald. *Professing Literature.* Chicago: U of Chicago P, 1987.

Irigaray, Luce. "When Our Lips Speak Together." *Signs* 6 (1980):69–79.

Kristeva, Julia. "Women's Time." *Signs* 7 (1981):13–35.

Lentricchia, Frank. *Criticism and Social Change.* Chicago: U of Chicago P, 1983.

Macdonell, Diane. *Theories of Discourse.* Oxford: Basil Blackwell, 1986.

Merod, Jim. *The Political Responsibility of the Critic.* Ithaca: Cornell UP, 1987.

Moi, Toril. *Sexual/Textual Politics.* London: Methuen, 1985.

Ohmann, Richard. "Use Definite, Specific, Concrete Language." *College English* 41 (1979):390–97.

Williams, Raymond. *Marxism and Literature.* London: Oxford UP, 1977.

Winterowd, Ross W. *Composition/Rhetoric: A Synthesis.* Carbondale: Southern Illinois UP, 1986.

11

AGAINST CLOSE READING

Peter J. Rabinowitz

THEME

When I first mentioned the title for this essay to one of my colleagues, he remarked that of course it must be ironic. The response suggests the magnitude of the problem I will be addressing; for the fact that an announcement of opposition to close reading would be read automatically as a signal of irony underscores the stature of close reading in our critical discourse. Indeed, commitment to close reading may well be the *cantus firmus* in the multivoiced canon of contemporary criticism, the nearest thing we have to a shared principle. Jonathan Culler recently argued that "whatever critical affiliations we may proclaim, we are all New Critics, in that it requires a strenuous effort to escape notions of the autonomy of the literary work, the importance of demonstrating its unity, and the requirement of 'close reading.' "[1] And though the strenuous effort behind contemporary revisions of critical practice has managed to break down New Critical notions of autonomy and (especially under the pressure of deconstruction) unity, the "requirement of close reading" seems to have us as firmly as ever in its grip. We tend to accept as a matter of course that good reading is slow, attentive to linguistic nuance (especially to figurative language), and suspicious of surface meanings.

Close reading is a fundamental link between the New Critics and the deconstructionists, at least the Yale School: J. Hillis Miller's claim that the "center of our discipline . . . is expertise in the handling of figurative language" and his insistence that our fundamental task in the "teaching of reading" is inevitably "the teaching of the interpretation of tropes"[2] could almost (except for its characteristic use of the word "trope") have come from the pen of Cleanth Brooks, who insisted that "the essence of poetry is metaphor."[3] Indeed, Miller went so far as to describe what he saw as Gerald Graff's attack on close reading as "a major treason against our profession."[4] Similarly, though it focuses on areas that have been "ignored by male critics," the revisionist feminist criticism that Naomi Schor dubbed the "clitoral" school is still intimately tied to close reading because of its "hermeneutics focused on the detail."[5] So is much reader-response criticism, especially Stanley Fish's once-influential "affective stylistics," which examines the text so closely (indeed, microscopically) that getting through even a single sentence is a major chore. And even while pleading for pluralism, Henry Louis Gates, Jr., insists on the necessity of close reading: it is a position on which "there can be no compromise."[6]

Despite its broad acceptance, though, close reading is neither the natural, the only, nor necessarily the best way to approach a text. I am not suggesting that close reading is always bad or that it should be neither taught nor used. What I *do* want to argue, though, is that close reading rests precariously on a number of shaky assumptions and that its centrality, especially in our classrooms, therefore needs to be questioned.

Take the assumptions about the way texts are produced. For critics who care at all about authors, for instance, close reading entails a questionable notion of the psychology of the creator: it tacitly assumes that authors can consciously or unconsciously maintain such control over the details of their texts that all those details can fit together and have meaning and that consequently, as Brooks puts it, "every word in a good poem counts."[7] It further assumes that the texts we have are the texts the authors wrote, thus conveniently ignoring the interference of publication as an economic and cultural institution, including the effects of both editorial intervention and simple error in transmission, which, as Hershel Parker has argued, can be considerable.[8] I am not talking simply about textual cruxes in historically distant works like *Hamlet* or the lyrics of Sappho. The problem comes up in current works as well, as I saw recently in my senior seminar, where we discovered that, among us, we had two slightly but significantly different texts for the final paragraph of Alice Walker's *Meridian* —although nothing on the jacket or title page prepared us for such a variation.

But defense of close reading depends not only on a number of questionable assumptions about how literature is produced; it depends also on faulty assumptions about how it is read, assumptions that, especially in the classroom, readily turn into prescriptions about how it *ought* to be read. These pedagogical prescriptions seriously influence the way we do read, and it is on the problematic nature of the consequent effects that I want to direct my attention here.

I start from the assumption that there are many different kinds of reading, which engage the reader in substantially different kinds of activity. In part, the kind of activity depends on the reader and his or her immediate situation, because to a certain extent, we read to satisfy our own needs and interests, and different initial concerns demand different kinds of interpretive practice: the act of teasing out the implicit homoerotic tendencies in Turgenev's *Asya*, for instance, is a substantially different process from looking for its contribution to the development of first-person narrative techniques. In part, too, the kind of activity will vary from text to text, at least to the extent that we are reading to extract the author's intended meaning, which is one of the ways (although far from the only way) in which many people read. Different authors, after all, expect and desire their readers (even their ideal readers) to process their texts through radically different procedures. Harold Robbins does not expect his readers to approach his texts in the same way that George Eliot does, and neither of them calls for the same kind of reading that Ngũgĩ wa Thiong'o does.

Reading, in other words, is a very general term for a vast number of significantly different kinds of activity. But by privileging close reading we profoundly reduce this multiplicity. Granted, not all close readers read in exactly the same way. A New Critical reading of a Donne poem in search of the structure that orders its imagery is a significantly different activity from a Derridean reading of Rousseau. Still, the various types of close reading have strong family resemblance to one another, and their continued dominance in the aristocracy of critical activities—a dominance barely diminished by the critical revolutions of the last twenty years—can skew evaluation, distort interpretation, discourage breadth of vision, and separate academics from both students and other nonprofessional readers.

VARIATION 1

First, evaluation. Close reading inevitably brings in its wake a questionable literary hierarchy—or, actually, a questionable series of interlocking hierarchies. David Daiches was not being eccentric or extreme when he argued that literary value depends on the "degree to which the work lends itself to" the "kind of treatment" that New Critical theory demands.[9] And though the specific critical schools in vogue may have changed since then, this circular process of assigning value to what fits our prior conceptions of reading remains firmly in place. To a large extent, the canon as we know it today (that is, the academically sanctioned canon represented by college reading lists, MLA sessions, and Norton anthologies) consists of a collection of those texts that respond well to a series of standardized reading strategies—specifically, to varieties of close reading.[10]

To say that evaluation is circular in this way is not to suggest that it is irrational. Indeed, such valorization could not possibly have wormed its way so deeply into American pedagogic practice were it not supported by sound pragmatic consequences. To give but one example: teachers quite reasonably like to teach texts they can *do* things with, and close reading has shown itself exceptionally well adapted to classroom use. Among other things, it allows the instructor both to teach a skill rather than to convey information (and hence accords well with our current notions of the liberal arts) and also to fill a class period even in contexts that necessitate short homework assignments. It is thus not surprising that we tend to gravitate toward congenial texts that work well with the technique.

But do we really want to make pedagogic convenience serve as the basis for a whole series of implicit evaluative claims? For if you privilege close reading, you also tend to privilege figurative writing over the realistic portrayal of material social conditions, deep meaning over surface meaning, form over content, the elite over the popular, and indirect expression over direct. In the realm of poetry, you privilege lyric over narrative; in the realm of fiction, symbolism and psychology over plot. These acts of privileging in turn devalue certain kinds of voices. A writer directly confronting brute oppression, for instance, is apt to be seen as "less good" than someone who has the luxury to explore minutely the details of middle-class crises. I do not want to suggest that *no* didactic political texts can make it into the canon: *Hard Times* and *Native Son* are hardly ignored. But you always have to work to justify serious consideration of such texts in a way that you do not need to work to justify studying texts that are linguistically richer. Thus, it takes effort to demonstrate that Harriet Wilson's *Our Nig,* with its straightforward, unresonant prose, is not automatically less of a novel than Henry James's more intricate and highly wrought *What Maisie Knew,* although there is good reason to believe that the racist brutality faced by the black indentured servant who serves as Wilson's heroine is more important for our culture—and thus more deserving of our consideration—than the middle-class sexual and marital merry-go-round that oppresses Maisie.

VARIATION 2

It would be bad enough if the preference for close reading simply warped the process of evaluation, causing us to chuck the inappropriate texts onto a noncanonical pile—for then, at least, the rebellious spirits among us could rummage peacefully through the rejects. But close reading also has an insidious effect on interpretation. We not only reject many of the works that do not fit, but, what is more damaging, we also twist many others until they *do* fit. As Wole Soyinka puts it, critics use language to "appropriate" literary production to serve the needs of their own social situations.[11] Yet somehow we fail to recognize the magnitude of the distortion: one of the major problems with much current critical practice is the tendency (in part an outgrowth of our New Critical heritage) to overestimate the coercive power of literary artifacts and to underestimate the extent to which texts can serve as mirrors, not mirrors of the external world but mirrors of the reader, who is apt to find in a text not what is really there but rather what he or she expects or wants to find.

Of course, the phrase "what is really there" may conjure up the notion of determinate meaning, a notion that has been coming increasingly under attack. It might thus initially appear as if the text's acquiescence in the reflection of the reader were only a problem for critics who aim at uncovering authorial intention. In fact, however, there are very few critics whose arguments do not depend, at some level, on the assumption that there are at least *some* interpretive truths that are not imposed on the text by the reader. Certainly the arguments of critics who aim at revealing hidden meanings—be they the male homosocial patterns that Eve Kosofsky Sedgwick finds in the British tradition or the "immasculation" that Judith Fetterley sees in the American canon[12]—depend fundamentally on the claim (even if it is only implied) that what is found is on some level "really" there. And even contextual critics who appear to be more radically committed to the principle that the situation of the reader more or less creates the text still often betray an underlying concern for what is "really" there. Thus, for instance, Jane Tompkins finds herself seeking out the "true subject of *The Last of the Mohicans.*"[13]

One might think that the tendency to read yourself into texts would be ameliorated by literary education, especially through the teaching of close reading. In fact, though, the vexing question of where the text ends and the reader begins is made all the more difficult when dealing with readers who have been academically trained. A trained reader can transform almost any text into the particular kind of poetic utterance that he or she expects or desires it to be. Any well-trained New Critic, in other words, can pick up virtually any lyric and, with sufficient labor, turn it into a pattern of resolved stresses; anyone well trained in deconstructive techniques can, even more readily, look closely at a text and find the cracks that, when pried apart, will turn the text around to say something other than what it appears on the surface to mean. Whatever your political position, it is possible—if you want—to reclaim the works of Shakespeare so that they conform to your beliefs.

The combination of malleable texts, on the one hand, and close readers, on the other, can have serious consequences for our literary health. One of the most common consequences, especially among New Critics and Yale deconstructionists, is a trope-ical disease that I call the "figurization" of content, a disease whose main symptom is the tendency to treat the concrete and specific as if they "stand for" (metaphorically or metonymically) some more general and abstract states. Thus, for instance, J. Hillis Miller can argue that "everything" in *What Maisie Knew* "stands for something else."[14] Among other things, this neutralizes the power of political discourse by treating the historical reality represented in literature merely as a medium for more abstract (and presumably more important) concerns. At the 1986 Ezra Pound conference at Hamilton, for instance, M. L. Rosenthal defused the political reality of Pound's fascism by symbolically equating it with Actaeon's invasion of Artemis's grove, which in turn became a symbol for "the free, exploring imagination." In the process, Pound's major flaw was transformed into a virtue, almost into an admirable form of heroism.[15] That may be an especially virulent case, but most college teachers of *Huckleberry Finn* have encountered students who read it in high school without ever considering slavery as a concrete, political, historical institution that has continuing ramifications for contemporary American life. Rather, slavery became one of a network of symbols in a novel dealing with such general and "universal" issues as growth and maturation.

The ability to spin tropes and figures the way that a silkworm spins silk is useful under certain circumstances, but those who engage in it exclusively risk trapping themselves in their own cocoons and shutting off the rest of the world. It does not really matter whether we engage in this practice naively (as some New Critics did) or whether (following Fish) we glory in the fact that with sufficient ingenuity we can hear whatever we want to hear in any text. In either case, the more we exercise the skill, the more solipsistic we become and the more we lose the ability to adjust our reading habits—our ability, for instance, to hear what the author really might have been trying to say, to perceive what his or her historical situation might really have felt like, or to recognize the real cultural constraints that might have operated on the text. Stanley Fish once said that interpretation was "the only game in town."[16] And close reading comes perilously close to turning interpretation precisely into a game, into a grab for debater's points: give me any text and I can show you that it really says whatever I want it to say.

In the past, this process has typically been used to mask the oppositional nature of certain canonical texts: to show, as I have suggested, that *Huckleberry Finn* was not centrally concerned with issues of race. But this process does not necessarily make literature appear more conservative. As Barbara Foley compellingly argues, any conservative modernist text, with close enough reading, can be made oppositional, too.[17] In either case, however, it effectively severs the relationship between literature and its specific and concrete relation to historical, cultural, and political reality.

Variation 3

As teachers of literature, we often justify our profession by arguing that literature can help us expand our horizons: we can encounter "people" and have experiences that lie outside our day-to-day lives, thus coming to examine the unspoken assumptions by which we live. I agree in principle. I also share Socrates' position that "the unexamined life is not worth living" (with the proviso that we do not assume that the only appropriate form of examination is that practiced by middle-class, white, Western males, and with the additional caveat that we understand that the unlived life is not worth examining, either);[18] I believe strongly, too, that one of the primary values of literature is that it can help raise consciousness. But does close reading necessarily help in this quest?

True, New Critical dogma, and much pedagogic practice in its wake, insists that, in the words of Brooks and Warren, "before extensive reading can be profitable, the student must have some practice in intensive reading."[19] But I suspect that the opposite is in fact the case: intensive reading may well be a nearly worthless skill for someone who has not already devoured a large and heterogeneous collection of texts. The best readers—at least among college students—tend to be those who were the most voracious readers as children, and I am not sure that we do them a favor by encouraging them to substitute intensive for extensive reading, as we do in high school AP classes and in college.

Anything that encourages the kind of self-imprisonment that figurization of content does, of course, discourages real exploration and hence diminishes the opportunities for developing breadth of vision. Indeed, at its worst, the reduction of all literature to a play of tropes ends up making the act of reading simply an act of repetition. Lest you think that I am exaggerating the problem, let me call once again on J. Hillis Miller. In the previously cited discussion of *What Maisie Knew* he insists not only that "everything stands for something else" (figurization with a vengeance, that!) but further that it all stands for the *same* something else ("the act of reading itself") and that "analogous results would universally follow" from the reading of other texts.[20] Miller has apparently so perfected the ability to hear what he wants to hear in texts that he feels comfortable interpreting them even before he has read them.

Furthermore, receptivity to new texts and new literary experiences does not depend solely on the care with which you approach them. Receptivity depends as well on the *range* of your reading and on the *variety* of interpretive strategies you have at your disposal. The comforting but false belief that close reading can unlock the doors of any text does more than just seduce you into carrying an inappropriately small interpretive keyring; because close reading means, among other things, slow reading, it reduces the *number* of texts with which a reader is liable to be familiar.

The effects are especially stifling when close reading is practiced exclusively on canonical texts, but the preference for tiny portions meticulously chewed leads to a deprivation of spiritual nutrition in other ways, too, even if your diet extends beyond the traditional canon. For instance, the more painstaking the reading process, the more alert you are to intertextual nuance—to the shadows of other texts that are cast over the one you are reading. In a sense, of course, this is a good thing, for one of the ways that texts communicate is through their conversations with other texts. But just as close readers can find the meanings they expect in texts, so they can find the allusions they anticipate.

This becomes an especially serious problem in any attempt—such as many teachers make these days—to escape from the hegemony of Western literature and to include non-Western texts in the curriculum. Of course, picking out one or two texts from an unfamiliar tradition, a virtually unavoidable practice in any world literature course based on close reading, inevitably leads to tokenization. But there is an additional, subtler difficulty as well. When readers approach texts from unfamiliar traditions, they are apt to seek—and to privilege—echoes of the texts they already know. The more closely they read, the more such echoes they find, even if they are not really there. As a result, the classic Western texts retain their centrality. In fact, their centrality is reinforced: because new literary experiences are appropriated *through* them, they seem to serve as a kind of universal source of literary practice.[21]

Another way in which close reading narrows perspectives is that it discourages students from doing certain kinds of research—indeed, we actively train them so that they *cannot* do it. My wife recently asked me about how much reading she could legitimately expect from a student who wanted to do a paper on forgotten nineteenth-century women authors. My first reaction was that the student needed to read lots of those novels, for there is no other way to sort out, for instance, their shared attributes from the specific characteristics of particular texts or particular novelists. But how could she do it? The novels tend to be long, and nowhere in our schooling do we teach people anything at all about how they might responsibly and efficiently handle such masses of text. We have taught them how to slow down, how to go back to reread passages that fail to make immediate sense, how to pay attention to nuance and reduce apparent contradictions through imputations of irony, but we have not taught them to skim, how to ignore the inessential. I am not even sure I know *how* to teach it.

VARIATION 4

Of course, like most academics, I am exaggerating the power teachers have over their students. If texts are not coercive, teachers are probably even less so. When reading for class, perhaps, many students engage dutifully in close reading, but even those who read well that way when carrying out assignments use other techniques to process the texts they read once they escape from the academy. In fact, most of us who really enjoy literature—teachers and nonteachers alike—recognize on some level that close reading is esoteric, the sort of reading that, as Gates puts it, "it is the especial province of the literary critic to render."[22] And whereas those who are professionally committed to literature are apt to make the distinction between real reading and "reading just for fun," those whose lives are centered elsewhere may well rephrase the distinction as one between real reading and "reading just for school." In either case, we are creating an artificial split between what goes on in the academy and what goes on in "real life," and we end up with models of reading and theories of textuality that either ignore or (perhaps even worse) devalue the kind of reading (and, as a consequence, the kinds of books) that engage most readers most of the time.

It is a sign of how deeply ingrained this distinction is that even the most progressive of our contemporary critics sometimes fall into the trap of elitism. I am not suggesting that we should abandon research into canonical texts: there is no reason to believe that a full-length study of Danielle Steele would be more useful, more valuable, or more interesting than even yet another book on Milton, and the study of Milton is not in and of itself elitist. But I do believe that critics who want to tackle theoretical issues (especially issues of reading and history) and who sidestep the popular run the risk of diluting their arguments. Barbara Foley's *Telling the Truth,* for instance, is one of the sharpest books of criticism to appear in years, one that offers an extremely powerful theory of how novels make assertions about the world. But Foley deals with the traditional historical novel as if it were a genre that had for all intents and purposes passed away—even though it remains (at Waldenbooks if not at the MLA) a remarkably viable genre. As a consequence, some of her historical claims are, at the very least, thrown into doubt.

But though I do not want to devalue "ordinary" reading, I do not want to overvalue it, either. I agree that most people know more about some kinds of reading than we give them credit for, but I cannot really find comfort in the populist assumption that, outside the classroom, people will independently discover either the most interesting texts (interesting in terms of their own perspectives and their own needs) or the most productive ways to read them. The stress on close reading may separate academic from nonacademic reading, but we cannot assume that this binary opposition is simply another form of the opposition between, say, false and true consciousness. Reading is a complicated activity; the fact that we teach it badly in school does not necessarily mean that people will learn it well on their own.

CODA

I could continue in this way, but I don't want to end in a minor key, so let me modulate into D major for my coda and conclude by answering the question: if I am against close reading, what am I *for?* Perhaps it is just my Chicago background coming out, but the alternative seems clear: pluralism. I need to clarify that term, though, especially given that I am appearing in a collection with Barbara Foley. I am certainly not proposing the kind of anything goes, reactionary-liberal noncommitment that seems to follow from the criticism of Stanley Fish. Recognition that there are multiple perspectives on a text does not preclude making rational choices among them, depending on the author involved or the particular needs of the reader, who is always situated in a particular cultural context and historical moment. Thus, for instance, those of us who are teachers can legitimately show our students that different writers in different social, historical, and economic contexts wrote for different purposes and with different expectations and that a polemical poem by Mayakovsky asks for an entirely different *kind* of reading than does a lyric by Mallarmé or a Native American chant or a poem by Rod McKuen. Likewise, we can legitimately teach our students that different readers (or the same readers under different circumstances) read for different reasons and that to unravel the racial and sexual politics in a thriller by Chester Himes requires a set of interpretive strategies entirely different from those we use when we want to get caught up in the sheer drama of his convoluted plots. But we need to do more than teach our students that there *are* these different ways of reading; we also have to give them actual practice in these alternative ways of reading. That means, for instance, that an introductory literature course ought to include many different kinds of texts: a thousand-page novel as well as lyric poems, explicitly referential (even didactic) literature as well as highly wrought symbolic texts, texts aimed at a broad audience as well as some aimed at a literate elite. It ought also to include many different kinds of tasks: that is, it ought to require students to treat a given text in several different ways, at least some of which ought to grow out of the particular needs that arise from their personal and cultural situations. Most important, I think, we have to teach students to be *self-conscious* about what they are doing when they are reading—to realize that every decision about how to read is a choice that opens up certain doors only by closing others.

It is not simply that learning new, less rigid, and more self-conscious ways of appropriating texts will increase the number of texts we can enjoy and learn from. More important, learning new ways of reading will allow us to enjoy a wider *range* of texts, texts that have the potential to give us precisely those new perspectives on our cultural assumptions that Socrates was pushing. Only in this way, I believe, can reading foster intellectual growth, for it is only this approach to teaching literature that can make us conscious of—and hence able to deal effectively with—the narrowness of our "standard" interpretive techniques.

NOTES

An earlier and very much condensed version of this essay appeared under the title "Our Evaluation of Literature Has Been Distorted by Academe's Bias Toward Close Readings of Texts," *Chronicle of Higher Education* 6 April 1988, A40.

1. Jonathan Culler, *The Pursuit of Signs* (Ithaca: Cornell UP, 1981) 3.
2. J. Hillis Miller, "The Function of Rhetorical Study at the Present Time,"

The State of the Discipline, 1970's–1980's, ADE Bulletin 62 (September/November 1979): 13.

3. Cleanth Brooks, *The Well Wrought Urn: Studies in the Structure of Poetry* (New York: Harcourt, Brace, and World/Harvest, 1947) 248. See also his insistence that "literature is ultimately metaphorical and symbolic" in "My Credo: The Formalist Critics," *Kenyon Review* 13 (Winter 1951): 72–81.

4. J. Hillis Miller, *Fiction and Repetition: Seven English Novels* (Cambridge: Harvard UP, 1982) 21.

5. Naomi Schor, "Female Paranoia: The Case for Psychoanalytic Criticism," *Yale French Studies*, no. 62 (1981): 216.

6. Henry Louis Gates, Jr., "Criticism in the Jungle," *Black Literature and Literary Theory*, ed. Henry Louis Gates (New York and London: Methuen, 1984) 4.

7. Brooks, *Well Wrought Urn*, 222.

8. See, in particular, Hershel Parker, *Flawed Texts and Verbal Icons: Literary Authority in American Fiction* (Evanston: Northwestern UP, 1984).

9. David Daiches, *Critical Approaches to Literature* (Englewood Cliffs: Prentice-Hall, 1956) 3.

10. For a fuller discussion of this process, with particular attention to the way that it helps masculinize the canon, see my *Before Reading: Narrative Conventions and the Politics of Interpretation* (Ithaca: Cornell UP, 1987), especially chap. 7.

11. Wole Soyinka, "The Critic and Society: Barthes, Leftocracy, and Other Mythologies," *Black Literature*, ed. Gates, 27–57.

12. Eve Kosofsky Sedgwick, *Between Men: English Literature and Male Homosocial Desire* (New York: Columbia UP, 1985); Judith Fetterley, *The Resisting Reader: A Feminist Approach to American Fiction* (Bloomington: Indiana UP, 1978).

13. Jane Tompkins, *Sensational Designs: The Cultural Work of American Fiction, 1790–1860* (New York: Oxford UP, 1985) 104.

14. J. Hillis Miller, "Is There an Ethics of Reading?" *Reading Narrative: Form, Ethics, Ideology*, ed. James Phelan (Columbus: Ohio State UP, 1989) 96.

15. M. L. Rosenthal, "Ideology, Passion, Poetry: Ezra Pound," address given at the Ezra Pound Centennial Conference, Hamilton College, 21 April 1985.

16. Stanley Fish, *Is There a Text in This Class?: The Authority of Interpretive Communities* (Cambridge: Harvard UP, 1980) 355.

17. See "Subversion and Oppositionality in the Academy," the third essay in this volume.

18. Thanks to Molly Lazarus for teaching me this in my early days of teaching.

19. Cleanth Brooks and Robert Penn Warren, *Understanding Fiction,* 2nd ed. (New York: Appleton-Century-Crofts, 1959) xi.

20. Miller, "Is There an Ethics of Reading?" 96, 98.

21. Thanks to Ketu Katrak for pushing my ideas on this point.

22. Gates 5.

CONTRIBUTORS

Maria-Regina Kecht teaches German and comparative literature at the University of Connecticut at Storrs. She is currently at work on a manuscript focusing on the intellectual responsibility of contemporary American literary critics.

Mas'ud Zavarzadeh, professor of English at Syracuse University, is the coeditor (with Donald Morton) of *Theory/Pedagogy/Politics: Texts for Change* (1991).

John Schilb teaches in the English Department of the University of Maryland at College Park and directs the Freshman Writing Program there. His essays on pedagogy and curriculum have appeared in several anthologies and various journals such as *PRE/TEXT Reader* and *Rhetoric Review.*

Barbara Foley, associate professor of English at Rutgers University at Newark, is the author of *Telling the Truth: The Theory and Practice of Documentary Fiction* (1986). She is now working on a manuscript provisionally entitled *Radical Representations: American Proletarian Criticism and Fiction.*

David Shumway, associate professor of English at Carnegie Mellon University, is the author of *Michel Foucault* (1989) and coeditor (with E. Messer-Davidow and D. J. Sylvan) of the forthcoming series *Knowledge: Disciplinarity and Beyond.*

Kathleen McCormick, associate professor of English at Carnegie Mellon University, has written the forthcoming book entitled *Reading: Cognition, Institutions, Ideology* and coedited (with E. Steinberg) the forthcoming MLA volume *Approaches to Teaching "Ulysses."*

Susan R. Horton is professor of English at the University of Massachusetts at Boston and editor of the *Journal of Urban and Cultural Studies.* Her recent publications include articles on Dickens and essays on literacy.

Jim Merod is professor of English and director of the Humanities Center at the National University, San Diego. Most recently he published *The Political Responsibility of the Critic* (1987).

Richard Ohmann is professor of English and director of the Humanities Center at Wesleyan University. His latest book is *Politics of Letters* (1987).

Reed Way Dasenbrock is associate professor of English at New Mexico State University. He is the editor of *Redrawing the Lines: Analytic Philosophy, Deconstruction, and Literary Theory* (1989) and the author of the forthcoming book *Imitating the Italians: Wyatt, Spenser, Synge, Pound, Joyce.*

John Clifford, associate professor of English at the University of North Carolina, Wilmington, edited *The Experience of Reading: Louise Rosenblatt and Reader Response Theory* (1991) and is presently compiling an anthology entitled *Writing Theory and Critical Theory* that will be published by the MLA.

Peter Rabinowitz, professor of comparative literature at Hamilton College, is the author of *Before Reading: Narrative and the Politics of Interpretation* (1987).

INDEX